MW00345595

HUNTER-GATHERER BEHAVIOR

Human Response during the Younger Dryas

HUNTER-GATHERER BEHAVIOR

Human Response during the Younger Dryas

Edited by Metin I. Eren

Walnut Creek, California

LEFT COAST PRESS, INC.
1630 North Main Street, #400
Walnut Creek, CA 94596
http://www.LCoastPress.com

Copyright © 2012 by Left Coast Press, Inc. First paperback edition 2013.

All rights reserved. No part of this publication may be reproduced, stored in a retrieval system, or transmitted in any form or by any means, electronic, mechanical, photocopying, recording, or otherwise, without the prior permission of the publisher.

ISBN 978-1-59874-602-0 hardback
ISBN 978-1-59874-603-7 paperback
ISBN 978-1-61132-786-1 institutional eBook
ISBN 978-1-61132-525-6 consumer eBook

Library of Congress Cataloging-in-Publication Data

Hunter-gatherer behavior : human response during the Younger Dryas / edited by Metin I. Eren.
    p. cm.
Includes bibliographical references.
ISBN 978-1-59874-602-0 (hardback : alk. paper)
ISBN 978-1-59874-603-7 (paperback : alk. paper)
ISBN 978-1-61132-786-1 (institutional eBook)
ISBN 978-1-61132-525-6 (consumer eBook)
1. Hunting and gathering societies. 2. Human beings—Effect of climate on. 3. Paleoclimatology—Quaternary. 4. Climatic changes—History. I. Eren, Metin I., 1982-
 GN388.H84 2012
 306.3'64—dc23
                                    2012001555

Printed in the United States of America

⊚™ The paper used in this publication meets the minimum requirements of American National Standard for Information Sciences—Permanence of Paper for Printed Library Materials, ANSI/NISO Z39.48–1992.

CONTENTS

ILLUSTRATIONS

TABLES

FIGURES

ON YOUNGER DRYAS CLIMATE CHANGE AS A CAUSAL DETERMINATE OF PREHISTORIC HUNTER-GATHERER CULTURE CHANGE

1

Metin I. Eren

Introduction

At the terminal end of the Pleistocene there was a sharp temperature downturn that briefly reversed the general warming trends that were evident prior to the Holocene (Straus and Goebel 2011:259). This climatic cooling event, called the Younger Dryas, has received considerable attention as of late, which is significant when one contemplates that "no event in the climate record has received more attention than the Younger Dryas" (Broecker et al. 2010:1078). It was within this context that the short-lived, extraterrestrial Younger Dyras, origins hypothesis generated substantial debate (e.g., Buchanan et al. 2008; Collard et al. 2008; Firestone et al. 2007; Haynes et al. 2010; Holliday and Meltzer 2010; Paquay et al. 2009; Surovell et al. 2009). However, even more plausible, traditional explanations for Younger Dryas origins (e.g., Alley 2007) have also recently been questioned (e.g., Broecker et al. 2010; Wunsch 2010). Nevertheless, despite a lack of consensus regarding the origins of the Younger Dryas, it is still evident that between 11,000 and 10,000 BP (12,900–11,600 cal BP)[1] a singular event affected climates around the world, which in turn impacted local environments. Yet it appears that these climatic and environmental changes were not globally ubiquitous, nor uniform in strength. Thus, for the archaeologist,

Hunter-Gatherer Behavior: Human Response during The Younger Dryas, edited by Metin I. Eren, 11–24. © Left Coast Press. All rights reserved.

two questions naturally arise. First, how dramatic was Younger Dryas climate and environmental change in different geographic locations? Second, in what ways did terminal Pleistocene hunter-gatherers have to adapt behaviorally and technologically during the Younger Dryas? It was these two questions that researchers specifically addressed in a symposium entitled "Hunter-gatherer Transitions through the Younger Dryas: A Global Perspective" at the 73rd Annual Meeting of the Society for American Archaeology in Vancouver, Canada (2008). And it is these two questions that researchers elaborate upon in this volume.

Before moving on to more specific topics, it is worth briefly reflecting upon why the latter two questions necessitate a book, and what the value of this book and the contributions within it ultimately entail. After all, it has been understood by archaeologists for some time that climatic and environmental change does not "determine" prehistoric cultural and technological change. But it is for that very reason, the lack of any direct one-to-one correlation between climate and culture change, that a comparative examination of prehistoric hunter-gatherer adaptations in a global context is useful. Only through juxtaposed, focused case studies of prehistoric hunter-gatherers can we understand the diversity of adaptive responses humans can espouse, which in turn allows us to establish boundaries of behavioral variability (Shea 2011). Comprehending how much behavioral variability humans are capable of, especially in relation to the context(s) in which that variability occurs, permits us to ask broader, fundamental questions about the mechanisms of human adaptation, survival, and evolution.

The inspiration for the symposium and this volume came from research I conducted during my first two years of graduate school (2005–2007). Having been invited to present a paper at the 2007 festschrift of my undergraduate advisor, Ofer Bar-Yosef, I wished to expand upon my nascent work in the late Pleistocene of the North American lower Great Lakes region. My graduate advisor, David Meltzer, recommended that I reexamine whether or not the Younger Dryas impacted Paleoindian behavior there, an appropriate topic for the festschrift given that Professor Bar-Yosef himself investigated the Younger Dryas impact on Levantine hunter-gatherers (e.g., Bar-Yosef 1998, 2002; Bar-Yosef and Belfer-Cohen 2002; Bar-Yosef and Meadow 1995). To my surprise, there did not appear to be any influence of Younger Dryas climate change upon Paleoindian culture change (Eren 2009). Looking back, as with any research project, there are some things in the paper that I would have done differently[2], although there are several conclusions still quite valid today (see the discussion below). Regardless, the experience was overall quite positive, and given the unexpected result,

I became curious as to whether or not the influence of Younger Dryas climate change upon hunter-gatherer adaptations was exaggerated in other regions of the world. Assembling some of the most innovative minds on the topic, including David Meltzer and Ofer Bar-Yosef, was the most fruitful and efficient way to attack the subject.

Demonstrating that the Younger Dryas Impacted Hunter-gatherer Behavior

Up-to-date syntheses on the causes of, and debates surrounding, the Younger Dryas itself can be found in Meltzer and Holliday (2010), Fiedel (2011), Alley (2007), Broecker et al. (2006), Broecker et al. (2010), and Wunsch (2010). The goal in this introductory chapter will be to explore a generalized, scientific framework for establishing climate and environmental change as a causal determinate of hunter-gatherer behavior.

There was great diversity of evolving hunter-gatherer adaptations between 11,000 and 10,000 BP (12,900–11,600 cal BP). Determining whether or not these changes were directly in response to Younger Dryas climate and environmental change is challenging, to say the least. How should a researcher who suspects Younger Dryas climate to be causal factor of hunter-gatherer culture change go about proving it? I suggest that the systematic examination of three increasingly complex "if-then" statements may be the most robust way to support prehistoric climate-induced, culture change. The implementation of such a program is no easy task, but required if one is to move beyond mere assertion.

If-then Statement I

If Younger Dryas climate change is influencing culture change, then there should be evidence of both environmental change and culture change.

This first expectation may appear simplistic, but it is the foundation upon which a casual relationship between Younger Dryas climate and terminal Pleistocene culture must rest. Demonstrating change, either environmental or cultural, can be a tricky endeavor. In terms of climatic and environmental change (or at least the establishment of change in ecological parameters *directly salient* to mobile hunter-gatherers), the fact of the matter is that the Younger Dryas does not currently appear to have been an invariable global force (in addition to papers in this volume, see Straus and Goebel 2011). In fact, it appears to have affected adjacent regions differently (compare Ellis et al. 2011 vs. Lothrop et al. 2011), and some regions not at all. As such,

Younger Dryas environmental change should never be taken as a given and should be explicitly demonstrated.

While determining a temporal scale of analysis for environmental change during the Younger Dryas is certainly challenging (i.e., should change be measured every 1000, 500, or 100 years?), archaeologists are in the difficult position of also inferring what level of environmental shift would have been perceptible enough to humans (consciously or unconsciously) to provoke long-term behavioral responses. For example, Meltzer and Holliday's (2010) exhaustive examination of environmental change and the archaeological record in the Rocky Mountains and Great Plains indicate that in those regions "Paleoindians were not constantly scrambling to keep up with Younger Dryas age climate changes" (p. 31). In those regions, climate and environmental change simply were not as extreme as in other locations. Thus, for a group of flexible hunter-gatherers who frequently responded to daily, weekly, and seasonal weather patterns, adapting to extended climatic and environmental variation "would have been nothing new to them" (Meltzer and Holliday 2010:31–32).

In addition to understanding the range of challenges inherent in studying Younger Dryas climate and environmental change, it is also important for researchers to understand differing scales and types of analyses in documenting hunter-gatherer culture change. In regard to late Pleistocene hunter-gatherers of the North American, lower Great Lakes region, I argued that there was no change in broad categories of tool classes from early to late Paleoindian times during the Younger Dryas (Eren 2009). Ellis et al. (2011:537) criticized the approach of using broad tool categories, arguing that "such gross categories could mask a wide range of activity variability." Although this may be so, categories that are too narrowly defined might mask important similarities as well. For an illustrative example, we can briefly look at Great Lakes Paleoindian toolstone procurement distances. Using a 50 km-scale of analysis, Ellis et al. (2011) show that the early Paleoindian record in the lower Great Lakes seems to be biased toward shorter average toolstone procurement distances than later times (e.g., Figure 1.1a). While small, biased sample sizes are certainly playing their part in this pattern, it is interesting to note that if the scale of analysis changes from 50 km to 100 km, some of the differences between early and middle Paleoindian groups nearly disappear (Figure 1.1b). The point here is not to say that any one scale of analysis is right or wrong, but instead that different scales of analysis are arbitrarily determined by the researcher and ultimately provide different types of information, be it for tool classes or toolstone procurement distances.

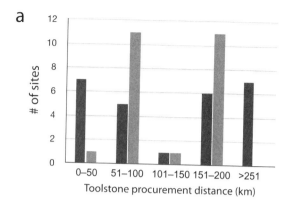

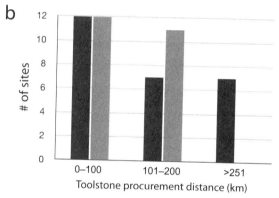

Figure 1.1 The number of early Paleoindian (black) and middle Paleoindian (grey) sites at varying toolstone procurement distances. When the toolstone, procurement distance scale is set at 50 km (a), early Paleoindian sites appear to be closer to toolstone sources (0–50 km), while middle Paleoindian sites do not (see Ellis et al. 2011:539). But when the toolstone procurement distance scale is set at 100 km (b), there is little to no difference between the number of early and middle Paleoindian sites in the 0–100 km- and 101–200 km-categories. Note that at either scale, only early Paleoindian sites appear to possess toolstone, procurement distances over 250 km (a) [recreated from Ellis et al. 2011: 539].

The perceived extent of Younger Dyras environmental change may be inaccurate due to the nature of proxy data or the collection of that data (Grimm et al. 2009; Wunsch 2010). Radiocarbon dating and calibration can be extremely problematic due to the well-known radiocarbon "plateau," making it difficult to chronologically covary hunter-gatherer adaptations with environmental change (Meltzer and Holliday 2010).

Likewise, the demonstration of culture change can be just as challenging as the demonstration of environmental change, in no small part due to the nature of late Pleistocene hunter-gatherer data. For instance, in my previous investigation of lower Great Lakes Paleoindians of the Younger Dryas Chronozone, I examined five material characteristics of Paleoindian behavior (Eren 2009): 1) the type composition of stone-tool assemblages; 2) site/assemblage sizes; 3) kinds of subsurface cultural features documented; 4) toolstone procurement distance; and 5) the geographic location of sites. Ellis et al. (2011) asserted that some of the selected traits I investigated were analytically frail in comparison to three they examined, which in addition to toolstone procurement distance included the frequency of Paleoindian site presence and the geographic distribution of Paleoindian sites. But in the same way that the identification of subsurface features may be influenced by postdepositional processes (explicitly acknowledged in Eren 2009), both frequency and distribution of Paleoindian sites can be severely skewed by collector bias, postdepositional processes, or misinterpretations of time-depth (all explicitly acknowledged by Ellis et al. 2011, but still taken at "face value," p. 539). The fact of the matter is that there is currently no empirical way to argue that any one of these traits is "more robust" than another. Indeed, while archaeologists studying Younger Dryas hunter-gatherers should always strive for rigor, if we start to selectively disdain the accumulated [archaeological] record because of its imperfections (Shott 1997), we eventually will end up with nothing left to analyze. A more positive and productive way forward, indeed the only way forward, is to explicitly acknowledge biases in any and all traits we wish to examine, rather than subjectively eschewing particular ones we believe to be problematic. Making conclusions from the data we have now does not prevent the collection of new data in future, nor does it hamper different conclusions to be made from that new data, whether we are talking about sub-plowzone features, site frequency, or some other analytical category.

In the event that researchers can demonstrate environmental and culture change during the Younger Dryas, they will be ready to tackle the next if-then statement.

If-then Statement 2

Assuming evidence of climate and culture change is demonstrated, if Younger Dryas climate change is influencing culture change, there should be tight temporal covariance of climatic/environmental events with behavioral changes.

Researchers who suspect Younger Dryas, climate change influenced hunter-gatherer culture change need to demonstrate chronological covariance between the two, in some cases taking into consideration time lags. However, covariance can be difficult to substantiate given that dates for geological, environmental, and archaeological events can be notoriously imprecise (Dillehay 2009). Such difficulty is exemplified by the meticulous work of Jones (2009), who examined climate change, patch choice, and subsistence intensification at the French terminal upper Paleolithic site of Pont d'Ambon. In the Dordogne River valley, she documented a decline in patch evenness between 13,000 and 9500 BP, resulting in increased grassland. In response, it appears that prehistoric hunter-gatherers over time intensified their use of the grassland patch, as evidenced by the increasing abundance of grassland fauna (specifically rabbits) in five stratigraphically distinct zooarchaeological assemblages. As such, she successfully fulfills the requirements of "if-then" statement 1. Jones (2009:376) thus concludes that "the inhabitants of Pont d'Ambon seem to have adapted to changing climate by efficiently exploiting new species available to them, and possibly, during the Younger Dryas, by intensifying their use of one of these new species, the European rabbit." Her interpretive caution is appropriate. The dates of the stratigraphic layers (couche) from which her zooarchaeological assemblages are derived include: Couche 4, 12,840 BP; Couche 3b, 12,130 BP; Couche 3a, 9830 BP; Couche 3, 10,350 BP and 9990 BP; Couche 2, 9640 BP. Thus, the zooarchaeological assemblages in question either precede the Younger Dryas by 1,000 radiocarbon years, or date to the very end of it. Thus her data seem to be signifying an important trend more relevant to the terminal Pleistocene as a whole, rather than to the Younger Dryas in particular. So, while cultural changes might have been occurring *during* the Younger Dryas, the lack of clear, explicit covariance between the Younger Dryas and culture change does not support the notion that cultural changes were *caused* by the Younger Dryas.

If-then Statement 3

Assuming covariance of Younger Dryas climate and culture change is demonstrated, if climate change is influencing culture change, then there should be evidence falsifying other possible influences of culture change.

Covariance between Younger Dryas climate change and hunter-gatherer behavioral change is not enough to indict the former as a causal, or even a contributing, factor to the latter. Once a convincing climate-culture covariation has been demonstrated, a researcher who suspects climate as a driving factor should begin to systematically falsify other possible nonclimate variables. The connection will rarely, if ever, be a clear-cut, for we can never rule out entirely unknown (to us) nonclimate factors (McGrew 1992:166). But with each falsification of a nonclimate factor, the association between climate and culture becomes more robust.

Recently, Newby et al. (2005) attempted to make a culture-climate connection for the Younger Dryas in the New England-Canadian maritimes region. They demonstrate that there were broad environmental and cultural (i.e., projectile points) changes during the Younger Dryas (reiterated recently by Lothrop et al. 2011). Specifically, according to Newby et al. (2005) the Younger Dryas fostered more open habitats of spruce woodlands, while abrupt warming at the end of the Younger Dryas increased closed deciduous forests. And there does appear to have been broad, projectile point changes occurring as well, from fluted to nonfluted forms. Therefore, the first if-then statement may be considered satisfied, because there are clearly both ecological and cultural changes evident. If we ignore for a moment thorny issues in projectile point systematics, as well as radiocarbon ranges and outliers, we can tentatively accept the covariance of the abandonment of fluting with the end of the Younger Dryas, which Newby et al. (2005) and Lothrop et al. (2011) proposed. With that said, we can provisionally consider the second if-then statement satisfied once this landmark is reached. Bradley et al. (2008), Newby et al. (2005), and Lothrop et al. (2011) suggest the following as their primary explanation for the covariance. Abrupt environmental changes at the end of the Younger Dryas caused a shift in caribou habitats, namely the northward migration of open tundra and spruce parklands. Assuming that fluted points were used for the hunting of "long distance migrating caribou herds" (Newby et al. 2005:152), they propose that bifacial fluting was abandoned as a result of this ecological change and nonfluted points were used to hunt more solitary animals, like moose and deer, in closed, mixed pine forests.

Is this argument scientifically robust and thus deserving center stage as a primary explanation as Bradley et al. (2008:152) boldly claim? Based on the framework set forth in if-then statement 3, the answer is "no," because other nonclimate-related reasons for culture change have yet to be falsified. Indeed, the early Paleoindian presence in the New England-Canadian maritimes region appears to represent a colonization pulse (Lothrop et al. 2011), and thus changes in projectile point form may just as likely be a result of factors such as "settling-in" (Meltzer 2002), or as others have acknowledged, stylistic drift (Hamilton and Buchanan 2008; Lothrop et al. 2011). Until these other factors are empirically eliminated, the declaration that Younger Dryas climate change was a determinate of culture change in this instance is unsupported. Indeed, as Lothrop et al. (2011:563) rightly note, analogous and possibly synchronous projectile point changes occur in the lower Great Lakes region of North America, but "most accompanying environmental changes in the Younger Dryas do not" (see also Ellis et al. 2011; Eren 2009). And the question remains as to why behaviorally flexible, highly mobile, late Pleistocene hunter-gatherers could not have hunted moose or deer with fluted points (or, for that matter, caribou with nonfluted points). Without any empirical justification as to why fluted or nonfluted points should perform better on different animal types, Bradley et al.'s (2008) claim lacks any sound basis. As such, Newby et al. (2005) and Lothrop et al. (2011) are on firmer ground when they exercise caution and acknowledge the covariation of point forms with Younger Dryas environmental change to be fortuitous.

Are these If-then Statements Too Much to Ask?

Tackling these if-then statements may be challenging, but they are certainly not too much to ask. Indeed, we must approach hypotheses that claim linkage, whether mundane or outrageous, in a similar fashion, and not dispose of rigor because a hypothesis for culture change, like climate change, appears to be "reasonable." Indeed, once all three if-then statements are tackled, a researcher *must*, as Meltzer explains (1991:237), link ecological or climatic stress "*directly* [original emphasis] to the human adaptive responses detected archaeologically." Meltzer continues, "too often efforts to link [...] climates with a human response do not go beyond showing that certain cultural patterns are roughly 'compatible'" with a model of climate or ecological change or stress.

We must also accept, when the time comes to tackle climate-culture connections, that the current resolution of our data, expectations, and tests may very well be equifinal. This is not to say that equifinality will be permanent since new ideas and methods may resolve interpretive deadlock. But until that time comes, it will be more productive—and responsible—to ask different questions of our data rather than uncritically promote an unsupported position.

The Younger Dryas Does not Currently Appear to Have Dramatically Affected Hunter-gatherer Adaptations and Behavior

As the papers in this volume broadly show, there is currently little evidence for a connection between Younger Dryas climate change and hunter-gatherer culture change. This is not to say that there were no environmental or culture changes, only that evidence robustly linking the former to the latter on a global scale is lacking. And, as Meltzer and Bar-Yosef point out in their discussant chapter, in many cases "*continuity* [of hunter-gatherer behavior] is more apparent in the archaeological record than change." As such, this volume not only expands upon earlier investigations coming to the same conclusion (Eren 2009; Meltzer and Holliday 2010), but is overwhelmingly corroborated by other recent examinations of the topic (Straus and Goebel 2011).

We might note in passing that some extreme northern regions, like the western Great Lakes of North America, do appear to have been abandoned by mobile hunter-gatherers during the Younger Dryas (e.g., see Ellis et al. 2011). Does "abandonment" constitute a behavioral or cultural change? Yes and no. The act of abandoning a landscape is certainly an alteration to a group's behavior that was not present beforehand. However, the reason a regional abandonment is undertaken by hunter-gatherers is ostensibly so they can then continue practicing their usual adaptations elsewhere without dramatically altering them, as might be necessary if they did not relocate (Eren 2009).

Acknowledgments

The author is financially supported by a Leverhulme Trust Early Career Fellowship; though during the preparation of the 2008 SAA symposium he was supported by a National Science Foundation Graduate Research Fellowship, Southern Methodist University, and Mustafa, Kathleen, and Nimet Eren. Thanks to Rebecca Catto, Stephen Lycett, and David Meltzer for reading over an early version of this chapter.

Notes

1. Throughout this volume, uncalibrated radiocarbon dates are indicated as "BP," while calibrated radiocarbon dates are indicated as "cal BP."
2. For example, as Ellis et al. (2011) point out, central tendencies may not be the most salient parameters to consider when comparing early and middle Paleoindian toolstone procurement distances. Further, their own statistical analysis raises some additional important points for consideration.

References

Alley, R.
   2007 Wally was Right: Predictive Ability of the North Atlantic "Conveyor Belt" Hypothesis for Abrupt Climate Change. *Annual Review of Earth and Planetary Sciences* 35:241–272.

Bar-Yosef, O.

1998 The Natufian Culture in the Levant, Threshold to the Origins of Agriculture. *Evolutionary Anthropology* 6:159–177.

2002 The Role of the Younger Dryas in the Origin of Agriculture in West Asia. In *The Origins of Pottery and Agriculture*, edited by Y. Yashuda, pp. 39–54. Lustre Press/Roli Books, New Delhi.

Bar-Yosef, O., and A. Belfer-Cohen

2002 Facing Environmental Crisis—Societal and Cultural Changes at the Transition from the Younger Dryas to the Holocene in the Levant. In *The Transition from Foraging to Farming in Southwestern Asia*, edited by R. Cappers and S. Bottema, pp. 55–67. Ex Oriente, Berlin.

Bar-Yosef, O., and R. Meadow

1995 The Origins of Agriculture in the Near East. In *Last Hunters, First Farmers: New Perspectives on the Prehistoric Transition to Agriculture*, edited by T. Douglas Price and A. Birgitte Gebauer, pp. 39–94. School of American Research Press, Santa Fe.

Bradley, J., A. Spiess, R. Boisvert, and J. Boudreau

2008 What's the Point? Modal Forms and Attributes of Paleoindian Bifaces in the New England-Maritimes Region. *Archaeology of Eastern North America* 36:119–172.

Broecker, W., G. Denton, R. Edwards, H. Cheng, R. Alley, and A. Putnam

2006 Was the Younger Dryas Triggered by a Flood? *Science* 313:1146–1148.

2010 Putting the Younger Dryas Cold Event into Context. *Quaternary Science Reviews* 29:1078–1081.

Buchanan, B., M. Collard, and K. Edinborough

2008 Paleoindian Demography and the Extraterrestrial Impact Hypothesis. *Proceedings of the National Academy of Sciences* 105:11651–11654.

Collard, M., B. Buchanan, and K. Edinborough

2008 Reply to Anderson et al.; Jones, Kennett, and West; Culleton; and D. Kennett et al.: Further Evidence against the Extraterrestrial Impact Hypothesis. *Proceedings of the National Academy of Sciences* 105:E112–E114.

Dillehay, T.

2009 Probing Deeper into First American Studies. *Proceedings of the National Academy of Sciences* 106:971–978.

Ellis, C., D. Carr, and T. Loebel

2011 The Younger Dryas and Late Pleistocene Peoples of the Great Lakes Region. *Quaternary International* 242:534–545.

Eren, M.

2009 Paleoindian Stability during the Younger Dryas in the North American Lower Great Lakes. In *Transitions in Prehistory: Papers in Honor of Ofer Bar-Yosef*, edited by John Shea and Daniel Lieberman, pp. 385–417. American School of Prehistoric Research Press and Oxbow Books, Oxford.

Fiedel, S.
2011 The Mysterious Onset of the Younger Dryas. *Quaternary International* 242:262–266.

Firestone, R., A. West, J. Kennett, L. Becker, T. Bunch, Z. Revay, P. Schultz, T. Belgya, D. Kennett, J. Erlandson, O. Dickerson, A. Goodyear, R. Harris, G. Howard, J. Kloosterman, P. Lechler, P. Mayewski, J. Montgomery, R. Poreda, T. Darrah, S. Que Hee, A. Smith, A. Stich, W. Topping, J. Wittke, and W. Wolbach
2007 Evidence for an Extraterrestrial Impact 12,900 Years Ago that Contributed to the Megafaunal Extinctions and the Younger Dryas Cooling. *Proceedings of the National Academy of Sciences* 104:16016–16021.

Grimm, E., L. Maher, Jr., and D. Nelson
2009 The Magnitude of Error in Conventional Bulk-sediment Radiocarbon Dates from Central North America. *Quaternary Research* 72:301–308.

Hamilton, M., and B. Buchanan
2008 The Accumulation of Stochastic Copying Errors Causes Drift and Culturally Transmitted Technologies: Quantifying Clovis Evolutionary Dynamics. *Journal of Anthropological Archaeology* 28:55–69.

Haynes, C. Vance, Jr., J. Boerner, K. Domanik, D. Lauretta, J. Ballenger, and J. Goreva
2010 The Murray Springers Clovis Site, Pleistocene Extinction, and the Question of Extraterrestrial Impact. *Proceedings of the National Academy of Sciences* 107:4010–4015.

Holliday, V., and D. Meltzer
2010 The 12.9ka ET Impact Hypothesis and North American Paleoindians. *Current Anthropology* 51:575–607.

Jones, E.
2009 Climate Change, Patch Choice, and Intensification at Pont d'Ambon (Dordogne, France), during the Younger Dryas. *Quaternary Research* 72:371–376.

Lothrop, J., P. Newby, A. Spiess, and J. Bradley
2011 Paleoindians and the Younger Dryas in the New England-Maritimes Region. *Quaternary International* 242:546–569.

McGrew, W.
1992 *Chimpanzee Material Culture: Implications for Human Evolution.* Cambridge University Press, Cambridge.

Meltzer, D.
1991 Altithermal Archaeology and Paleoecology at Mustang Springs, on the Southern High Plains of Texas. *American Antiquity* 56:236–267.

2002 What Do You Do When No One's Been There Before? Thoughts on the Exploration and Colonization of New Lands. In *The First Americans: The Pleistocene Colonization of the New World*, edited by N. Jablonski, pp. 27–58. Wattis Symposium Series in Anthropology, Memoirs of the California Academy of Sciences Number 27, San Francisco.

Meltzer, D., and V. Holliday
2010 Would North American Paleoindians Have Noticed Younger Dryas Age Climate Changes? *Journal of World Prehistory* 23:1–41.

Newby, P., J. Bradley, A. Spiess, B. Shuman, and P. Leduc
2005 A Paleoindian Response to Younger Dryas Climate Change. *Quaternary Science Reviews* 24:141–154.

Paquay, F., S. Goderis, G. Ravizza, F. Vanhaeck, M. Boyd, T. Surovell, V. Holliday, C. Vance Haynes, Jr., and P. Claeys
2009 Absence of Geochemical Evidence for an Impact at the Bølling-Ållerød/Younger Dryas Transition. *Proceedings of the National Academy of Sciences* 106:21505–21510.

Shea, J.
2011 *Homo Sapiens* Is as *Homo Sapiens* Was: Behavioral Variability versus "Behavioral Modernity" in Paleolithic Archaeology. *Current Anthropology* 52:1–35.

Shott, M.
1997 Variation in Great Lakes Paleoindian Assemblages. *Midcontinental Journal of Archaeology* 22:197–236.

Straus, L., and T. Goebel (editors)
2011 Human and the Younger Dryas: Dead End, Short Detour, or Open Road to the Holocene? *Quaternary International* 242(2):259–584.

Surovell, T., V. Holliday, J. Gringerich, C. Ketron, C. Vance Haynes, Jr., I. Hilman, D. Wagner, E. Johnson, and P. Claeys
2009 An Independent Evaluation of the Younger Dryas Extraterrestrial Impact Hypothesis. *Proceedings of the National Academy of Sciences* 106:18155–18158.

Wunsch, C.
2010 Towards Understanding the Paleocean. *Quaternary Science Reviews* 29:1960–1967.

2

CLIMATE, TECHNOLOGY, AND SOCIETY DURING THE TERMINAL PLEISTOCENE PERIOD IN SOUTH AMERICA

Tom D. Dillehay

Introduction

Current paleoecological evidence from South America suggests that the cooler Younger Dryas (YD) period (~13,000–12,200 cal BP) of the northern hemisphere was not a major event in the southern hemisphere, and if it occurred in a few regions, it probably only had a minor affect on human adaptations. Although many local and regional cultural transformations during this period are understood in terms of different climate and environmental changes, others are not. For example, in some instances when cooler or arid climatic conditions are not thought to be favorable in some areas, people developed certain initial pulses toward hunter-gatherer complexity, such as the transition from mobile foraging to less mobile or semisedentary strategies and the beginning of plant and possibly animal domestication (Bonavia 1991; Dillehay 2000; Lavallée 2000; Piperno 2006). Contrarily, in other areas where more temperate and ameliorating climatic conditions at the end of the Pleistocene favored more complex socioeconomic changes, people continued to practice a mobile-forager lifestyle. How do we explain these changes and paradoxes, and are climate, social, or other factors accountable? Presently, the congruities and incongruities between climatic and archeological records in South America

Hunter-Gatherer Behavior: Human Response during The Younger Dryas, edited by Metin I. Eren, 25–56. © Left Coast Press. All rights reserved.

do not allow us to answer this question. Several difficulties are the offsetting chronologies, scales of analyses, and vagaries of preservation of these records, as well the spatial and temporal extrapolations made by researchers in attempting to reconcile sampling biases in the databases. However, some regional records are becoming clear enough whereby reasonable explanations and new hypotheses can be offered. In this paper, I review general patterns in the paleoecological and archeological records of South America, and what we know and do not know about the relationship between human adaptation and climate change during the YD period. The focus is not just pattern identification but problems and prospects in reconciling and making sense of the records.

Archeologists studying the initial peopling of South America have given considerable attention to the interaction among humans, climates, and paleoenvironments in their respective research areas. Yet, the YD event is rarely considered in the archeological literature of South America. I see two reasons for this absence. First, the YD is presently documented as a possible event in only a few areas of the continent's northern Neotropic ecozones. Until recently, the YD in South America had not received as much attention from paleoecologists as it had in North America and elsewhere (e.g., Rodbell 2000), and it is not generally perceived as a comparable cooling event in the southern hemisphere (cf. Ackert et al. 2008; Bradley 1999; Bush et al. 2006a, 2006b, 2007; Lovell and Kelly 2008; Rodbell and Seltzer 2000; Van Veer et al. 2000; Weng et al. 2004). Second, except in reference to human adaptations to high latitudes and high altitudes, some South American archeologists do not consider climate to have been a strong factor in determining most human distributions and thus have given little attention to specific climatic episodes such as the YD (e.g., Borrero 1999; Bryan 1973; Dillehay 2000; cf. León 2007). Based on these reasons and on discussions below, the position in this paper is that the YD was not a widespread climatic event in South America. This does not imply that other climatic changes during the terminal Pleistocene were not important to human adaptations. The idea is that climates and environments determined local resource patterns and influenced human uses of resources, especially food. However, humans created the conditions and organizations in which they lived, which largely dictated their responses to climatic changes.

In general, paleoecological studies for the period around 13,000–12,200 cal BP in South America are not evenly concentrated across the continent. Some areas such as southern Patagonia, the central Andes, the high plains or savanna of Bogotá, Colombia, and the eastern highlands of Brazil are probably best represented. Proxy climatic records from these and other regions are drawn from a wide variety of source materials, including stratified ice-cores in the high Andes, marine isotope studies, atmospheric CO_2, pollen, molecular phylogenies, microfauna (i.e., snails), and others. Ideally, it would be useful to review all of the types of evidence offered by these records, how they are biased and constrained, and the kinds of climatic changes they reflect, while taking into consideration such variables as temperature, precipitation, latitude, altitude, wind patterns, and so forth. It would also be useful to employ these records to establish broad biogeographical regions across the continent for the YD period. This would allow researchers to discuss the evidence for climatic and environmental changes within each region, correlate the chronologies of these changes with human events, deduce their significance at different local and regional scales of analyses, and hypothesize what, if any, impact these changes might have had on human populations and the resources upon which they depended. Such inquiry would no doubt identify interesting patterns in the distribution of humans and the kinds of interactions open to them in particular environments. However, such a presentation would involve the massing and scrutiny of a considerable amount of data, which is beyond the scope of this paper. Instead, I present a synopsis of the kinds of proxy records available and what they inform us about climatic patterns across the major regions of the continent. I also attempt to reconcile differences and prospects among those records while providing a general understanding of human and environmental interactions across the continent (Figure 2.1) during the YD period.

Figure 2.1 refers to the major biogeographic regions of South America that are discussed in the text. These include the coastal plains, sabana or high plains of Bogotá, Orinoco lowlands, and the Guyana highlands of the northern rim (Figure 2.2). Other regions—shown below—include the Amazonian lowlands, llanos, and Brazilian highlands of the eastern tropics, the Andean chain and altiplano, and the Gran Chaco, La Plata basin, Pampas and Patagonia of the southern cone.

A Younger Dryas Period in South America?

Current paleoecological studies suggest that 14,000 cal BP years ago, temperature and precipitation increased substantially in many parts of the northern hemisphere. This warming trend in the north was interrupted by a return of glacial conditions and cooler climates during the YD period from around 13,000 to 12,200 cal BP (e.g., Bush et al. 2007; Haug et al. 2001; Mayle and Beerling 2004; Mayle et al. 2004; Mayle and Cwynar 1995; Rodbell 2000). The cause of this cooling is unresolved,

Figure 2.1 Map showing the location of the major biogeographical zones in South America.

Figure 2.2 General view of low tropical forest canopy and hills in Guyanas.

but hypotheses focus on whether it was a global or a North Atlantic event. Termination of the YD around 12,200 cal BP roughly corresponds to the boundary between the Pleistocene and Holocene periods.

In South America, the YD is perceived differently than in North America. Signals of climatic amelioration are strongly evident from approximately 18,500 to 15,000 cal years ago in the central and southern regions of South America, when, for example, some Andean pollen records show there was a sudden shift to moister, dryer and possibly slightly cooler conditions in northern, tropical South America (cf. Bush et al. 2005, 2006a, 2006b, 2007; Grabandt 1985; Van der Hammen and Hooghiemstra 1995; Van Veer et al. 2000). By roughly 12,500 cal years ago, there were further rapid increases in temperature and rainfall. In the northern areas of the Neotropics, it appears that the YD is best represented by slight increases in precipitation rather than temperature changes. Farther south, fossil pollen studies by Seltzer and his colleagues (e.g., Seltzer et al. 2002a, 2002b) in the highlands of Bolivia and Peru and by Haug (2001; cf. Bush et al. 2007) and his colleagues in Venezuela suggest that tropical Andean glaciers retreated rapidly throughout much of the YD period. Even farther south, the paleoclimatic records from Antarctic ice-cores and from fossil pollen records in southern Chile and Argentina between about 18,500 and 15,000 cal BP suggest that deglaciation and warming in the southern hemisphere may have occurred 2,000 to 3,000 years earlier than in the northern hemisphere and that the southern grasslands were characterized by a subhumid, dry climate. Specifically in southern Patagonia, Ackert et al. (2008) show that while some mountain glaciers on the eastern side of the Andes re-advanced during the YD period, those on the western side did not. They conclude from pollen studies that easterly re-advances resulted from an increase in local precipitation rates caused by changes in wind circulation patterns and not from regional cooling. Also based on pollen studies, Markgraf et al. (1991; cf. Bennett et al. 2000; Heusser 2003; Heusser and Rabassa 1987; Villagrán 2001) believe that the YD period in southern Patagonia was marked by a transitional climate of warm, dry, species-rich, shrubby grasslands and not cold, moor species grasslands. These collective data generally agree with the paleoecological evidence from Australia (De Deckker 2003) and New Zealand (McGlone 1995), and also indicate that there was little or no cooling in most areas of the southern hemisphere. Instead, a steady rise in temperature is indicated by these collective data, which is generally consistent with results of other studies from South America (e.g., Baker et al. 2001; Blunier et al. 1998; Bush et al. 2007; Rodbell 2000). These findings differ from those of previous studies in highland Ecuador (Clapperton et al. 1997; McCulloch et al. 2000) and studies of glacier advances and isotope paleotemperature data from ice-cores from the higher central Andes (Thompson et al. 1995, 1998). The combined data of Clapperton et al. (1997) and Thompson et al. (1995, 1998) suggest only a slight cooling of 2–3 degrees in the higher altitudes of the Andes (cf. Dornbusch 2002).

In reviewing the paleoecological evidence for shifts in biota regimes, many environments of the terminal YD period may have been similar to ecotones (e.g., Bush et al. 2004, 2006a, 2006b; Clapperton 1993; Goodman et al. 2001; Stocker 1998), where biotic mixtures from adjacent zones were present. This may have been most marked in certain elevations of the north and central Andes and in the eastern lowland tropics of the Amazon basin, as suggested by several fossilized pollen records (e.g., Behling et al. 2002, 2005; Bush and Flenley 2006). In these regions, rainforest taxa are more abundant in pollen profiles, suggesting expansion and reconstitution outward from hypothesized glacial refugia; forest expansion at higher altitudes is also evident in the Neotropics of Ecuador, Peru, and parts of western Amazonia (Bush 1991; Paduano et al. 2003; Seltzer and Rodbell 2005). Previous notions that the Amazon was a refugia of forests scattered among a vast savanna during the late Pleistocene period no longer applies. Pollen studies in the Amazon basin now show no clear fragmentation of the rainforest during the YD period but its expansion along margins and probably a drier forest than today (Bush 2005; Bush et al. 2006a, 2006b, 2007). Current studies also indicate that no single biotic description can be correctly provided for the entire basin; however, it can be suggested that "intermediate forests" largely comprised of woody savanna and mesic foliage best characterize the region during the YD period (Bush et al. 2006a, 2006b; Colinvaux et al. 2001; Haffer and Prance 2001).

Lake levels and river activity increased in many parts of the continent during the terminal Pleistocene, and the expansion of the montane forests along the eastern slopes of the Andes occurred by around 14,200 cal BP (Bush et al. 2005, 2006a, 2006b; Weng et al. 2004). Fossil-pollen cores from Lake Titicaca and the highlands of Peru and Ecuador support the case for repeated climatic oscillations about 500 years before the YD in North America (Paduano et al. 2003; Rodbell and Seltzer 2000). Most paleobotanical data from these areas suggest that widespread warming trends were underway by at least 12,300 cal years ago, although some cooling trends may have occurred in high altitudes and high latitudes of the Andes, as noted above. On the other hand, other pollen records suggest that some environments such as the grasslands of Argentina and the arid coastal plains of Peru and Chile were fairly stable by 13,000 cal years ago, although characterized by fluctuating precipitation rates and temperatures (Ariztegui et al. 1997; McCulloch et al. 2000; Moreno and

Leon 2003; Moreno et al. 2001). The Argentine Pampas during the YD were extensive, temperate, subhumid, and dry grasslands with a variety of herbivores, such as guanaco, glyptodont, that people hunted (Markgraf 1993; Prieto 1996; Quattrocchio et al. 1995).

It also is important to briefly consider the different impacts that human activities had on local and regional environments, including the burning of vegetation, overexploitation of animal and plant resources, and the transport of plant species into new environments. For instance, archeological, pollen and charcoal evidence from northern South America, especially the lowland tropics of Colombia, suggests that people were manipulating certain plant and possibly animal species since at least 13,000 cal BP, including the clearing of forests and the use and possible expansion of naturally cleared areas by burning and possibly by transferring economically exploitable plants (e.g., *Lagenaria* spp. and *Solanum* spp.) from one biome to another (see Gnecco and Aceituno 2006). Similar instances of the human use of fire, whether accidental or intentional, producing increased vegetation clearing is documented in south-central Chile between 14,000 and 13,000 cal BP (Moreno 2004; Moreno and Leon 2003) and in south Brazil (Behling et al. 2002, 2005), as evidenced by the sudden and continued increase of charcoal in local pollen records. As discussed below, humans also potentially altered landscapes by possibly causing the extinction of some megafauna and by taming or domesticating camelids (i.e., vicuna, paleo-llama) as early as 11,500 to 10,500 cal years ago (cf. Bonavia 1996; Nunez and Dillehay 1979).

In sum, two issues are important here. First, paleoecological records and chronologies based on radiocarbon dates for climate changes across many areas of South America are not well understood (Lovell and Kelly 2008). Thus, a blanket interpretation of the YD period cannot be applied across the Americas. Current evidence suggests that YD cooling in the North Atlantic area was a regional, rather than a hemisphere-long phenomenon. Although, there may have been some areas of South America (e.g., high Andes) that experienced slight cooling. Second, whether there were cooler or wetter conditions in South America and whether they were caused by the YD or other climatic events, people still had to adapt to the changing conditions. It is important to know which climatic condition affected people in each region, because it would have differently structured the biota resources exploited by people and influenced the degree of mobility they practiced. Based on these understandings, I view the YD as only a temporal period and not a widespread cooling event in the southern hemisphere. I focus the remaining discussions on patterns and prospects related to selected paleoecological and archeological regional records.

Reconciling Archeological and Paleoecological Records

In reconstructing human and environmental interactions in the late Pleistocene period in South America, archeologists run the risk of over-relying on the ecological settings of contemporary environments or the continent's general biogeography (Figure 2.1). To offset this bias, archeologists attempt to relate the archeological data to regional paleoecological records in specific geographical settings, such as the western Amazon rainforest, the central Andean mountains (Figure 2.3), the Gran Chaco, or the southern Patagonian grasslands (Figure 2.4), and how they changed over time. They also attempt to understand local databases exclusively in terms of reconstructed, late Pleistocene landscapes and their associated resource structures (*sensu* Binford 1980; Kelly 1995), the latter of which is difficult to achieve, given the scarcity of detailed and reliable paleoecological information for many regions of the continent. As more information becomes available from paleoecological analyses, archeologists should be able to interpret their data within more local and regional frameworks. For now, however, we must extrapolate from one proxy record to another not only in reconstructing past climates and environments but in identifying the reactions of past forager societies to them.

Figure 2.3 General view of the cold, puna grassland and distant cordillera of the Andes in central Peru.

Figure 2.4 View of the Patagonian grasslands and hills south of Bariloche, Argentina.

Although this approach seems overly reductionist and environmentally deterministic, it makes some sense in light of contemporary and historically known foragers in South America (e.g., Hill and Hurtado 1996; Politis 2007) and elsewhere (e.g., Gamble 1999) who utilized their knowledge of their natural worlds for surviving and for procuring food. It is also recognized that the content and distribution of resources in the environment have an impact on the way people behave, although they are clearly not the only factors influencing people's behavior. Study of the impact of the natural world is essential; it often provides archeologists with the most empirical approach we have to understanding the economy and diet of past peoples through the archeological record and indirectly past, local environments. Thus, we are reduced to looking at what comprises this record, and the relationship between site location and past environments, stone tools and other artifacts, and floral and faunal remains.

Although all archeological sites dating to the late Pleistocene relate in one way or another to the YD period, not all floral and faunal records from sites are reliably indicative of local and regional climates, because food species are selected by humans making choices about what they procure or exchange for foods. Thus, archeologists know that archeological records alone cannot always be taken as accurate proxy records for local conditions, unless they have been specifically earmarked as climatic and environmental indicators and studied as such in comparison to regional paleoecological data, which often is not the case (earmarked meaning that the floral [e.g., pollen, charcoal, phytoliths], faunal [e.g., diatoms, snails, mammal species], and sediment records from archeological sites are sampled to qualitatively and quantitatively match similar proxies from regional paleoecological sites). Archeologists also realize that climatic changes during the terminal Pleistocene and early Holocene must have affected animal and plant species differently in different biomes, producing mosaics of coexisting species not found in the present-day records. In an attempt to counter these biases, many proxy reconstructions of local archeological environments by archeologists are extrapolated from the spatially closest paleoecological records. This often can lead to misleading or only partial reconstructions of past environments and human lifestyles.

Other approaches to reconstructing past lifestyles include demographic and social considerations. However, so little systematic archeological survey work has been carried out in many regions of South America that it is too speculative to comment on population density and on broad settlement, subsistence, and social patterns during the late Pleistocene. Though site density is low in many regions, largely due to sampling biases and possibly to low human densities at times, enough patterning is evident in the central Andes, eastern Brazil, and southern Patagonia, for example, to suggest a rise in the number of sites between approximately 13,000 and 11,700 cal BP (e.g., Dillehay 2000; Flegenheimer et al. 2006; Kipnis 1998; León 2007). The central Andes, in particular, perhaps present a clearer picture, reflecting more intensive archeological fieldwork and, along the arid desert coast, better conditions for dating and organic preservation. There is also evidence suggestive of a wider range of environments as climates ameliorated across South America during this period (Baker et al. 2001; Bush and Flenley 2006; Clapperton 1993). It also is worth considering that denser human populations probably led to more social contact and the establishment of social networks for the exchange of partners and material goods, especially in high density coastal areas (Dillehay 2000) and probably the open grasslands of the southern cone, where the concentration of certain resources occurred (e.g., shellfish, fish, and guanaco, respectively). However, a problem with this consideration is the difficulty of identifying the archeological correlates of networks and exchange. The spread of people and goods may result from geographic drift, deliberate migration, and/or exchange. At present, however, we do not have enough sophisticated methodologies in archeology to always distinguish between these causal variables.

A further issue concerns the scale of events observed in the archeological and paleoecological records. Purely social factors are difficult if not impossible to prove for the late Pleistocene era. Perhaps more helpful in the short-term are explanations that relate the organization of technology, settlement-subsistence strategies, and exchange with local economies (cf. Aschero 2000; Borrero 2007; Correal 1986; Gnecco and Aceituno 2006; Vialou 2005). For instance, increasingly plentiful resources might have led to a rupture in earlier patterns of mobility and raw material exchange, encouraging more use of locally available rocks for stone artifacts that then conditioned observed changes in flake tools and scraper sizes. This argument seems supported at some sites in lowland Colombia (Lopez 1999) and in various areas of Argentina (Aschero 2000; García 2003), but fails to explain situations where, as on the north coast of Peru, raw materials for stone-tool production changed little over time, even when climatic change is documented (Dillehay et al. 2003a; Maggard 2009). By focusing on changing environments and environmental mosaics and attempting to relate them to human demographic changes on a local level, we can begin to better accommodate issues of scale both spatially and temporally. Until more investigations are carried out on the relationship between human demography and changing climates and environments, we must rely heavily on aspects of the archeological record that afford comparative analyses across multiple localities. Currently, these are site location, stone-tool industries, and when preserved, faunal and floral assemblages and their comparison with spatially proximal paleoecological studies.

Site Location, Stone-tool Industries, and Implications for Human and Environmental Interaction during the YD Period

The current archeological evidence from South America indicates that by at least 14,500 cal BP early South Americans were diversified general foragers, specialized highland hunters, maritime gatherers and hunters, and other combinations in a wide variety of environmental contexts (Ardila and Politis 1989; Borrero 2007; Bryan 1973; Dillehay 2000; Dillehay et al. 1992; Kipnis 1998; Lavallée 2000). These diverse economies entailed different degrees of technological innovation, planning, uncertainty and risk management, resource sharing, mobility and territoriality, and social interaction, which eventually led to different regional developments during the subsequent early Holocene period. It is important to recognize that these developments took place in many different types of environments ranging from excessively coastal habitats and dry deserts to humid, tropical forests and that they did not fully emerge until plant and/or animal domestication and a semisedentary lifestyle occurred, especially in the Andean region (Aldenderfer 1999; Bonavia 1991, 2008; Dillehay 1999; Lavallée 2000). How did climatic changes affect the distribution of humans, the economic strategies they developed, and the types of environments they colonized at the end of the Pleistocene period? South America's relatively low to moderate density of archeological research in comparison to North America means that there are good data to work with in some areas, but there are still many regional and thematic lacunae. Many of the best observations, for example, come from coastal situations, such as Brazil, Peru, and Chile (Dillehay 2000; Kipnis 1998; León 2007). In these areas, changes in ecology and subsistence parallel inland regions where different closely juxtaposed mountain environments exist within a short distance, and southern Patagonia where much corresponding archeological and paleoecological research has occurred (Borrero 2007; Massone 2005; Miotti and Salemme 2004).

In these and other areas (e.g., Orinoco lowlands, Brazilian highlands, Argentine Pampa), archeologists have tried to explain changes in terminal Pleistocene environments, technology, and subsistence practices into a coherent scene. Fieldwork in north-coastal Peru, for example, has conceptualized changes in systematic terms, with late Pleistocene and early Holocene climatic changes seen as homeostatic plateaus separated by brief episodes of more rapid organizational readjustments on the part of hunters and gatherers as they move toward greater socio-economic complexity (Lavallée 2000; Moseley 1992). Others have recognized lags in the transition to climatic amelioration (cf. Chauchat et al. 2003; Metivier 1998). Others have explained social networks and population movements as people adapting to changing cultural and climatic conditions (Dillehay et al. 2003a, 2003b). None of these studies fully addresses the discontinuous nature of archeological time and space gaps in both local and regional records and whether they are associated with social changes or short-term, climatic change and thus possible shifts in local resource structures. Current data cannot resolve these problems. Independently identifying environmental and human-population stressors on changing resource structures also remains problematic.

For the study of the terminal Pleistocene, human adaptations to climate change, site location and density, and stone-tool industries are arguably the most widely spread and best represented archeological databases. In the most general terms, interassemblage variability in stone artifacts across time and space is most heavily employed by archeologists to identify human mobility and economic practices (e.g., Aldenderfer 1999; Gnecco and Salgado 1989; Kipnis 1998; Salemme and Miotti 2003; Schmitz 1987). Faunal and floral records are also important, but they are not always well preserved in many early sites. Specifically, the interest is not so much in stone-tool technologies but what they imply about human population dynamics and whether people changed, as reflected in shifting technologies, when climates change. The basic notion in relating stone tools to mobility is that in a given landscape, more formal stone tools tend to be associated with mobile hunting and gathering adaptations, because such tools were highly reliable, maintainable, and transportable. More expedient or less formal stone tools, such as flakes and other unifaces, tend to be associated with collectors and an increasingly sedentary lifestyle. In some areas, there are recurring combinations of formal and/or informal tools associated with a subset of traits (e.g., ground stone tools, permanent structures, plant remains, and grinding stones) generally attributed to hunter-gatherer or collector lifestyles, respectively. The study of stone-tool industries and site locations do not provide enough data, however, to determine whether there were resource imbalances in a given area and whether changes in stone-tool technology represent responses to climate change or to technological and social innovations. As noted above, more local faunal and floral data and local reconstructions of past environments are needed to document whether technology and site location changes (or continuities) temporally correspond to climate change and to shifts in resource structures.

To provide a more specific and brief case of some of the above issues, the earliest records of stone-tool industries in the central Andes are best represented by the Fishtail and Paijan projectile-point industries, which are both roughly dated to the YD period. The former is slightly earlier (~13,000–12,300 cal BP: Dillehay 2000; Flegenheimer et al. 2006) and found throughout a wide variety of environments of South America, including the humid, dry grasslands of the Brazilian; Uruguyan and Argentine Pampas; the cooler and wetter grasslands of southern Patagonia; the arid foothills and desert coastal plains of the western Peruvian Andes; the high, cold, puna grasslands of northern Chile; and the humid highlands and subtropical lowlands of northwestern South America. Paijan is present primarily in both humid and dry highland and coastal areas of the north and central Andes and dates later (~12,800–11,400 cal BP: Dillehay et al. 2003a, 2003b). Differences between Fishtail and Paijan are striking in some areas. The latter is defined by points with concave stems and weak shoulders (like a fish tail) and occasionally a longitudinal thinning flake on the basal stem. Larger flakes were favored along with coarser rocks such as crystal and quartzite. No blade elements are currently known. Stemmed points with barbed shoulders, large scrapers, and long-backed, cutting tools (*limaces*) are among the few formal tools of Paijan. Both industry types occur in the same environmental settings on the north coast of Peru and at times in the same buried stratum in sites, indicating that the coexistence of and differences between these two industries cannot be explained by environmental factors, at least not by those identifiable on a regional and local level. Several regional variants have also been defined for both industries, mostly reflecting differences in the usage of raw material rather than more localized adaptations.

In some localities, research on a microlocal level of analysis can relate climatic and environmental change to specific stone-tool industries and human responses. For instance, between 12,000 and 11,200 cal BP, the compression of early Paijan and later people into several circumscribed habitats from the coastal plains to the western Andean slopes in the Zana and Jequetepeque valleys in northwestern Peru probably led to increased contact and promoted the later development of more complex social relationships (Chauchat et al. 2003; Dillehay et al. 2003a, 2003b; Moseley 1992). The pollen, staple isotope, and floral and faunal evidence from the valleys do not reflect a YD cooling in the area. However, there is archeological evidence that late Paijan groups began to decrease their mobility, aggregate, and establish more permanent camps at the edge of a dry, thorn forest near active springs and within equidistance of a desert coast to the west and a montane, humid forest to the east. These sites were highly localized as indicated by the presence of local lithic, raw material and by various floral and faunal foods indigenous to the dry forest. Later sites of the Las Pircas and early Tierra Blanca cultures, dated between around 11,000 and 7500 cal BP (Dillehay 2011), were associated with a more stable environment for people to prolong social contact and exchange, which led to enhanced conditions for population growth and greater cultural complexity. These developments are represented by the presence of large and numerous grinding stones, irrigation canals and crop production, and several permanent domestic structures forming small, aggregated foraging/horticultural communities. Though people still relied on foraging for some items during this period, the rich resources of the dry forest ecotone, combined with a few food crops (i.e., squash, peanuts, quinoa) allowed for a more settled way of life (Dillehay et al. 2007). During this period, several new, sociocultural traits were likely developed to handle more complex planning and decision making; risk management; resource sharing between different groups; and technological innovations. And this happened during the peak aridity of the South American hypsithermal between around 9500 and 6200 cal BP.

Summarizing the data from these two valleys, small-scale changes combining short-distance, environmental moves, development of irrigation and crop technologies, and continued reliance on some hunting and gathering in a specific ecotonal setting among various households of a small, aggregated community made significant advances and created the potential for change elsewhere. In this case, interdisciplinary research on a very specific and small scale environmental setting allowed archeologists to pinpoint specific human and environmental parameters as people not only adjusted to local climate changes over a long period of time, but they also transformed their social and economic practices to benefit from them (cf. Credou 2006). However, evidence shows that similar developments did not take place in neighboring areas, even some as close as 2–5 km within the two valleys, where similar suitable climatic and environmental conditions existed. Although we cannot point directly to climate changes as the catalysts for these social and cultural changes, there must have been choices and preferences by local communities in responding to them, with some deciding to change, others possibly deciding to move elsewhere, and others maintaining a status quo.

More poorly defined or less formal stone-tool industries occurred farther east and south on the continent (Aldenderfer 1999; Crevelli et al. 1996, 1997; Santoro 1989; Schmitz 1987), often making the relationship between these industries and environmental change even more difficult to ascertain. For instance, the Amazon basin continues to remain largely enigmatic, with few significant and well-documented early sites. Overall, the impression of early stone industries in many areas of the basin, as well as the Brazilian highlands and the Orinoco lowlands, is one of considerable expediency, though formal tools do become more common after 12,000 to 11,000 cal years ago (Dillehay 2000; Lavallée 2000). Portions of the lowland, tropical forests and other areas of South America where there also is no paleoecological evidence of a YD period, varying degrees of hunting and gathering persisted, despite many richly productive ecological areas and opportunities for more intensified hunting and plant manipulation (e.g., Borrero 2007; Johnson et al. 2007; Kipnis 1998; Núñez et al. 2002; Roosevelt et al. 1996).

Although some areas of the continent were abandoned, and settlement in others was sporadic, some regions offered the best ecological stability, and which supported large, persistent, human populations. Generally speaking, I believe that those people who lived closest to the northern and mid-latitude, Pacific and Atlantic coastlines and to the Equator may fit this scenario best, because oceanic variables and continental-wide rainfall and temperature changes, in these areas probably had the least effect on the environment. Further, many coastal areas probably provided year-round availability, if not abundance, of food sources. If equatorial rainforests are difficult for foragers to colonize

(Bailey and Headland 1991; see Colinvaux and Bush 1991 and Piperno and Pearsall 1998 for responses and further discussion), then the expansion of more open, mosaic forest, environments in the Amazon basin and neighboring tropical regions could have had the reverse effect on human settlement during the terminal Pleistocene period; not least because such environments probably favored the growth of key plant foods. The presence of forest and savanna environments in these regions also would have provided numerous ecotonal situations that would have been major attractions for sustaining human populations. Such settings may have been best for the exploitation of a wide variety of plant and animal biota. A widespread, enduring, human presence in these environments seems likely, but supportive archeological evidence is presently lacking. A few rockshelters and open-air sites are located near the margins and in the heart of the present-day Amazon forest and along major tributaries, but the data are too sparse to draw any conclusions (Kipnis 1998; Lopez 1999; Roosevelt et al. 1996).

Turning to a more specific exemplary area, the interior-central highlands of Brazil, recent studies have brought to light similar cultural characteristics and human and environmental interactions. Hunter-gatherers produced lithic industries focused on fine unifacial and a few bifacial tools and exploited a wide range of large and small modern-day faunal species during the terminal Pleistocene. However, in the subsequent early Holocene phase, the lithic industry was poorly developed and characterized by expedient, unifacial, stone tools. The diet also shifted from a primary dependency on game to terrestrial mollusks, small game species, fruits, and other plants (Prous 1991; Prous and Fogaca 1999). Similar patterns are observed in nearby regions (Bryan and Gruhn 1993; Kipnis 1998; Schmitz 1987). No megafaunal remains appear in sites. Many of these dietary and technological shifts are more directly related to profound environmental modifications in the region between 14,000 and 11,000 cal BP when there was a marked increase of humidity in a cool climate. There also seems to have been much seasonal movement by humans, which provided increased contact and sharing of technologies and other cultural traits.

In Patagonia, the Pampa of the southern cone, and northern tropics of the continent, as well as some pockets of the Andes, hunting and gathering also continued well into the historic period (Borrero 2007; Johnson et al. 2006; Salemme and Miotti 2002). In the Argentine grasslands, groups initially had broad-spectrum (but meat-based), subsistence patterns, but they later developed from generalized forager into specialized hunters. Not known is the extent to which changing climatic regimes influenced these shifts (Politis et al. 2003;

cf. Crivelli et al. 1997). Similar observations have been made in the high, puna grasslands of Peru and northern Chile (Santoro 1989). The evident similarities of stone-tool assemblages in Patagonia or in the Argentine pampas suggest that these areas formed parts of broad regional interaction networks that stretched across many shifting environments and climates in the terminal Pleistocene. Not yet studied is what these cross-cutting networks say about YD period climate change and its impact on human developments. Defining more connections and patterns requires much more sustained fieldwork to complement the scattered observations currently available.

Ideally speaking, the best test for human and environmental interactions during the YD period is in the Neotropical region of northern South America where there are some hints in the paleoecological record of a slight cooling event (Grabandt 1980; Van Veer et al. 2000). However, so few systematically excavated sites of the terminal Pleistocene exists in the lowland tropics of Colombia, Venezuela, and Guyanas that it is highly speculative to comment on such interactions at his time (cf. Ardila and Politis 1989; Dillehay 2000; Jaimes 1999). The northern Neotropics are particularly important, because some of the earliest documented cultigens appear in archeological sites dated around 11,500 cal BP in Ecuador and perhaps slightly later in Colombia (Piperno and Stothert 2003). Not understood are the specific climatic and environmental conditions under which plant domestication occurred in this region.

Plant Manipulation and Climates

The availability of plants and animals must have been altered considerably throughout the Pleistocene and Holocene transition. But at this time depth, only infrequent evidence of plant consumption survives in the archeological record. At least in favorable localities, appreciable use of certain technologies seems to have been made of plant foods, including the domestication of squash (*Cucurbita moschata*) and possibly other plants by 11,500 cal BP (Piperno 2006; Piperno and Stothert 2003). The regularity of the spread and the degree to which domestication and adoption largely resulted from cultural diffusion as opposed to the dispersion of human populations and to what extent climate change spurred these developments are not known. The use of plant foods and technologies over the span of time and at selected localities set the stage for later, successive waves of development of agriculture in the early to middle Holocene and the rapid appearance of towns and pyramid societies by 7,000 cal years ago (Lavallée 2000; Moseley 1992).

Once climates became stabilized after ~12,000 to 11,000 cal years ago, many human populations shifted to long-distance exchange relations that afforded opportunities for more social and economic development beyond simple hunting and gathering, especially in the northern and central Andes and in the eastern tropical lowlands. Given the early development of complex societies in South America, with specific reference to the presence of semisedentary to sedentary lifestyles by 11,000 to 9500 cal BP in parts of the central Andes (Lavellée 2000; Moseley 1992), we should look more specifically to the importance of early plant manipulation and early human-induced landscape modification (e.g., forest clearance, introduction of new plants and animals to environments). The processes involved in the origins of agriculture (and of sedentism), mainly viewed here as subsistence intensification, are many and complex. The domestication, spread, and adoption of crops must have been patchy and sporadic across many northern and central tropical to semitropical latitudes in the continent where many domesticates were probably first developed (Dillehay 2011; Piperno 2006); but it is not known whether social or climatic factors determined these patterns. However, there is evidence for the long-term persistence of foraging alongside the use of domesticates in Colombia and Ecuador (Piperno 2006; Piperno and Stothert 2003) and in Peru (Dillehay et al. 2008), and there seems little reason to suppose that elsewhere in South America similar events were not taking place, although hunting and gathering did not give way to agricultural systems in some areas of the southern cone until much later.

On a global scale, most authors have pointed to climate change, coevolution of human subsistence strategies, plant and animal domesticates, population pressures, and the combination of these and other correlates as explanatory variables related to the rise of social complexity. As noted by Richerson et al. (2001; cf. Balter 2007), much of our recent understanding of these processes is derived from the historical details of particular localized archeological and paleoecological cases. Thinking primarily of the northern hemisphere, Richerson and his colleagues have proposed that agriculture was impossible during the Last Glacial Maximum, and in the long run, was compulsory in the early to middle Holocene. Their belief is that because agricultural subsistence systems are vulnerable to weather extremes, and because the cultural evolution of the specialized use of plant resources probably occurred relatively slow, agriculture could not have evolved during the variable, cool, and dry YD climates of the terminal Pleistocene in the northern latitudes. In contrast, stable, early to middle Holocene climates allowed the development of agriculture in vast areas with relatively warm, wet climates.

This was not necessarily the case in South America where deglaciation appears to have occurred slightly earlier than in North America, and where warm, stable climates characterized many areas by 15,000–13,000 cal BP, and where broad-spectrum economies were practiced at least by 12,500 cal BP (Bryan 1973; Dillehay 1999, 2000; León 2007; Piperno 2006). In terminal Pleistocene times, when climate conditions were generally warm and stable, deliberate plant manipulation seems to have been underway in a few areas, primarily in the Neotropics and the northern and central Andes (Piperno 2006). The best documented examples of plant domestication are the presence of at least two varieties of squashes in Colombia, Ecuador, and Peru by 11,300 cal BP (Dillehay et al. 2008; Piperno et al. 2004) and the use of palm nuts and other plants in Colombia by 10,500 cal BP (Gnecco and Aceituno 2006; Lopez 1999). Macrobotanical and microbotanical evidence from lower Central America, Colombia, and Ecuador indicate that human manipulation of Neotropical plant species—including squash, gourd, arrowroot, manioc, lerén, yam, and probably maize—likely led to their domestication between 11,200 and 8000 cal BP. In eastern Brazil, palm nuts are present in sites as early as 11,500 cal BP (Kipnis 1998).

In addition to the Neotropical areas mentioned above, in the Zana Valley (Dillehay et al. 2003a, 2003b, 2007), the adoption of cultigens took place during the terminal YD and intensified in early to middle Holocene times. From 10,500 to 8700 cal BP, increased crop production occurred in the valley during the hypsithermal's peak period of aridity, which has been documented in other regions of South America as well (Piperno 2006; Piperno and Pearsall 1998). However, local paleoecological data from the valley do not reflect a period of severe aridity associated with the hypsithermal. Instead, a warm, stable environment existed, suggesting that the area was largely unaffected by excessive warming. This may not be the case for other small-scale, localized, gardening groups in other parts of the Andes and South America. It is probable that some groups shifted in and out of an increased reliance on plants as they found themselves in climatic crises, subsistence crises, and/or social crises. It also is probable that social conditions, such as settlement aggregation, shared inventions, and cultural transmission, were important factors determining economic and dietary choices. In these and other cases, terminal Pleistocene hunter-gatherers apparently solved complex nutritional and scheduling problems associated with nondomesticated plant rich diets by continuing to rely on animals and, in some cases, a few cultivated plants while coping with any short-term, climatic changes.

In sum, the bottom line is regardless of favorable or unfavorable climatic patterns, there is no doubt that people were manipulating certain species of plants in various areas of the continent during the terminal Pleistocene. We must remember, however, that plant-food diets took considerable amounts of time to develop and adapt, and probably were not very cost effective at first, thus prompting most groups to continue a foraging lifestyle well into the middle Holocene period. Further, the long timeframe of most climatic changes may not be directly relevant to the origins and spread of agriculture, because they occurred so slowly compared to the likely more rapid rate at which humans were adapting through sociocultural mechanisms. However, regional short-term, climatic changes (e.g., excessive drought, El Nino flooding) may have been relevant, but they are currently difficult to identify and correlate in local archeological and paleoecological records.

Extinction and Animal Domestication

In many parts of the world, the late Pleistocene witnessed a wave of large mammal extinctions, an event that has provoked much debate over the relative causes for it, such as human hunting, anthropogenic landscape change, and climate (cf. Barnosky et al. 2004; Grayson and Meltzer 2003; Martin and Klein 1984). South America experienced extinctions across the Pleistocene and Holocene transition. The role of climate change in the extinction of some large mammals and the survival of others well into the Holocene period is not well understood in South America. In Argentina, for instance, there is evidence to suggest that some large animals survived in the early Holocene era (Hubbe et al. 2007).

From the perspective of faunal records across the continent, the period immediately after the YD witnessed a shift in many areas toward a diet in which hunting smaller game became more important, but much variability is apparent among sites and regions (cf. Bonavia 1991; Lavallée 2000; Moseley 1992). Increased exploitation of more predictable animals present in larger numbers but smaller packages, such as guanaco and deer, occurred on the puna grasslands of Peru, Bolivia, and Chile and in the Pampa and Patagonian grasslands of the southern cone. Early sites along the Peruvian and Chilean coasts show intensive shellfish, fish, sea mammals, and seabird exploitation beginning around 13,000 cal BP, but this probably reflects coastline regression as much as new patterns of hunting and foraging behavior (cf. Jackson et al. 2007; Keefer et al. 1998; Lavallée et al. 1999; Sandweiss et al. 1998). Similar but later developments occurred along the Atlantic coast as well (Kipnis 1998).

Evidence also shows that early Andean people experimented with controlling and manipulating wild camelids and other animals (e.g., guinea pigs). The more controversial evidence comes from the puna or high grasslands of Peru where a number of researchers (Wheeler in Lavallée et al. 1985; cf. Bonavia 1996; Lavallée et al. 1985; Rick 1981; Yacobaccio 1995) argue for the transition from specialized hunting to incipient domestication of camelids from terminal Pleistocene to middle Holocene times, primarily based on settlement data and faunal remains. Other studies have attempted to demonstrate early camelid domestication on the basis of changing bone morphologies in various species of camelids (e.g., Wheeler 1988). No studies, however, show convincing signs of morphological change in camelid bones and skeletons consequent upon exploitation and steps toward domestication in terminal Pleistocene and early Holocene times (Bonavia 1996). Arguments that domestication occurred in the early Holocene are largely ecological ones. However, hunters and incipient pastoralists could have changed the behavior of animals by herding them into opportunistic grazing areas or corrals (Nunez and Dillehay 1979).

Conclusions

There is little to no major paleoecological evidence that the cool, dry, YD period of the northern hemisphere occurred at the same scale and with the same intensity in the southern hemisphere; but if it did, it seems to have had less impact on the adaptive patterns of early South Americans than it did on people in the northern latitudes. Continental climates ameliorated relatively quickly from 18,000 to 15,000 cal years ago, and this amelioration may have been punctuated in some places by a YD stadial in high altitudes of the Andes and perhaps elsewhere. Once this period terminated, around 12,000 cal years ago, temperature and rainfall increased significantly in some areas, forests expanded in many areas, and people settled more regularly into previously drier and inhospitable lands. Limited but locally important loses of land to rising seas, the extinction of some large mammals, and the cultivation of some plants suggest that the change to a warmer, wetter climate around 12,000 cal BP may have been positive in many areas. Associated with these and other climatic and environmental shifts were human migration, abandonment and resettlement, possibly sedentism, subsistence change, and technological continuity and discontinuity throughout South America.

At present, it is difficult to correlate specific types of human adaptations, such as sedentism and broad-spectrum diets or high mobility and big-game hunting, to specific types of climatic and environmental patterns. As noted at the outset, paradoxes exist in the proxy records whereby favorable and staple environments were associated with prolonged high mobility of hunter-gatherer and unsuitable environments were related to advanced hunter-gatherers and incipient horticulturalists. As more detailed knowledge of the continent's paleoenvironments and first inhabitants is built up, more detailed understandings of these phenomena will be possible.

References

Ackert, R., Jr., R. Becker, B. Singer, M. Kurz, M. Caffee, and D. Mickelson
  2008 Patagonian Glacier Response During the Late Glacial-Holocene Transition. *Science* 321:392–395.

Aldenderfer, M.
  1999 The Pleistocene/Holocene Transition in Peru and its Effects upon Human use of the Landscape. *Quaternary International* 53–54:11–19.

Ardila, G., and G. Politis
  1989 Nuevos Datos para un Viejo Problema: Investigacion y Discussion en turno del Poblamiento de America del Sur. *Revista de Museo del Oro* 23:2–45.

Ariztegui, D., M. Bianchi, J. Masaferro, E. Lafargue, and F. Niessen
  1997 Interhemispheric Synchrony of Late-glacial Climatic as Recorded in Proglacial Lake Mascardi, Argentina. *Journal of Quaternary Sciences* 12:333–338.

Aschero, C.
  2000 El Poblamiento del Territorio. In *Nueva Historia Argentina*, Tomo 1, edited by M. Tarrago, pp. 19–59. Editorial Sudamericana, Buenos Aires.

Bailey, R., and T. Headland
  1991 The Tropical Rain Forest: Is it a Productive Environment for Human Foragers? *Human Ecology* 19:261–285.

Baker, P., G. Seltzer, S. Fritz, R. Dunbar, M. Grove, P. Tapia, S. Cross, H. Rowe, and J. Broda
  2001 The History of South American Tropical Precipitation for the Past 25,000 Years. *Science* 291:640–643.

Balter, M.
  2007 Seeking Agriculture's Ancient Roots. *Science* 29:1830–1835.

Barnosky, A., M. Kaplan, and M. Carrasco
  2004 Assessing the Effect of Middle Pleistocene Climate Change on Marmota Populations from the Pit Locality. In *Biodiversity Response to Climate Change in the Middle Pleistocene: The Porcupine Cave Fauna from Colorado*, edited by A. Barnosky, pp. 332–340. University of California Press, Berkeley.

Behling, H., H. Arz, J. Patzold, and G. Wefer
  2002 Late Quaternary Vegetation and Climate Dynamics in Southeastern Brazil: Inferences from Marine Cores GeoB-3229-2 and GeoB-3202-1. *Palaeogeography, Palaeoclimatology, Palaeoecology* 179:227–243.

Behling, H., V. Pillar, L. Orloci, and S. Bauermann

2005 Late Quaternary Grassland (Campos), Gallery Forest, Fire and Climate Dynamics, Studied by Pollen, Charcoal and Multivariate Analysis of the Sao Francisco de Assis core in Western Rio Grande do Sul (southern Brazil). *Review of Paleobotany and Palynology* 133:235–248.

Bennett, K., S. Haberle, and S. Lumley

2000 The Last Glacial-Holocene Transition in Southern Chile. *Science* 290:325–328.

Binford, L.

1980 Willow Smoke and Dog's Tails: Hunter-gatherer Site Systems and Archeological Site Formation. *American Antiquity* 45:4–20.

Blunier, T., J. Chappellaz, J. Schwander, A. Dällenbach, B. Stauffer, T. Stocker, D. Raynaud, J. Jouzel, H. Clausen, C. Hammer, and S. Johnsen

1998 Asynchrony of Antarctic and Greenland Climate Change during the Last Glacial Period. *Nature* 394:739–743.

Bonavia, D.

1991 *Peru: Hombre e Historia de los Origenes al Siglo XV*. Edubanco, Lima.

1996 *Los Camélidos Sudamericanos: Una Introducción a su Estudio*. IFEA, Lima.

2008 *South American Camelids*. Cotsen Institute of Archaeology, University of California, Los Angeles.

Borrero, L.

1999 The Prehistoric Exploration and Colonization of Fuego-Patagonia. *Journal of World Prehistory* 13:321–355.

2007 Paleoindians without Mammoths and Archaeologists without Projectile Points? The Archaeology of the First Inhabitants of the Americas. In *Paleoindian Archaeology: A Hemispheric Perspective*, edited by J. Morrow and C. Gnecco, pp. 9–20. University Press of Florida, Gainesville.

Bradley, R. J.

1999 *Paleoclimatology: Reconstructing Climate of the Quaternary*. Harcourt/ Academic Press, San Diego.

Bryan, A.

1973 Paleoenvironments and Cultural Diversity in Late Pleistocene South America. *Quaternary Research* 3:237–256.

Bryan, A., and R. Gruhn

1993 *Archeological Investigations in Six Caves or Rockshelter in Interior Bahía, Brazil*. Brazilian Studies, University of Oregon, Crovalle.

2003 Some Difficulties in Modeling the Original Peopling of the Americas. *Quaternary International* 109–110:175–179.

Bush, M.
1991 Modern Pollen-rain Data from South and Central America: A Test of the Feasability of Fine-resolution Lowland Tropical Palynology. *The Holocene* 1:162–167.
2005 Of Orogeny, Precipitation, Precession, and Parrots. *Journal of Biogeography* 32:1301–1302.

Bush, M., and J. Flenley (editors)
2006 *Tropical Rainforest Responses to Climatic Change*. Springer, Berlin.

Bush, M., W. Gosling, and P. Colinvaux
2006a Climate Change in the Lowlands of the Amazon Basin. In *Tropical Rainforest Responses to Climatic Change*, edited by M. Bush and J. Flenley, pp. 55–76. Springer, Berlin.

Bush, M., J. Hanselmann, and H. Hooghiemstra
2006b Andean Montane Forests and Climate Change. In *Tropical Rainforest Responses to Climatic Change*, edited by M. Bush and J. Flenley, pp. 55–76. Springer, Berlin.

Bush, M., B. Hansen, D. Rodbell, G. Seltzer, K. Young, B. León, M. Silman, M. Abbott, and W. Gosling
2005 A 17,000 Year History of Andean Climatic and Vegetation Change from Laguna de Chochos, Peru. *Journal of Quaternary Science* 20:703–714.

Bush, M., M. Listopad, and M. Silman
2007 A Regional Study of Holocene Climate Change and Human Occupation in Peruvian Amazonia. *Journal of Biogeography* 34:1342–1356.

Bush, M., M. Silman, and U. Dunia
2004 48,000 Years of Climate and Forest Change in a Biodiversity Hot Spot. *Science* 303:827–829.

Chauchat, C., J. Pelegrin, C. Mora, R. Becerra, and R. Esquerre (editors)
2003 *Projectile Point Technology and Economy: A Case Study of Paijan, North Coastal Peru*. Texas A&M University Press, College Station.

Clapperton, C.
1993 *Quaternary Geology and Geomorphology of South America*. Elsevier, Amsterdam.

Clapperton, C., M. Hall, P. Mothes, M. Hole, J. Still, K. Helmens, P. Kuhry, and A. Gemmell
1997 Younger Dryas Icecap in the Equatorial Andes. *Quaternary Research* 47:13–28.

Colinvaux, P., and M. Bush
1991 The Rain-forest Ecosystem as a Resource for Hunting and Gathering. *American Anthropologist* 93:153–160.

Colinvaux, P., G. Irion, M. Rasanen, M. Bush, and J. de Mello
2001 A Paradigm to be Discarded: Geological and Paleoecological Data Falsify the Haffer and Prance Refuge Hypothesis of *Amazonian* Speciation. *Amazoniana* 16:609–646.

Correal, U.
1986 Apuntes Sobre el Medio Ambiente Pleistocénico Andino y el Hombre Prehistórico en Columbia. In *New Evidence from the Pleistocene Peopling of the Americas*, edited by A. Bryan, pp. 115–131. Center for the Study of Early Man, University of Maine, Orono.

Credou, J.
2006 *Resources Marines et Subsistance des Paijániens à la Transition Pléistocène-Holocène (Désert du Cupisnique Pérou)*. Mémoire de master 2. Direction P. Bearez. Spécialité: Préhistoire et Quaternaire. Museum de Histoire Naturelle de Paris, Paris.

Crivelli, E., E. Eugenio, U. Pardiñas, and M. Silveira
1997 Archaeological Investigation in the Plains of the Province of Buenos Aires, Llanura Interserrana Bonaerense. *Quaternary of South America and Antarctic Penninsula* 10:167–207.

Crivelli, E., U. Pardiñas, M. Fernández, M. Bogazzi, A. Chauvin, V. Fernandez, and M. Lezcano
1997 Cueva Epullán Grande (Pcia. Del Neuquén): Informe de avance. *Praehistoria* 2:185–265.

De Deckker, P.
2003 Late Quaternary Cyclic Aridity in Tropical Australia. *Palaeogeography, Palaeoclimatology, and Palaeoecology* 70:1–9.

Dillehay, T. D.
1999 The Late Pleistocene Cultures of South America. *Evolutionary Anthropology* 7:206–216.

2000 *The Settlement of the Americas: A New Prehistory*. Basic Books, New York.

2011 *From Foraging to Farming in the Andes*. Cambridge University Press, Cambridge.

Dillehay, T. D., G. Ardila, G. Politis, and M. Beltrão
1992 Earliest Hunters and Gatherers of South America. *Journal of World Prehistory* 6:145–204.

Dillehay, T. D., J. Rossen, G. Magaard, K. Stackelbeck, and P. Netherly
2003a Localization and Possible Social Aggregation in the Late Pleistocene and Early Holocene on the North Coast of Peru. *Quaternary International* 109–110:3–11.

Dillehay, T. D., J. Rossen, P. Netherly, G. Magaard, and K. Stackelbeck
2003b New Evidence of the Paijan Culture on the North Coast of Peru and its Importance in Early Andean Prehistory. In *Where the South Winds Blow: Ancient Evidence of Paleo South Americans*, edited by L. Miotti, M. Salemme, and N. Flegenheimmer, pp. 13–15. Center for the Study of the First Americans, Texas A&M University, College Station.

Dillehay, T. D., J. Rossen, T. Andres, and D. Williams
2007 Preceramic Adoption of Peanut, Squash and Cotton in Northern Peru. *Science* 316:1890–93.

Dillehay, T. D., C. Ramirez, M. Pino, M. Collins, J. Rossen, and D. Pino–Navarro
2008 Monte Verde: Seaweeds, Food, and Medicine and the Peopling of the Americas. *Science* 325:1287–1289.

Dornbusch, U.
2002 Pleistocene and Present Day Snowlines Rise in the Cordillera Ampato, Western Cordillera, Southern Peru (15°15´?15°45´ S and 77°30´?77°15´ W). *Neues Jahrbuch fuer Geologie und Palaeontologie Abhandlungen* 225:103–126.

Flegenheimer, N., C. Bayon, and A. Pupio
2006 *Llegar a un Nuevo Mundo: La Arqueologia de los Primeros Pobladores del Actual Territorio Argentino.* Museo y Archivo Historico Municipal, Bahia Blanca.

Gamble, C.
1999 *The Paleolithic Societies of Europe.* Cambridge University Press, Cambridge.

García, A.
2003 *Los Primeros Pobladores de los Andes Centrales Argentinos.* Zeta Editores, Mendoza.

Gnecco, C., and J. Aceituno
2006 Early Humanized Landscapes in Northern South America. In *Paleoindian Archaeology: A Hemispheric Perspective*, edited by J. Morrow and C. Gnecco, pp. 86–104. University Press of Florida, Gainesville.

Gnecco, C., and H. Salgado
1989 Adaptaciones Pre–cerámicas en el Suroccidente de Colombia. *Boletín del Museo del Oro* 24:35–55.

Goodman, A., D. Rodbell, G. Seltzer, and B. Mark
2001 Subdivision of Glacial Deposits in Southeastern Peru Based on Pedogenic Development and Radiometric Ages. *Quaternary Research* 56:31–50.

Grabandt, R.
1980 *Pollen Rain in Relation to Vegetation in the Colombian Cordillera Oriental.* University of Amsterdam, Amsterdam.

Grayson, D., and D. Meltzer
2003 A Requiem for North American Overkill. *Journal of Archaeological Science* 30:585–593.

Haffer, J., and G. Prance
2001 Climatic Forcing of Evolution in Amazonia during the Cenozoic: On the Refuge Theory of Biotic Differentiation. *Amazoniana* 16:579–608.

Haug, G., K. Hughen, D. Sigman, L. Peterson, and U. Röhl
2001 Southward Migration of the Intertropical Convergence Zone through the Holocene. *Science* 293:1304–1308.

Heusser, C.
2003 *Ice Age Southern Andes: A Chronicle of Paleoecological Events.* Elsevier, Amsterdam.

Heusser, C., and J. Rabassa
1987 Cold Climate Episode of Younger Dryas Age in Tierra del Fuego. *Nature* 328:609–611.

Hill, K., and A. Hurtado
1996 *Ache Life History: The Ecology and Demography of a Foraging People.* Aldine Press, New York.

Hubbe, A., M. Hubbe, and W. Neves
2007 Early Holocene Survival of Megafauna in South America. *Journal of Biogeography* 34:1642–1646.

Jackson, D., C. Méndez, R. Seguel, A. Maldonado, and G. Vargas
2007 Initial Occupation of the Pacific Coast of Chile during Late Pleistocene Times. *Current Anthropology* 48:725–731.

Jaimes, A.
1999 Nuevas Evidencias de Cazadores-recolectores y Aproximación al Entendimiento del uso del Espacio Geográfico en el Noroccidente de Venezuela: Sus Implicaciones en el Contexto Sudamericano. *Arqueología del Área Intermedia* 1:83–120.

Johnson, E., G. Politis, M. Gutierrez, G. Martínez, and L. Miotti
2006 Grassland Archaeology in the Americas: From the U. S. Southern Plains to the Argentinian Pampas. In *Paleoindian Archaeology: A Hemispheric Perspective*, edited by J. Morrow and C. Gnecco, pp. 44–68. University Press of Florida, Gainesville.

Keefer, D., S. de France, M. Moseley, J. Richardson III, D. Satterlee, and A. Day-Lewis
1998 Early Maritime Economy and El Niño Events at Quebrada Tacahuay. *Science* 281:1833–1835.

Kelly, R.
1995 *The Foraging Spectrum: Diversity in Hunter-gather Lifeways.* Smithsonian Institution Press, Washington, D.C.

Kipnis, R.
1998 Early Hunter-Gatherers in the Americas: Perspectives from Central Brazil. *Antiquity* 72:581–592.

Lavallée, D.
2000 *The First South Americans.* University of Utah Press, Salt Lake City.

Lavallée, D., M. Julien, P. Béarez, P. Usselmann, M. Fontugne, and A. Bolaños
1999 Pescadores-recolectores Arcaicos del Extremo Sur Peruano. Excavaciones en la Quebrada de los Burros (Tacna, Perú). Primeros Resultados 1995–1997. *Bulletin de l'Institut Français d'Études Andines* 28:13–52.

Lavallée, D., M. Julien, J. Wheeler, and C. Karlin
1985 *Telarmachay Chasseurs et Pasteurs Préhistoriques des Andes-I. Tome I & II. Synthèse 20. Éditions Recherche surles Civilisations.* Institut Français des Études Andines, Paris.

León Canales, E.
2007 *Orígenes Humanos en los Andes del Perú.* Universidad San Martín de Porres, Lima.

Lopez, C.
1999 *Ocupaciones Tempranas en las Tierras Bajas Tropicales del Valle Medio del Rio Magdalena, Sitio 05-YON-002, Yondó-antioquia.* FIAN, Bogota.

Lovell, T., and M. Kelly
2008 Was the Younger Dryas Global? *Science* 321:348–349.

Maggard, G.
2009 Late Pleistocene Colonization and Regionalization in South America: Fishtail and Paijan Settlement Patterns on the North Coast of Peru. Unpublished Ph.D. dissertation, Department of Anthropology, University of Kentucky, Lexington.

Markgraf, V.
1991 Younger Dryas in Southern South America? *Boreas* 20:63–69.
1993 Climatic History of Central and South America since 18000 yr BP: Comparison of Pollen Records and Model Simulations. In *Global Climates since the Last Glacial Maximum*, edited by H. Wright, Jr., J. Kutzbach, T. Webb III, and W. Ruddiman, pp. 357–385. University of Minnesota Press, Minneapolis.

Martin, P., and R. Klein
1984 *Quaternary Extinctions*. University of Arizona Press, Tucson.

Massone, M.
2005 *Los Cazadores Después del Hielo*. Centro Diego Barros Arana, Santiago.

Mayle, F., and D. Beerling
2004 Late Quaternary Changes in Amazonian Ecosystems and Their Implications for Global Carbon Cycling. *Palaeogeography, Palaeoclimatology, Palaeoecology* 204:11–24.

Mayle, F., D. Beerling, W. Gosling, and M. Bush
2004 Responses of Amazonian Ecosystems to Climatic and Atmospheric Carbon Dioxide Changes since the Last Glacial Maximum. *Philosophical Transactions of the Royal Society of London B* 359:499–514.

Mayle, F., and L. Cwynar
1995 A Review of Multi-proxy Data for the Younger Dryas in Atlantic Canada. *Quaternary Science Reviews* 14:813–821.

McCulloch, R., M. Bentley, R. Purves, N. Hulton, D. Sugden, and C. Clapperton
2000 Climatic Inferences from Glacial and Palaeoecological Evidence at the Last Glacial Termination in Southern South America. *Journal of Quaternary Sciences* 15:409–417.

McGlone, M.
1995 Late Glacial Landscape and Vegetation Changes and the Younger Dryas: Climatic Oscillations in New Zealand. *Quaternary Science Review* 14:867–881.

Metivier, S.
1998 *A Reconstruction of Glacial Extent, Temperature and Precipitation in South America at the Time of the Last Glacial Maximum*. Master's thesis, Syracuse University, Syracuse.

Miotti, L., and M. Salemme
2004 Problamiento, Movilidad y Territories Entre las Sociedades Cazadores-recolectoras de Patagonia. *Complutum* 15:177–206.

Moreno, P.
2004 Millennial-scale Climate Variability in Northwest Patagonia over the Last 15,000 yr. *Journal of Quaternary Science* 19:35–47.

Moreno, P., G. Jacobson, T. Lowell, and G. Denton
2001 Interhemispheric Climate Links Revealed from a Late Glacial Cool Episode in Southern Chile. *Nature* 409:804–808.

Moreno, P., and A. Leon
2003 Abrupt Vegetation Changes during the Last Glacial-Holocene Transition in Mid-latitude South America. *Journal of Quaternary Science* 18:787–800.

Moseley, M.
1992 *The Inca and Their Ancestors*. Thames and Hudson, London.

Nunez, L., and T. D. Dillehay
1979 *Movilidad Giratoria y Armonia Social: El Desarollo SocioEconomico PreHispanico en los Andes Merionales*. Universidad Norte de Chile and the Museo Arqueologico de San Pedro de Atacama. Antofagasta, Chile.

Núñez, L., M. Grosjean, and I. Cartajena
2002 Human Occupations and Climate Change in the Puna de Atacama, Chile. *Science* 298:821–824.

Paduano, G., M. Bush, P. Baker, S. Fritz, and G. Seltzer
2003 A Vegetation and Fire History of Lake Titicaca since the Last Glacial Maximum. *Palaeogeography, Paleoclimatology, Palaeoecology* 194:259–279.

Piperno, D.
2006 The Origins of Plant Cultivation and Domestication in the Neotropics: A Behavioral Ecological Perspective. In *Foraging Theory and the Transition to Agriculture*, edited by D. Kennett and B. Winterhalder, pp. 137–166. University of California Press, Berkeley.

Piperno, D., and D. Pearsall
1998 *The Origins of Agriculture in the Lowland Neotropics*. Academic Press, San Diego.

Piperno, D., and K. Stothert
2003 Phytolith Evidence for Early Holocene Cucurbita Domestication in Southwest Ecuador. *Science* 299:1054–1057.

Piperno, D., E. Weiss, I. Holst, and D. Nadel
2004 Processing of Wild Cereal Grains during the Upper Paleolithic Revealed by Starch Grain Analysis. *Nature* 430:670–673.

Politis, G.
2007 *Nukak: Ethnoarchaeology of an Amazonian People*. Publications of the Institute of Archaeology, University of London.

Politis, G., E. Johnson, M. Gutierrez, and W. Hartwell
2003 Survival of Pleistocene Fauna: New Radiocarbon Dates on Organic Sediments from La Moderna (Pampean Region, Argentina). In *Where the South Winds Blow: Ancient Evidence of Paleo South Americans*, edited by L. Miotti, M. Salemme, and N. Flegenheimer, pp. 45–50. Center for the Study of the First Americans, Texas A&M University, College Station.

Prieto, A.
1996 Late Quaternary Vegetational and Climatic Changes in the Pampa Grassland of Argentina. *Quaternary Research* 49:129–148.

Prous, A.
1991 Les Fouilles de la Lapa do Boquete. *Journal de la Societe des Americanistes* 77:77–109.

Prous, A., and E. Fogaca
1999 Archaeology of the Pleistocene-Holocene Boundary in Brazil. *Quaternary International* 53/54:21–41.

Quattrocchio, M., A. Borromei, and S. Grill
1995 Cambios Vegetacionales y Fluctaciones Paleoclimaticos Durante el Pleistoceno Tardio-Holoceno en el Sureste de la Provincial de Buenos Aires (Argentina). *Actas del VI Congreso Argentino de Paleonotologia y Bioestratigrafia*, pp. 221–229. Trelew.

Richerson, P., R. Boyd, and R. Bettinger
2001 Was Agriculture Impossible during the Pleistocene but Mandatory during the Holocene? A Climate Change Hypothesis. *American Antiquity* 66:387–411.

Rick, J.
1981 *Prehistoric Hunters of the High Andes.* Academic Press, New York.

Rodbell, D.
2000 The Younger Dryas: Cold, Cold Everywhere? *Science* 290:285–286.

Rodbell, D., and G. Seltzer
2000 Rapid Ice Margin Fluctuations during the Younger Dryas in the Tropical Andes. *Quaternary Research* 54:328–338.

Roosevelt, A., M. Lima da Costa, C. Lopes Machado, M. Michnab, N. Mercier, H. Vallada, J. Feathers, W. Barnet, M. Imazio da Silveira, A. Henderson, J. Silva, B. Chernoff, D. Reese, J. Holman, N. Toth, and K. Schick
1996 Paleoindian Cave Dwellers in the Amazon: The Peopling of the Americas. *Science* 272:373–384.

Salemme, M., and L. Miotti (editors)
2002 South America: Long and Winding Roads for the First Americans at the Pleistocene/Holocene Transition. *Quaternary International* 109–110:1–179.

Sandweiss, D., H. McInnis, R. Burger, A. Cano, B. Ojeda, R. Paredes, M. Sandweiss, and D. Glascock
1998 Quebrada Jaguay: Early South American Maritime Adaptations. *Science* 281:1830–1832.

Santoro, C.
1989 Antiguos Cazadores de la Puna (9.000 a 6.000 A.C.). In *Culturas de Chile: Prehistoria, Desde sus Orígenes Hasta los Albores de a Conquista*, edited by J. Hidalgo, pp. 33–55. Editorial Andrés Bello, Santiago.

Schmitz, P.
1987 Prehistoric Hunters and Gatherers of Brazil. *Journal of World Prehistory* 1:53–126.

Seltzer, G., and D. Rodbell

2005 Delta Progradation and Neoglaciation, Laguna Parón, Cordillera Blanca, Perú. *Journal of Quaternary Science* 20:715–722.

Seltzer, G., D. Rodbell, P. Baker, S. Fritz, P. Tapia, H. Rowe, and R. Dunbar

2002a Early Deglaciation in the Tropical Andes. *Science* 298:1685–1686.

2002b Early Warming of Tropical South America at the Last Glacial-interglacial Transition. *Science* 296:1685–1687.

Stocker, T.

1998 The Seesaw Effect. *Science* 282:61–62.

Thompson, L., M. Davis, E. Mosely-Thompson, T. Sowers, K. Henderson, V. Zagorodnov, P-N Lin, V. Mikhalenko, R. Campen, J. Bolzan, J. Cole-Dai, and B. Francou

1998 A 25,000-year Tropical Climate History from Bolivian Ice Cores. *Science* 282:1858–1864.

Thompson, L., E. Mosley-Thompson, M. Davis, P-N Lin, K. Henderson, J. Cole-Dai, J. Bolzan, and K. Liu

1995 Last Glacial Stage and Holocene Tropical Ice Core Records from Huascarán, Peru. *Science* 269:46–50.

Van der Hammen, T., and H. Hooghiemstra

1995 The El Abra Stadial: A Younger Dryas Equivalent in Colombia. *Quaternary Science Reviews* 14:841–851.

Van Veer, R., G. Islebe, and H. Hooghiemstra

2000 Climatic Change during the Younger Dryas Chron in Northern South America: A Test of the Evidence. *Quaternary Science Reviews* 19:1821–1835.

Vialou, Á.

2005 *Pré-história do Mato Grosso, Volume 1: Santa Elina.* Editora da Universidade São Paulo, São Paulo.

Villagrán, C.

2001 Un Modelo de la Historia de la Vegetación de la Cordillera de la Costa de Chile Central-sur: La Hipótesis Glacial de Darwin. *Revista Chilena de Historia Natural* 74:793–803.

Weng, C., M. Bush, and M. Silman

2004 An Analysis of Modern Pollen Rain on an Elevational Gradient in Southern Peru. *Journal of Tropical Ecology* 20:113–124.

Wheeler, J.

1988 *Origin and Evolution of the South American Camelidae.* Western Veternarian Conference, Las Vegas.

Yacobaccio, H.

1995 Biomasa Animal y Consume en el Pleistoceno-Holoceno sur Andino. *Arqueología* 4:43–71.

3

THE HUMAN COLONIZATION OF THE HIGH ANDES AND SOUTHERN SOUTH AMERICA DURING THE COLD PULSES OF THE LATE PLEISTOCENE

Luis Alberto Borrero

Introduction

When the process of human dispersal into the Americas during the Pleistocene is analyzed, one of the first considerations is whether the timing of human movement co-varies with climatic phases. It is known that the expansion into areas north of Siberia probably occurred during warm pulses before the Last Glacial Maximum (Goebel et al. 2008). The first humans moving into North America, on the other hand, experienced very dramatic climatic instability in Beringia, including cold and warm phases (Clague et al. 2004). However, archaeological evidence suggests that the proliferation of people in North America at approximately 11,500 BP was probably related to an intra-Ållerød, cold interval (Haynes 2002). The panorama is less controversial for tropical America. In northern South America and Panamá, the evidence of early colonization clearly indicates the use of a variety of environments, including the tropical forests (Mora and Gnecco 2003; Ranere and Cooke 2003), and the Andean plateaus (Correal Urrego and Van der Hammen 1977). But association between human movement there and the climate is not completely understood (Colinvaux 1999; Van der Hammen and Correal Urrego 2001).

Hunter-Gatherer Behavior: Human Response during The Younger Dryas, edited by Metin I. Eren, 57–78. © Left Coast Press. All rights reserved.

The supposed influence of climate upon human movement and adaptations reappears in the discussion of the peopling of the high Andes and southern South America. The impression was that not only were Andean and Fuego-Patagonian populations living in adverse environments, but that during the initial period of occupation they faced even worse conditions related to late Pleistocene cold spells. Such adverse conditions were thought to be present in several locations in the Andes, where extensive glaciers precluded human occupation, and altitude obligated individuals to resort to different physiological (Aldenderfer 1997; Cocilovo and Guichón 1986) and cultural mechanisms in order to survive (Borrero 1995; Rick 1980). Thus, it has been suggested many times that it was not possible for humans to colonize the southern end of the continent under such inclement circumstances (Borrero 1996), but little climatic evidence has ever been offered to support this hypothesis.

The Younger Dryas (YD) and other cold climatic pulses occur within the Pleistocene/Holocene transition (Straus 1996), a period that witnessed the first clear evidence of human occupation in South America. The question this paper explores is whether these pulses were dramatic enough in South America to hinder human mobility or affect behavioral adaptations. With extensive plateaus reaching approximately 4,000 m asl, or more, the Andean mountains, and the southern tip of the continent are among the places where cold intervals were expected to produce a substantial impact on human populations. Did the early explorers of the high Andes and lands below 50° S need to adapt to cold environments? For several reasons, which I elaborate below, I suspect that they did not have to innovate many new mechanisms for survival. It is clear that the early colonizers of South America had a veritable library of tactics and strategies for survival under a variety of environments, ranging from the arctic to tropics. It is generally accepted that the first settlers of America surely had a command of essential skills for life in the high Arctic (Bettinger and Young 2004:243). Circulation through the plains of North America and the geographic bottleneck of Panamá under changing climate conditions surely added other skills (Cooke 2005; Haynes 2002). By the time humans approached the Andes and southern South America, they were probably prepared with a flexible suite of technological and subsistence strategies to deal with climatic instability. Even though most of the Andes are largely tropical to semitropical, the high altitude Andean environments were subject to extreme changes in climate. It is worth mentioning that the southern latitudes (ca. 56° S) discussed here are not very high in comparison with the latitudes of Beringia and Alaska (ca. 70° N). Additionally, the close proximity of the Atlantic and Pacific oceans in southern South America created a milder, maritime climate, much different than what would have been experienced at the same latitudes in the northern hemisphere.

Thus, one of the most important issues related to the archaeology of the first peopling of South America concerns the basic climatic and environmental conditions under which this process took place (Borrero 1996; Bryan 1973; Dillehay 2000; Gnecco 1999; Lynch 1983, 1990; Nuñez et al. 2005). Salient and archaeologically relevant characteristics of the YD are the abruptness of its beginning and end (Taylor et al. 1997). Consequently, understanding how dramatic the YD was in the southern hemisphere is central for those researchers who suggest that people had to adapt to new conditions. The high Andes and Fuego-Patagonia are the places where this question becomes most relevant, because these are regions characterized by relatively harsh environments, even during interstadial times.

The Younger Dryas

There were several cold episodes recorded in northwestern Europe that punctuated "the overall warming trend that brought about deglaciation" (Bradley 1999:271). Lasting more than 1,000 ^{14}C years (Alley et al. 1993), the YD was the coldest of those events, and it is well recorded at several places in the northern hemisphere. Many explanations for the beginning of the YD exist, but at present there is no consensus on the mechanisms involved (Bradley 1999).

Interest for the existence of global climatic mechanisms prompted scrutiny in several regions in South America (Clapperton 1993; Clapperton and McEwan 1985; Heine 1993; Moreno et al. 2001; Schreve-Brinkman 1978). It was with the work of palynologist, Calvin Heusser, that the presence of a YD signal began to be considered for Fuego-Patagonia (Heusser 1966, 2003). Working with pollen columns in the Lake region of Chile at 41° S, Heusser inferred the existence of a cold interval between 11,000 and 10,000 BP. Geologist, John Mercer disputed the existence of the YD in southern South America, based on the lack of glacial features related to a late glacial advance (Mercer 1976). Other studies by Heusser continued to produce evidence used as proof of a YD event. A cooling event was identified at several places in Tierra del Fuego, such as Caleta Róbalo on Navarino Island, and Puerto Harberton on Isla Grande of Tierra del Fuego. An important reduction in *Nothofagus* pollen was identified at these sites during the interval 13,000–10,000 BP, a reduction that was taken to signal cooling (Heusser and Rabassa 1987).

However, not all palynologists accepted this evidence, because the decrease in *Nothofagus* pollen was not evident in many other pollen columns (Markgraf 1991; Villagrán 1985). Markgraf considered an alternative explanation for the changes seen in Caleta Robalo. "The four radiocarbon dates in these segments indicate substantial changes in sedimentation rate, which imply that in this record, sedimentological changes are responsible for the influx changes, and not climate" (Markgraf 1989:429). This is a convincing explanation and one that takes into account the vagaries of preservation and deposition in "representative" temporal columns. In other words, she argued that the completeness of the time series on which the palynological identification of the YD was identified might have been compromised (Behrensmeyer et al. 2000).

A Younger Dryas Event in the Southern Cone?

A study of beetle faunas from the Central Lake region of Chile produced results that caused a major objection to the existence of a YD advance. It was found that the "taxa composition of the pre-14,000 BP assemblages was different from that of the post-14,000 BP assemblages" (Ashworth and Hoganson 1993:266). No significant change in the biota is observed between 11,000 and 10,000 BP. Working west of the Andes, Massaferro and Brooks (2002) found that chironomids indicated cooling and drying at Lake Stibnite during the YD. Analyzing the evidence, the synthesis by Raymond S. Bradley concluded that "studies of late glacial sites in Chile suggest that there was no YD episode in that area" (Bradley 1999:345).

But it was the absence of strong geological evidence that played a key role in disputing the existence of a YD event in South America (Heusser 2003:179). Late glacial advances of ice were recorded at several places. Even evidence obtained in Ecuador and Peru in more tropical settings was related to late glacial advances of ice (Clapperton and McEwan 1985; Clapperton et al. 1997; Mercer and Palacios 1977), though their chronology was not completely settled (Heine 1993, 1994). Focusing on the southern cone, in the north of Patagonia, there is evidence of a glacier advance—referred to as the Huelmo-Mascardi cold reversal—preceding YD times at Mire Huelmo and Lake Mascardi (Ariztegui et al. 1997; Hajdas et al. 2003; Moreno et al. 2001). However, at the same latitude on the channels of the Pacific side of the Andes, the YD signal was not identified (Ashworth and Hoganson 1993; Ashworth and Markgraf 1989; Ashworth et al. 1991; Bennett et al. 2000). Further south, a late Pleistocene advance of the ice indicated by the Punta Banderas Moraine, Lago Argentino, is seen as a response to "dramatically increased precipitation rather than dramatic cooling" (Ackert et al. 2008:394). Marden (1993) initially believed that the late glacial re-advancement of the Grey Glacier in Torres del Paine indicated the YD. However, recent research at Torres del Paine (Fogwill and Kubik 2005) shows no concordance with the YD. Studies by McCulloch and Davies (2001) in the region of the Strait of Magellan showed the existence of a cold climate after deglaciation, "with no evidence of a temperature reversal during the YD" (Sugden et al. 2005:282). As such, "the advance recognized in latitude 41° S [the Huelmo-Mascardi Cold Reversal] could represent the most southerly influence of the Younger Dryas" (Sugden et al. 2005:285).

An intensive research program in southern South America showed that the late glacial ice advance recorded at the Strait of Magellan "coincides with the ACR [Antarctic Cold Reversal] recognized in the Vostok core" (McCulloch et al. 2005:309). One "implication is that this part of southernmost South America was responding to an antiphase Antarctic climatic signal during the late glacial" (Fogwill and Kubik 2005:407), known as the Antarctic cold reversal (Blunier et al. 1997). Finally, it is relevant to mention that in other places in the southern hemisphere, the panorama is equally ambiguous. The much discussed presence of a YD advance in New Zealand, particularly at the Franz Josef Glacier, was not sustained by the chronology of the Waiho Loop advance (Barrows et al. 2007). In sum, the now growing consensus is that any YD ice advance would have been of minor significance in South America (Sugden et al. 2005) compared to earlier advances.

Human Peopling and Charcoal Microparticles in Southern Patagonia

The discussion about climatic conditions and the existence of a cold signal in high latitudes underscores the importance of dry conditions at the end of the Pleistocene. This aspect is relevant for the discussion of the earliest presence of humans in southern South America. In Heusser's (1994) view, changes in charcoal concentrations recorded at pollen columns are related to human activities and constitute a good proxy for their presence, even in the absence of classic markers like lithics, pottery, or bones. However, Heusser takes this idea to the extreme by suggesting that charcoal hiatuses during MIS 2 (Marine Isotope Stage 2) at several columns in Chile are the result of "cold climatic conditions at the LGM [Last Glacial Maximum] that forced Paleoindians to retreat equatorward" (Heusser 2003:74). On the basis of radiocarbon dates, Coronato et al. (1999:88) suggested that humans were present in the north of Tierra del Fuego at approximately 13,000 BP, at least

2,000 years before any known archaeological evidence. The point is that widespread archaeological evidence for Patagonia supports the presence of hunter-gatherers at 11,000 BP, but no earlier (Bird 1988; Borrero 2008; Miotti et al. 2003; Nami and Nakamura 1995; Paunero 2003a, 2003b; Steele and Politis 2009), and specifically in Tierra del Fuego at 10,500 BP (Massone 2004). We are talking of an area located some 1,000 km south of Monte Verde, the earliest archaeological site on the continent where occupations around 12,000 BP have been identified (Dillehay 1997). Using isolated radiocarbon dates some authors are also suggesting older ages for southern Patagonia, but those dates have not yet been replicated (Miotti et al. 2003). Nevertheless, the evidence for the earlier Patagonian sites indicates very low human demography with only ephemeral use of most sites. The charcoal argument implies that the earlier human settlers, with such a low population, produced a higher impact in the environment than the more numerous inhabitants of Fuego-Patagonia during the Holocene, a time for which there is no substantive increase in known charcoal. Therefore, this argument is not strong enough to support the tenet of human presence in southern South America before the end of the Pleistocene.

Radiocarbon analyses by Moreno (2000) and Abarzúa and Moreno (2008) on samples from the region of temperate rainforests around 42° S, in south-central Chile, showed peaks of charcoal microparticles that postdate human occupations at Monte Verde (Dillehay 1997) and are probably related to a human presence in the region. In this case, the arguments made by Abarzúa and Moreno is different than that of Heusser (2003) and Coronato et al. (1999), because the presence of humans is already based on independent evidence, like that obtained at Alero Marifilo (Adán et al. 2004).

More recently Markgraf (1993a:65) attributed the pattern of intense late Pleistocene deposition of microparticles charcoal observed by Heusser and others to "repeated fire disturbances and short-term plant successions"—in other words a local, rather than a global, cause for the increase in microcharcoal. This explanation makes better sense of the extreme variation in the charcoal records. Markgraf discussed the correlation between major events recorded by charcoal particles at different columns and a decrease in *Nothofagus* (Markgraf 1993b), but found that deposition of charcoal appears to postdate indications for the disappearance of *Nothofagus* pollen. A role for volcanoes cannot be excluded (Markgraf et al. 2007), but the most widely accepted explanation relates the evidence of fires to variation in storm tracks (Markgraf et al. 2007; Whitlock et al. 2007). Specifically, Whitlock et al. (2007) examined the geographic and temporal patterns in thirty-one radiocarbon-dated, charcoal records in southern South America. They detected a multimillennial pattern and proposed that meridianal shifts in the Westerlies, coupled with obliquity-driven, positive anomalies in summer insolation, could account for the intensified occurrence of fires during the early Holocene; but increased use of fire by humans could also have been a factor. Villa Martinez and Moreno (2007) and Moreno et al. (2009) argue that the abundance of charcoal microparticles is related to a wider availability of fuel, which is influenced by climate changes.

It is worth mentioning that charcoal concentrations recorded at the isolated Malvinas/Falkland islands in the Atlantic Ocean led to a suggestion that they were peopled during the middle Holocene (Buckland and Edwards 1998), an interpretation that must also be taken with caution. The absence of any independent marker for the presence of humans makes this interpretation suspect. It appears that even when their interpretation is not clear, charcoal particles cannot be automatically taken to indicate the early presence of humans. Finally, even though it seems plausible that the presence of humans could have produced an increase of fire, when no other evidence is available, it is not advisable to exclusively use microscopic charcoal particles as a viable signal for human presence.

Implications

The duration of late Pleistocene cold pulses, be it the YD, the Huelmo-Mascardi, or the ACR, is too short to expect any specific biological adaptation of animals or humans. Any adaptation to cold climates observed in animals is probably related to previous, longer glacial periods. The extinction of the Pleistocene megafauna is a process that occurred during the end of the late Pleistocene across South America (Borrero 2008). Much has been written concerning the role of climate in the extinction process with explanations ranging from redistribution of resources (Graham and Lundelius 1984), to forced changes in diet (Markgraf 1985). The general chronological coincidence between this phenomenon and the presumed evidence for climatic deterioration in the south of the continent and the Andes suggests the possibility of a causal correlation. However, extinctions are not confined to the high altitudes and latitudes. The hinterland and the lowlands of the Pacific and Atlantic coasts, as well as the tropical and the subantarctic zones were equally impacted (Barnosky et al. 2004; Steadman et al. 2005). For that reason, any role the YD or the ACR played in the process of extinction needs to be carefully evaluated.

In addition to extinction, other changes in faunal regimes should also be considered. Morphometric studies of guanaco (*Lama guanicoe*) bones demonstrate that body size in guanacos diminishes in the southern portion of the continent throughout the Holocene, while in Tierra del Fuego, ancestral size is retained up to late Holocene times (L'Heureux 2005). However, any correlation of this pattern with the Antarctic climatic signal fails to suggest a causal argument (L´Heureux 2008). Studies of the peculiarities of the morphology of Patagonian Pleistocene horses (*Hippidion saldiasi*) also failed to find an explanation in cold conditions (Alberdi and Prado 2004).

If we accept that the climate in southern South America was in sync with the ACR, it is the time to ask what this event implies for humans expanding into this unknown, previously uninhabited country. Humans do not react to changes in temperature in predictable ways. Several studies of human responses to a climatic change, like the Medieval Climatic Anomaly in western USA, showed a variety of responses ranging from human dispersal to concentration (Jones et al. 1999). The global assessment of the impact of the LGM on human populations (Gamble and Soffer 1990) provides further examples of varied human adaption to cold. The post-glacial climate in the southern latitudes was always cold (McCulloch and Davies 2001), and the high Andean environments always ranked among the most difficult to inhabit. However, conditions were never adverse enough to produce a significant drop in productivity, as indicated by the availability of megamammals (Martin 2008a, 2008b; Prevosti and Vizcaino 2006; Ubilla 2006). Yet, even when there was greater faunal diversity at the end of the Pleistocene, humans were not taking advantage of that diversity (Miotti and Salemme 1999).

Also, there is no evidence of substantial ice advances on the eastern steppes (Coronato et al. 1999), which according to current archaeological evidence was the initial area colonized by humans (Bird 1988; Borrero and Manzi 2007; Borrero and Miotti 2007; Miotti 1996; Paunero 2003a, 2003b). In the high Andes, the situation was not very different. As Rick explained, "it seems probable that human adaptations allowed *puna* occupation even when the ice was present in some areas" (Rick 1980:332). Because much of South America—including Patagonia— was not significantly covered by glaciers, circulation for humans and animals was not a major problem (Dillehay 2000). In biogeographical terms, even the highest Andes were accessible for hunter-gatherers. Archaeological evidence from Bolivia (Aldenderfer 1999), Perú (Rick 1980), Chile (Nuñez et al. 2005), and Argentina (García 2003; Yacobaccio 1996) indicates human use since the late Pleistocene. This is not to say that settlement conditions were easy, since a number of biological and cultural adaptations were required in altitudes above 3,000 m asl, but that the area was not prohibitive for humans. Other potential barriers of movement, like rivers, were not much of a problem during cold pulses such as the ACR, because these were the times during which freezing of the rivers facilitated human circulation in a landscape otherwise difficult to traverse. If anything, human dispersal toward the south appears to have been easier during cold intervals.

As already mentioned, it is impossible to attribute biological adaptations to the influence of short-term, climatic pulses. For example, it is clear that physiological adaptations to high altitude cannot be the result of short-term habitation, only long-term habitation. But humans have cultural responses at their disposal, which can change quite quickly. These responses can be triggered in shorter time periods and might have allowed humans to adapt to changing social and physical environments. The question that remains is if there is any evidence of those adaptations in the archaeological record during the YD in South America?

One potential effect of climate change is the extinction of human demes. This was conceivable in the late Pleistocene given the patchy distribution of the early colonizers in South America. For example, there is minimal evidence of human presence north of Tierra del Fuego, except for indications of ephemeral use of a small rockshelter around 10,500 BP (Massone 2004). Alternatively, there is widespread evidence of people living on the island during the last 2,000 ^{14}C years (Borrero and Barberena 2004). The extinction of late Pleistocene settlers on Tierra del Fuego might be plausibly explained by the inundation of the Strait of Magellan, which cut people off from the continent (Borrero 1997). This interpretation is heavily dependent on visibility and preservation that only now are beginning to be explored (Morello et al. 2008). It must be noted, however, that the pattern is not restricted to Tierra del Fuego. The archaeological record of several South American regions can be used to suggest a lack of human occupation during the middle Holocene as well (Zárate et al. 2005), in what is regionally known as the "archaeological silence" (Nuñez et al. 2005).

The relevance of this pattern is that it implies that some human populations may have not survived the Pleistocene/Holocene transition. Judging from the comparatively low frequencies of artifacts in the lower levels at any of these sites, it must be accepted that human populations were small and dispersed at the time. If we add the climatic and environmental instability into the mix (Clapperton 1993)—much of which was in early successional stages (Pisano 1975)—then we must conclude that many populations were probably barely viable at the end of the Pleistocene. It is conceivable that there were failed adaptations that occurred during the harsher conditions of the initial period of human colonization of South America. But human populations have many ways to react to adverse conditions, including migrations or reorganization of settlement over the landscape. These were surely alternative responses probably taken before the appearance of any real danger of extinction, and they can produce similar archaeological patterns to those resulting from discontinuous settlement at a micro-regional or even regional scale. In other words, they can produce situations difficult to distinguish from those produced by local extinction. This problem of equifinality must be solved before we accept the "archaeological silence" as proof of the extinction of human demes.

All that we can say is that there is a pattern of discontinuous use of landscape within several South American regions and that discontinuity is indicated by the depositional gaps in the early records (Borrero 1999; Borrero and Franco 1997). It is difficult to relate those gaps in human occupation to any YD or ACR cold spell. Not only is the time lag between cold spells and the evidence for abandonment too large, most of these areas had strong early Holocene archaeological signals; but the magnitude of the climatic changes was not dramatic. In order to discuss this particular aspect, it is important to examine if any of the classic responses to intense cold are observed in the archaeological record of the early South American colonizers of the high Andes and Fuego-Patagonia. Human occupation of high, cold latitudes is heavily dependent on shelter and insulation technologies (Jochim 1981). The limited evidence of shelters does not indicate the development of any sophisticated technology. No evidence of postholes or any human-constructed shelter has been found in the early record of the extreme south or in the high Andes. The bulk of the information for the early colonization of South America comes from natural caves, but this is probably more of a sampling effect than a human predilection for caves as shelters. In fact, the older, and in many ways more sophisticated, evidence of open-air shelters is from Monte Verde, a site used during a warm interval at around 41° S (Dillehay 1997) and located along the channels of Chinchihuapi Creek, some 50 km from the modern coast of the Pacific Ocean, in a patchy deciduous and coniferous forest.

Also, there is no evidence of clothing for that early period, and it is notable that there is a lack of bone technology—for example, needles—usually associated with textile production. Evidence of naked hunters has been observed in archaeological sites in Tierra del Fuego that date to the last part of the Little Ice Age (i.e., Darwin 1860), suggesting that people were well adapted to deal with cold conditions in that region. Using bones or dung for fuel is one classic adaptation to very cold climates (Soffer 1985). But evidence for use of bone as fuel is restricted to Paso Otero 5 (10,400–10,200 BP) in the Pampas, where 91% of the megamammal bones are burned (Joly et al. 2005). It must be noted that the site is located 38° S, in an area that probably experienced cold winters, but not year-long, extreme environments (Gutiérrez and Martínez 2008).

Another usual tactic to deal with cold environments relates to the intense degree animal resources were used (Binford 1978). The use of animal bones, including marrow cracking, is well represented in the earlier records, but it rarely implicates the kind of intense fragmentation related with rendering grease from the bones. Only in the very high Andes is there any evidence of "highly fractured but noncrumbly" bones at Pachamachay, in the Peruvian Puna (Rick 1980:236). In this and other high altitude sites, bone assemblages display some signatures that can be associated with cold adaptations—like intensive use of faunal remains—but these characteristics do not differ from the evidence of the Holocene. In other words, it cannot be accepted as evidence for adaptation to differential cold pulses during the late Pleistocene. Also, the typical, early, bone assemblage in Patagonia indicates the nonintensive consumption of animals, including megamammals (Borrero 2008). In fact, the most fragmented Patagonian bone assemblages belong in the middle Holocene (Barberena et al. 2007).

Thus, the demands of making a living in harsh, cold environments suggest that any human population should have clear fossil signals of this adaptation to cold temperatures, including food shortages. However, nothing in the archaeological record indicates any sort of specific adaptation to cold climates in South America. Further, no specialization of the tool kits is evident. The Fell Cave projectile points (also known as "fishtail" points), temporally limited to the late Pleistocene, are not restricted in their distribution to the south, but are also present in the Pampas (Flegenheimer 1980) and in Panamá (Cooke 2005). Finally, there is no evidence for early human use of the Patagonian coastlines, many of which are now submerged (Miotti 2003), and it is only in mid-Holocene times that this environment was intensively exploited in Tierra del Fuego (Orquera and Piana 1999).

Conclusion

No evidence of systematic, widespread use of special tactics against very cold conditions is present in the archaeological record in South America. Cold or warm pulses appear to make no real difference for late Pleistocene, human adaptations on the continent. Instead climatic changes, specifically cold temperatures, may have only affected the rate of the colonization, because the freezing of rivers may have been an important facilitating factor for human movement into the south.

As previously mentioned, "in most regions, the transition produced no impact on human populations, since [at that time] they were slowly beginning their process of adjustment to new environments" (Borrero 1996:347). Short-term camps, use of local rocks, and a subsistence base fastidiously focused on a few resources repeatedly indicate the hardships of exploration, not adaptations to extreme conditions.

References

Abarzúa, A., and P. Moreno
2008 Changing Fire Regimes in the Temperate Rainforest Region of Southern Chile over the Last 16,000 yr. *Quaternary Research* 69:62–71.

Ackert, R., R. Becker, B. Siunger, M. Kurz, M. Caffee, and D. Mickelson
2008 Patagonian Glacier Response during the Late Glacial–Holocene Transition. *Science* 321:392–395.

Adán, L., R. Mera, M. Becerra, and M. Godoy
2004 Ocupación arcaica en territorios boscosos y lacustres de la región pericordillerana (IX y X Regiones): el sitio Marifilo 1 de la localidad de Pucura. *Chungara* 11:1121–1136.

Alberdi, M., and J. Prado
2004 *Caballos Fósiles de América del Sur. Una Historia de Tres Millones de Años.* INCUAPA-Olavarría.

Aldenderfer, M.
1997 *Montane Foragers: Asana and the South-Central Andean Archaic.* University of Iowa Press, Iowa City.

1999 The Pleistocene/Holocene Transition in Peru and its Effects upon Human Use of the Landscape. *Quaternary International* 53/54:11–19.

Alley, R., D. Mecse, C. Shuman, A. Gow, K. Taylor, P. Grootes, J. White, M. Ram, E. Waddington, P. Mayewski, and G. Zielinski
1993 Abrupt Increase in Greenland Snow Accumulation at the End of the Younger Dryas Event. *Nature* 362:527–529.

Ariztegui, D., M. Bianchi, J. Masaferro, E. Lafargue, and F. Nissan
1997 Interhemispheric Synchrony of Late–Glacial Climatic Instability as Recorded in Proglacial Lake Mascardi, Argentina. *Journal of Quaternary Sciences* 12:133–138.

Ashworth, A., and J. Hoganson
1993 The Magnitude and Rapidity of the Climate Change Marking the End of the Pleistocene in the Midlatitudes of South America. *Palaeogeography, Palaeoclimatology, Palaeoecology* 101:263–270.

Ashworth, A., and V. Markgraf
1989 Climate of the Chilean Channels between 11,000 to 10,000 yr BP Based on Fossil Beetle and Pollen Analyses. *Revista Chilena de Historia Natural* 62:61–74.

Ashworth, A., V. Markgraf, and C. Villagrán

1991 Late Quaternary Climatic History of the Chilean Channels Based on Fossil Pollen and Beetle Analysis, and Analysis of the Modern Vegetation and Pollen Rain. *Journal of Quaternary Science* 6:279–291.

Barberena, R., F. Martin, and L. Borrero

2007 Estudio Biogeográfico de Conjuntos Faunísticos: Sitio Cóndor 1 (Pali Aike). In *Arqueología de Fuego-Patagonia*, edited by F. Morello, A. Prieto, M. Martinic, and G. Bahamonde, pp. 139–150. Fundación CEQUA, Punta Arenas.

Barnosky, A., P. Koch, R. Feranec, S. Wing, and A. Shabel

2004 Assessing the Causes of Late Pleistocene Extinctions on the Continents. *Science* 306:70–75.

Barrows, T., S. Lehman, L. Fifield, and P. Deckker

2007 Absence of Cooling in New Zealand and Adjacent Ocean During the Younger Dryas Chronozone. *Science* 318:86–89.

Behrensmeyer, A., S. Kidwell, and R. Gastaldo

2000 Taphonomy and Paleobiology. In *Deep Time: Paleobiology's Perspective*, edited by D. Erwin and S. Wing, pp. 103–147, *Paleobiology* 26(4), Supplement.

Bennett, K., S. Haberle, and S. Lumley

2000 The Last Glacial-Holocene Transition in Southern Chile. *Science* 290:325–328.

Bettinger, R., and D. Young

2004 Hunter-gatherer Population Expansion in North Asia and the New World. In *Entering America, Northeast Asia and Beringia before the Last Glacial Maximum*, edited by D. Madsen, pp. 239–251. University of Utah Press, Salt Lake City.

Binford, L.

1978 *Nunamiut Ethnoarchaeology*. Academic Press, New York.

Bird, J.

1988 *Travels and Archaeology in South Chile*. University of Iowa Press, Iowa City.

Blunier, T., J. Schwander, B. Stauffer, T. Stocker, A. Dällenbach, A. Indermühle, J. Tschumi, J. Chappellaz, D. Raynaud, and J. M. Barnola

1997 Timing of the Antarctic Cold Reversal and the Atmospheric CO_2 Increase with Respect to the Younger Dryas Event. *Geophysical Research Letters* 24:2683–2686.

Borrero, L.

1995 Arqueología de la Patagonia. Palimpsesto. *Revista de Arqueología* 4:9–69.

1996 The Pleistocene Holocene Transition in Southern South America. In *Humans at the End of the Ice Age: The Archaeology of the Pleistocene Holocene Transition*, edited by L. Straus, B. Eriksen, J. Erlandson, and D. Yesner, pp. 339–354. Plenum Press, New York.

1997 The Origins of Ethnographic Subsistence Patterns in Fuego-Patagonia. In *Natural History, Prehistory and Ethnography at the Uttermost End of the*

Earth, edited by C. McEwan, L. Borrero, and A. Prieto, pp. 60–81. British Museum Press, London.

Borrero, L.
1999 The Prehistoric Exploration and Colonization of Fuego-Patagonia. *Journal of World Prehistory* 13:321–355.

2008 The Elusive Evidence: The Archeological Record of the South American Extinct Megamammals. In *American Megafaunal Extinctions at the End of the Pleistocene*, edited by Gary Haynes, pp. 145–168. Springer, New York.

Borrero, L., and R. Barberena (editors)
2004 *Arqueología del Norte de la Isla Grande de Tierra del Fuego*. Editorial Dunken, Buenos Aires.

Borrero, L., and N. Franco
1997 Early Patagonian Hunter-Gatherers: Subsistence and Technology. *Journal of Anthropological Research* 53:219–239.

Borrero, L., and L. Manzi
2007 Arqueología Supra-regional y Biogeografía en la Patagonia Meridianal. In *Arqueología de Fuego-Patagonia*, edited by F. Morello, M. Martinic, A. Prieto, and G. Bahamonde, pp. 163–171. Ediciones CEQUA, Punta Arenas.

Borrero, L., and L. Miotti
2007 *La Tercera Esfinge Indiana: La Edad del Poblamiento de Argentina*. Relaciones de la Sociedad Argentina de Antropología 32, Buenos Aires.

Bradley, R.
1999 *Paleoclimatology: Reconstructing Climate of the Quaternary*. Harcourt/Academic Press, San Diego.

Bryan, A.
1973 Paleoenvironments and Cultural Diversity in Late Pleistocene South America. *Quaternary Research* 3:237–256.

Buckland, P., and K. Edwards
1998 Palaeoecological Evidence for Possible Pre-European Settlement in the Falkland Islands. *Journal of Archaeological Science* 25:599–602.

Clague, J., R. Mathewes, and T. Ager
2004 Environments of Northwest North America before the Last Glacial Maximum. In *Entering America: Northeast Asia and Beringia before the Last Glacial Maximum*, edited by D. Madsen, pp. 63–94, University of Utah Press, Salt Lake City.

Clapperton, C.
1993 *Quaternary Geology and Geomorphology of South America*. Elsevier Science Publisher, Amsterdam.

Clapperton, C., M. Hall, P. Mothe, M. Hole, J. Still, K. Helmens, P. Kuhry, and A. Gemmell
1997 A Younger Dryas Icecap in the Equatorial Andes. *Quaternary Research* 47:13–28.

Clapperton, C., and C. McEwan
1985 Late Quaternary Moraines in the Chimborazo Area, Ecuador. *Arctic, Antarctic, and Alpine Research* 17:135–147.

Cocilovo, J., and R. Guichón
1986 Propuesta para el Estudio de las Poblaciones Aborígenes del Extremo Austral de Patagonia. *Anales Instituto de la Patagonia (Serie Ciencias Sociales)* 16:111–123, Universidad de Magallanes, Punta Arenas, Chile.

Colinvaux, P.
1999 Quaternary Environmental History and Forest Diversity in the Neotropics. In *Evolution and Environment in Tropical America*, edited by J. Jackson, A. Budd, and D. Coates, pp. 359–405. The University of Chicago Press, Chicago.

Cooke, R.
2005 Prehistory of Native Americans on the Central America Land Bridge: Colonization, Dispersal, and Divergence. *Journal of Archaeological Research* 13:129–187.

Coronato, A., M. Salemme, and J. Rabassa
1999 Paleoenvironmental Conditions during the Early Peopling of Southernmost South America (Late Glacial–Early Holocene, 14-8 ka B.P.). *Quaternary International* 53/54:77–92.

Correal Urrego, G., and T. Van der Hammen
1977 *Investigaciones Arqueológicas en los abrigos Rocosos de Tequendama*. Banco Popular, Bogotá.

Darwin, C.
1860 *Journal of Researches into the Natural History and Geology of the Countries Visited during the Voyage of H.M.S. Beagle Round the World*. John Murray, London.

Dillehay, T. D. (editor)
1997 *Monte Verde: A Late Pleistocene Settlement in Chile*, Vol. 2. Smithsonian Institution Press, Washington, D.C.

Dillehay, T. D.
2000 *The Settlement of the Americas: A New Prehistory*. Basic Books, New York.

Flegenheimer, N.
1980 Hallazgos de Puntas "Cola de Pescado" en la Provincia de Buenos Aires. *Relaciones* 14:169–176.

Fogwill, C., and P. Kubik
2005 A Glacial Stage Spanning the Antarctic Cold Reversal in Torres del Paine (51°S), Chile, Based on Preliminary Cosmogenic Exposure Ages. *Geografiska Annaler* 87A:403–408.

Gamble, C., and O. Soffer
1990 Introduction, Pleistocene Polyphony: The Diversity of Human Adaptations at the Last Glacial Maximum. In *The World at 18,000 B.P., Vol. 1*, edited by O. Soffer and C. Gamble, pp. 1–23. Unwin Hyman, London.

García, A.
2003 Exploitation Territory at Agua de la Cueva (Southern Area) Site (11,000–9000 RCYBP). In *Where the South Winds Blow: Ancient Evidence of Paleo South Americans*, edited by L. Miotti, M. Salemme, and N. Flegenheimer, pp. 83–86. Center for the Study of the First Americans, Texas A&M, College Station.

Gnecco, C.
1999 An Archaeological Perspective of the Pleistocene/Holocene Boundary in Northern South Americañ. *Quaternary International* 53–54:3–9.

Goebel, T., M. Waters, and D. O'Rourke
2008 The Late Pleistocene Dispersal of Modern Humans in the Americas. *Science* 319:1497–1502.

Graham, R., and E. Lundelius
1984 Coevolutionary Disequilibrium and Pleistocene Extinctions. In *Quaternary Extinctions*, edited by R. Klein and P. Martin, pp. 223–249. The University of Arizona Press, Tucson.

Gutiérrez, M., and G. Martinez
2008 Trends in the Faunal Human Exploitation during the Late Pleistocene and Early Holocene in the Pampean Region (Argentina). *Quaternary International* 191:53–68.

Hajdas, I., G. Bonani, and P. Moreno
2003 Precise Radiocarbon Dating of Late-glacial Cooling in Mid-latitudes South America. *Quaternary Research* 59:70–78.

Haynes, G.
2002 *The Early Settlement of North America: The Clovis Era*. Cambridge University Press, Cambridge.

Heine, J.
1993 A Reevaluation of the Evidence for a Younger Dryas Climate Reversal in the Tropical Andes. *Quaternary Science Reviews* 12:769–779.

1994 Comments on C.M. Clapperton's Glacier Readvances in the Andes at 12,500–10,000 yr BP: Implications for Mechanism of Late-glacial Climatic Change. *Journal of Quaternary Science* 9:87.

Heusser, C.
1966 Late-Pleistocene Pollen Diagrams from the Province of Llanquihue, Southern Chile. *Proceedings American Philosophical Society* 110:269–305.

1994 Paleoindians and Fire during the Late Quaternary in Southern South America. *Revista Chilena de Historia Natural* 67:435–443.

2003 *Ice Age Southern Andes: A Chronicle of Paleoecological Events*. Elsevier, Amsterdam.

Heusser, C., and J. Rabassa
1987 Cold Climatic Episode of Younger Dryas Age in Tierra del Fuego. *Nature* 328:609–611.

Jochim, M.
1981 *Strategies for Survival*. Academic Press, New York.

Joly, D., R. March, and G. Martinez

2005 Les os Brûlés de Paso Otero 5: Un Temoignage Possible de l'Utilisation de l'os Comme Combustible par des Chasseurs–Cueilleurs de la Fin du Pleistocene en Argentine. *Archeosciences, Revue d'Archéométrie* 29:83–93.

Jones, T., G. Brown, L. Raab, J. McVickar, W. Spaulding, D. Kennett, A. York, and P. Walker

1999 Environmental Imperatives Reconsidered: Demographic Crises in Western North America during the Medieval Climatic Anomaly. *Current Anthropology* 40:137–170.

L'Heureux, G.

2005 Variación Morfométrica en Restos Óseos de Guanaco de Sitios Arqueológicos de Patagonia Austral Continental y de la Isla Grande de Tierra del Fuego. *Magallania* 33:81–94.

2008 *El Estudio Arqueológico del Proceso Evolutivo entre las Poblaciones Humanas y las Poblaciones de Guanaco en Patagonia Meridional y Norte de Tierra del Fuego.* BAR International Series 1751, Archaeopress, Oxford.

Lynch, T.

1983 The Paleoindians. In *Ancient South Americans*, edited by J. Jennings, pp. 87–137. W. H. Freeman, New York.

1990 Glacial-age Man in South America? A Critical Review. *American Antiquity* 55:12–36.

Marden, C.

1993 Late Quaternary Glacial History of the South Icefield at Torres del Paine, Chile. Unpublished Ph.D. dissertation, University of Aberdeen, Aberdeen.

Markgraf, V.

1985 Late Pleistocene Faunal Extinctions in Southern Patagonia. *Science* 228:1110–1112.

1989 Reply to C. J. Heusser's "Southern Westerlies during the Last Glacial Maximum". *Quaternary Research* 31:426–432.

1991 Younger Dryas in South America? *Boreas* 20:63–69.

1993a Paleoenvironments and Paleoclimates in Tierra del Fuego and Southernmost Patagonia, South America. *Palaeogeography, Palaeoclimatology, Palaeoecology* 102:53–68.

1993b Younger Dryas in Southernmost South America—An update. *Quaternary Science Reviews* 12:351–355.

Markgraf, V., C. Whitlock, and S. Haberle

2007 Vegetation and Fire History during the Last 18,000 cal yr B.P. In Southern Patagonia: Mallín Polux, Coyhaique, Provincia Aisén (45° 41′ 30″S, 71° 50′ 30″ W, 640 m elevation). *Palaeogeography, Palaeoclimatology, Palaeoecology* 254:492–507.

Martin, F.
2008a Tafonomía y Paleoecología de la Transición Pleistoceno-Holoceno en Fuego-Patagonia. Interacción entre Poblaciones Humanas y de Carnívoros y su Importancia Como Agentes en la formación del Registro Fósil. Tesis Doctoral, Universidad Nacional de La Plata.
2008b Bone Crunching Felids at the End of the Pleistocene in Fuego-Patagonia. *Journal of Taphonomy* 6 (3–4):337–372.

Massaferro, J., and S. Brooks
2002 Response of Chironomids to Late Quaternary Environmental Change in the Taitao Peninsula, Southern Chile. *Journal of Quaternary Science* 17:101–111.

Massone, M.
2004 *Los Cazadores Después del Hielo*. Centro Diego Barros Arana, Santiago.

McCulloch, R., and S. Davies
2001 Late-glacial and Holocene Palaeoenvironmental Change in the Central Strait of Magellan, Southern Patagonia. *Palaeogeography, Palaeoclimatology, Palaeoecology* 173:143–173.

McCulloch, R., C. Fogwill, D. Sugden, M. Bentley, and P. Kubik
2005 Chronology of the Last Glaciation in Central Strait of Maggallanes and Bahía Inútil, Southernmost South America. *Geografiska Annaler* 87A:289–312.

Mercer, J.
1976 Glacial History of Southernmost South America. *Quaternary Research* 6:125–166.

Mercer, J., and O. Palacios
1977 Radiocarbon Dating of the Last Glaciation in Perú. *Geology* 5:600–604.

Miotti, L.
1996 Piedra Museo. Nuevos Datos para la Ocupación Pleistocena en Patagonia. In *Arqueologia, Sólo Patagonia*, edited by J. Gómez Otero, pp. 27–38. CENPAT, Puerto Madryn.
2003 Patagonia: A Paradox for Building Images of the First Americans during the Pleistocene/Holocene Transition. *Quaternary International* 109–110:147–173.

Miotti, L., and M. Salemme
1999 Biodiversity, Taxonomic Richness and Specialists-generalists during Late Pleistocene/Early Holocene Times in Pampa and Patagonia (Argentina, Southern South America). *Quaternary International* 53/54:53–68.

Miotti, L., M. Salemme, and J. Rabassa
2003 Radiocarbon Chronology at Piedra Museo Locality. In *Where the South Winds Blow: Ancient Evidence of Paleo South Americans*, edited by L. Miotti, M. Salemme, and N. Flegenheimer, pp. 99–104. Center for the Study of the First Americans, Texas A&M, College Station.

Mora, S., and C. Gnecco
2003 Archaeological Hunter-Gatherers in Tropical Forests: A View from Colombia. In *Under the Canopy: The Archaeology of Tropical Rain Forests,*

edited by J. Mercader, pp. 271–290. Rutgers University Press, New Brunswick.

Morello, F., M. Massone, M. Arroyo, E. Calas, J. Torres, R. McCulloch, L. Borrero, M. Lucero, I. Martínez, and G. Bahamonde

2008 Evaluando el Registro Arqueológico de Tierra del Fuego durante el Holoceno Temprano y Medio: Lo Posotivo de los Balances Negativos. Paper presented at the VII Jornadas de Arqueología de la Patagonia, Ushuaia.

Moreno, P.

2000 Climate, Fire, and Vegetation between about 13,000 and 9200 ^{14}C yr B.P. in the Chilean Lake District. *Quaternary Research* 54:81–89.

Moreno, P., J. Francois, R. Villa-Martinez, and C. Moy

2009 Millennial-scale Ariability in Southern Hemisphere Westerly Wind Activity over the Last 5000 Years in SW Patagonia. *Quaternary Science Reviews* 28:25–38.

Moreno, P., G. Jacobson, T. Lowell, and G. Denton

2001 Interhemispheric Climate Links Revealed by a Late–Glacial Cooling Episode in Southern Chile. *Nature* 409:804–808.

Nami, H., and T. Nakamura

1995 Cronología Radiocarbónica con AMS Obre Muestras de Hueso Procedentes del Sitio Cueva del Medio (Ultima Esperanza, Chile). *Anales del Instituto de la Patagonia* 23:125–134.

Nuñez, L., M. Grosjean, and I. Cartajena

2005 *Ocupaciones Humanas y Paleoambientes en la Puna de Atacama.* Universidad Católica del Norte-taraxacum, San Pedro de Atacama.

Orquera, L., and E. Piana

1999 *Arqueología de la Región del Canal Beagle* (Tierra del Fuego, República Argentina). Publicaciones de la SAA, Buenos Aires.

Paunero, R.

2003a The Presence of a Pleistocene Colonizing Culture in La Maria Archaeological Locality, Casa del Minero 1. In *Where the South Winds Blow: Ancient Evidence of Paleo South Americans*, edited by L. Miotti, M. Salemme, and N. Flegenheimer, pp. 127–132. Center for the Study of the First Americans, Texas A&M, College Station.

2003b The Cerro Tres Tetas (C3T) Locality in the Central Plateau of Santa Cruz, Argentina. In *Where the South Winds Blow: Ancient Evidence of Paleo South Americans*, edited by L. Miotti, M. Salemme, and N. Flegenheimer, pp. 133–140. Center for the Study of the First Americans, Texas A&M, College Station.

Pisano, E.

1975 Características de la Biota Magallánica Derivadas de Factores Especiales. *Anales del Instituto de la Patagonia* 6:126–137.

Prevosti, F., and S. Vizcaino

2006 Paleoecology of the Large Carnivore Guild from the Late Pleistocene of Argentina. *Acta Palaeontologica Polonica* 51:407–422.

Ranere, A., and R. Cooke
2003 Late Glacial and Early Holocene Occupations of Central American Tropical Forests. In *Under the Canopy: The Archaeology of Tropical Rain Forests*, edited by J. Mercader, pp. 219–248. Rutgers University Press, New Brunswick.

Rick, J.
1980 Prehistoric Hunters of the Highlands. Academic Press, New York.

Schreve-Brinkman, E.
1978 A Palynological Study of the Upper Quaternary Sequence in the E1 Abra Corridor and Rock Shelters (Colombia). *Palaeogeography, Palaeoclimatology, Palaeoecology* 25:1–109.

Soffer, O.
1985 *The Upper Palaeolithic of the Central Russian Plain*. Academic Press, Orlando.

Steadman, D., P. Martin, R. MacPhee, A. Jull, and H. McDonald
2005 Asynchronous Extinction of Late Quaternary Sloths on Continents and Islands. *Proceedings of the National Academy of Sciences* 102:11763–11768.

Steele, J., and G. Politis
2009 AMS [14]C Dating of Early Human Occupation of Southern South America. *Journal of Archaeological Science* 36:419–439.

Straus, L.
1996 The World at the End of the Last Ice Age. In *Humans at the End of the Ice Age: The Archaeology of the Pleistocene Holocene Transition*, edited by L. Straus, B. Eriksen, J. Erlandson, and D. Yesner, pp. 3–9. Plenum Press, New York.

Sugden, D., M. Bentley, C. Fogwill, N. Hutton, R. McCulloch, and R. Purves
2005 Late-glacial Glacier Events in Southernmost South America: A Blend of 'Northern' and 'Southern' Hemispheric Climatic Signals? *Geografiska Annaler* 87A:273–288.

Taylor, K., P. Mayewski, R. Alley, E. Brook, A. Gow, P. Grootes, D. Meese, E. Saltzman, J. Severinghaus, M. Twicker, J. White, S. Whitlow, and G. Zielinski
1997 The Holocene/Younger Dryas Recorded at Summit Greenland. *Science* 278:825–827.

Ubilla, M.
2006 Late Pleistocene of South America. In *Encyclopedia of Quaternary Sciences*, edited by S. Elias, pp. 3175–3189. Elsevier, Amsterdam.

Van der Hammen, T., and G. Correal Urrego
2001 Mastodontes en un Humedal Pleistocenico en el Valle del Magdalena (Colombia) con Evidencias de la Presencia del Hombre en el Periglacial. *Boletín de Arqueología* 16:4–36.

Villa Martinez, R., and P. Moreno
2007 Pollen Evidence for Variations in the Southern Margin of the Westerly Winds in SW Patagonia over the Last 12,600 Years. *Quaternary Research* 68:400–409.

Villagrán, C.

1985 Análisis Palinológico de los Cambios Vegetacionales durante el Tardiglacial y Postglacial en Chiloé. *Revista Chilena de Historia Natural* 58:57–69.

Whitlock, C., P. Moreno, and P. Bartlein

2007 Climatic Controls of Holocene Fire Patterns in Southern South America. *Quaternary Research* 68:28–36.

Yacobaccio, H.

1996 The Evolution of South Andean Hunter-gatherers. Proceedings of the XIII Congress of the International Union of Prehistoric and Protohistoric Sciences, pp. 389–394. Forli.

Zárate, M., G. Neme, and A. Gil

2005 Mid-Holocene Palaeoenvironments and Human Occupation in Southern South America. *Quaternary International* 132:81–94.

4

KELP FORESTS, COASTAL MIGRATIONS, AND THE YOUNGER DRYAS: LATE PLEISTOCENE AND EARLIEST HOLOCENE HUMAN SETTLEMENT, SUBSISTENCE, AND ECOLOGY ON CALIFORNIA'S CHANNEL ISLANDS

Torben C. Rick and Jon M. Erlandson

Introduction

As the earth warmed at the close of the Pleistocene, coastal regions around the world underwent extensive ecological and biotic reorganization. Sea levels rose rapidly during the terminal Pleistocene and early Holocene, drowning vast, lowland landscapes where numerous, early coastal settlements may now lie on the continental shelves (see Bard et al. 1990, 1996; Erlandson 2001; Fairbanks 1989; Richardson 1998). This sea level rise, coupled with changes in sea surface temperature and marine productivity between the glacial and interglacial periods, posed new opportunities and challenges for coastal peoples (Binford 1968; Graham et al. 2003). Rising seas created highly productive estuaries in many areas around the world, and kelp forests and other marine ecosystems also changed in the face of new environmental regimes (Graham et al. 2003; Kinlan et al. 2005; Yesner 1980).

Although some scholars once argued that coastal regions around the world were intensively occupied only as recently as the middle Holocene (e.g., Osborn 1977; Yesner 1987), global sea level rise poses fundamental problems for archaeologists and paleoecologists trying to understand the nature of early coastal societies and environments, ancient migration routes, the antiquity of marine fisheries, and the

Hunter-Gatherer Behavior: Human Response during The Younger Dryas, edited by Metin I. Eren, 79–110. © Left Coast Press. All rights reserved.

history of human impacts on ancient coastal ecosystems (Bailey et al. 2007; Erlandson 2001; Erlandson and Fitzpatrick 2006). Although, in some parts of the world we can look to last interglacial shorelines for evidence of early coastal societies, this is not possible in the Americas, which may have been first settled shortly after the end of the Last Glacial Maximum (LGM), around 16,000 ± 1000 cal BP. Despite these limitations, knowledge of early New World coastal archaeology is rapidly growing, with sites in Alaska, British Columbia, Oregon, California, Baja California, Ecuador, Peru, and Chile are now known to contain evidence of human settlement during the terminal Pleistocene or onset of the Holocene, beginning as much as 14,200 calendar years ago at Monte Verde (Davis 2006; Davis et al. 2004; de France 2005; de France et al. 2001; Des Lauriers 2006; Dillehay et al. 2008; Erlandson 2002; Erlandson et al. 1996, 2007a, 2011a; Fedje and Christensen 1999; Fedje et al. 2004, 2005a, 2005b; Johnson et al. 2002; Keefer et al. 1998; Rick et al. 2005; Sandweiss et al. 1998; Stothert et al. 2003).

These New World sites add to a growing body of evidence around the world indicating that coastal regions were important places of early human settlement (Bailey 2004; Erlandson 2001; Klein et al. 2004; Marean et al. 2007). Along with recent genetic data and evidence for Pleistocene seafaring in the western Pacific, these sites also lend support to the coastal migration theory that maritime peoples migrating from Northeast Asia into the New World contributed to the initial peopling of the Americas (Dillehay et al. 2008; Erlandson 2002; Erlandson et al. 2007a, 2008a; Fedje et al. 2005a, 2005b; Fladmark 1979).

The relatively rapid environmental and climatic changes of the Younger Dryas may have been particularly pronounced for coastal peoples, but much remains to be learned about the archaeology and paleoecology of this time period. Several islands in the Mediterranean appear to have been colonized during the Younger Dryas (Broodbank 2006), as well as the first secure evidence for human settlement on California's Channel Islands (Erlandson et al. 2008a, 2011a; Johnson et al. 2002; Kennett et al. 2008; Reeder et al. 2011), Haida Gwaii in British Columbia (Fedje and Mathewes 2005), and Isla Cedros in Baja California (des Lauriers 2006). The earliest coastal sites in these regions may not have been identified yet, especially since much of the early archaeological record may lie submerged on the continental shelves. But there may be interesting connections between island colonization, the rapid cooling of the Younger Dryas, sea level rise, and changes in marine and terrestrial ecosystems.

In this paper, we discuss the archaeological and ecological records of the terminal Pleistocene and earliest Holocene from around 13,000 to 11,000 cal BP on California's Channel Islands. We expand on a recent summary of Younger Dryas environmental and cultural developments for the west coast of the United States and Baja California (Reeder et al. 2011) and the discovery of three terminal Pleistocene Channel Island sites (Erlandson et al. 2011a). Much of our focus is on work at several coastal archaeological sites that are among the oldest in the Americas with calibrated radiocarbon dates ranging between about 13,000 and 11,300 cal BP, roughly corresponding to the Younger Dryas (12,900 to 11,500 cal BP) (Figure 4.1). The archaeological record for this period is sparse and limited to interior or pericoastal sites located some distance from now submerged Younger Dryas shorelines, making many of our interpretations preliminary. Nevertheless, when placed in the context of recent models (including models of kelp forest productivity) of near-shore-marine environmental changes from the Pleistocene to the Holocene (Graham et al. 2003; Kinlan et al. 2005), and high-resolution marine climate records and pollen sequences from the Santa Barbara Basin (Hendy et al. 2002, 2004; Heusser 1998; Kennett et al. 2007, 2008), these data provide important lessons on human responses to rapid and dynamic environmental changes in coastal regions.

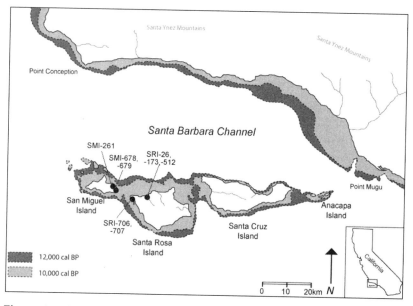

Figure 4.1 Map of the Santa Barbara Channel, ancient shorelines, and sites discussed in the text (Drafted by Leslie Reeder). Sea level reconstruction follows Porcasi et al. (1999).

Environmental and Cultural Background

The eight Channel Islands (northern group: Anacapa, Santa Cruz, Santa Rosa, and San Miguel; southern group: San Clemente, Santa Catalina, San Nicolas, and Santa Barbara) contain distinct insular ecosystems and biota that were available to early colonists. Ranging in size from about 2.6 to 249 km², the Channel Islands are currently between about 20 and 98 km from the mainland coast. All the islands have a Mediterranean climate, with mild summers and cool, wet winters. The relatively arid climate and generally alkaline archaeological soils have promoted good preservation of most archaeological remains, although erosion by waves, wind, and running water has affected many sites (Rick et al. 2006).

The Channel Islands contain a limited terrestrial fauna and flora, lacking many animals and plants common on the mainland (Schoenherr et al. 1999). The largest endemic land mammal, the diminutive island fox (*Urocyon littoralis*), occurs as a discrete subspecies on all the islands except Anacapa and Santa Barbara, and the island spotted skunk (*Spilogale gracilis*) is found only on Santa Rosa and Santa Cruz. During the late Pleistocene, pygmy mammoths (*Mammuthus exilis*) lived on the northern Channel Islands. The earliest dates for humans and latest dates for mammoths overlap statistically (Agenbroad 1998; Agenbroad et al. 2005), but some of these dates (i.e., those on human bone collagen) still await accurate corrections and calibration. Until the Historic period, the islands were devoid of the many terrestrial herbivores, carnivores, and rodents common along the mainland coast. The islands contain a diverse suite of marine resources, however, including an array of sea and shore birds, marine fishes, pinnipeds (seals and sea lions), cetaceans, and shellfish species.

During the last 20,000 years, the geography of the Channel Islands has changed dramatically. Sea level was considerably lower during the late Pleistocene and early Holocene, making the islands larger in area and somewhat closer to the mainland, but none of the islands were connected to the mainland during the Quaternary (Johnson 1983; Kennett et al. 2008; Porcasi et al. 1999). At the height of the last glacial, around 18,000 years ago, the northern islands formed a single land mass (Santarosae), the eastern end of which was only about 7–8 km from the mainland at the LGM. The islands moved toward their current configuration during the middle Holocene (see Figure 4.1). A number of additional islets were also located throughout the area, most of which are now submerged (Kinlan et al. 2005; Porcasi et al. 1999). Several studies have reconstructed ancient shorelines for the late Pleistocene through the Holocene in southern California (e.g., Inman 1983; Inman et al. 2005; Kennett et al. 2008; Kinlan et al. 2005; Masters and Aiello 2007; Nardin et al. 1981; Porcasi et al. 1999). More recent studies rely on global, sea-level curves (e.g., Bard et al. 1990, 1996; Fairbanks 1989) that suggest sea levels were roughly 120 m below present about 19,500 years ago, 50 m below present approximately 13,000 years ago, and 30–20 m below present about 9,000 years ago (see Inman et al. 2005; Kennett et al. 2008; Masters and Aiello 2007; Porcasi et al. 1999). Kennett et al. (2008) argue for a sequential breakup of Santarosae, with Anacapa separating around 10,900 cal BP, Santa Cruz from Santa Rosa around 9300 cal BP, and Santa Rosa from San Miguel around 9000 cal BP. These data suggest that all the northern islands remained connected until about 11,000 cal BP— after the end of the Younger Dryas.

Kinlan et al. (2005) noted that dramatic changes in shoreline length, island area, and reef area followed the end of the LGM, causing re-organization of marine habitats, particularly kelp forests that may have influenced Native American demography and subsistence strat-egies. Northern Channel Island reef areas and kelp forests remained productive throughout the Holocene, but were roughly 25% more ex-tensive during the terminal Pleistocene than today, after which they decreased gradually in size through the early to middle Holocene (Graham et al. 2003; Kinlan et al. 2005). Because kelp forests are a major source of near-shore productivity and biological diversity— supporting or sheltering a variety of shellfish, fish, seabirds, and sea mammals—used by both ancient and historic peoples, this re-structuring of marine habitats undoubtedly affected early, coastal foragers.

In addition to extensive climatic records, the Channel Islands con-tain thousands of archaeological sites with a nearly continuous record of hunter-gatherer occupation spanning 13,000 years. These sites were home to some of the most densely populated and complex late Holocene hunter-gatherers known (Arnold et al. 2004; Kennett 2005; Rick et al. 2005). Determining when humans first reached the islands and how the earliest peoples adapted to island environments is challenging. With relatively steep offshore bathymetry and comparatively limited lateral movement of shorelines, the Channel Islands have emerged as one of the best areas for documenting early New World maritime adap-tations and the implications for an initial coastal migration into the Americas (Cassidy et al. 2004; Erlandson 2002; Erlandson et al. 2007a, 2007b, 2008a, 2011a; Johnson et al. 2002; Kennett 2005; Reeder et al. 2008; Rick et al. 2001, 2005). However, many sites likely remain sub-merged under the ocean. No Clovis or Folsom points have been found on the Channel Islands, but a few isolated Paleoindian fluted points have been found on the coastal mainland (see Rondeau et al. 2007). The earliest Channel Island sites contain unique, stemmed points and crescents (Erlandson et al. 2011a). About fifty Channel Island sites appear to be securely dated between about 13,000 and 8000 cal BP, indicating that at least five of the eight Channel Islands were occupied during the early Holocene or earlier (Erlandson et al. 2008a; Rick et al. 2005). Most of these sites are on the northern Channel Islands, where more archaeological research has been accomplished and greater effort has been made to identify early sites. For the southern Channel Islands, the only well-documented early site is at Eel Point (SCLI-43) on San Clemente Island, which is dated to about 8400 cal BP (Cassidy et al. 2004; Raab and Yatsko 1992). Chipped-stone crescents, widely considered to be diagnostic of early Holocene or terminal Pleistocene occupations, have also been found on Santa Catalina and San Nicolas islands (Davis et al. 2010), however, suggesting that all the islands may have been visited or colonized by early maritime peoples. Below we focus on the earliest archaeological evidence from San Miguel and Santa Rosa islands, because the greatest amount of research on early island archaeology has been conducted there, and they contain the only well-documented sites older than 10,000 cal BP.

Terminal Pleistocene/Younger Dryas Sites on the Channel Islands

Since terminal Pleistocene shorelines on the Channel Islands have all been submerged and eroded by rising seas, we have searched for interior localities such as caves, rockshelters, springs, and lithic outcrops that may have drawn coastal peoples to interior locations (Erlandson et al. 2008a, 2011a). Currently seven archaeological sites, four on Santa Rosa and three on San Miguel, have produced evidence for human occupations that date between about 13,000 and 11,500 cal BP. These sites date within or close to the Younger Dryas, with one falling near the onset of the Younger Dryas and six falling near the end. Although the available data from these sites is still limited, they include some of the earliest shell middens in North America and provide a rare opportunity to examine human adaptations in a coastal setting during the dynamic Younger Dryas period. Several other sites have produced chipped-stone crescents and Arena points (also known as Channel Islands Barbed points), artifacts that may date to this same time period, but also may date to the early Holocene (especially Arena points; Erlandson and Braje 2007, 2008; Reeder et al. 2011; Rick 2008) (Figure 4.2). Our research is ongoing, and much of the work is preliminary. However, the available data provide a framework for

Figure 4.2 Arena point, crescents, and biface from early sites on Santa Rosa Island (adapted from Reeder et al. 2008).

building testable models focused on explaining terminal Pleistocene lifeways and environments on the Channel Islands (see also Kennett et al. 2008).

Arlington Springs, Santa Rosa Island

In 1959, Phil Orr (1968) recovered three human bones exposed in situ at the Arlington Springs site (CA-SRI-173), located adjacent to a freshwater spring and stream flowing over a bedrock sill along the northwest coast of the island. These human remains (two femora and a patella) were exposed in a steep cutbank along Arlington Creek, embedded in a refilled arroyo sequence approximately 11 m below the modern ground surface. At the time the human remains were deposited, the site was several kilometers from the shoreline at an interior locality people may have been drawn to by the presence of freshwater—especially in the dry summer season. Orr's initial research suggested an age of roughly 10,000 BP (uncalibrated), with recent redating and work at the site suggesting an age closer to 13,000 cal BP, making these among the oldest human remains in the Americas and the oldest well-documented archaeological site on the Channel Islands (Johnson et al. 2002).

A team led by John Johnson of the Santa Barbara Museum of Natural History (SBMNH) has conducted additional fieldwork at the site, including ground penetrating radar, excavation, soils studies, mapping, and other analyses designed to provide a better context for Orr's find and help define the antiquity and geoarchaeological context of the human remains, which Orr had stored intact in a block of sediment at the SBMNH. Although the final report is pending, several radiocarbon dates suggest a most likely date of approximately 11,000 BP (uncalibrated; Johnson et al. 2002). Depending on the corrections used for calibrating the dates, the calendar age of the Arlington Man remains could be anywhere between about 13,000 and 11,500 cal BP (see Erlandson et al. 2011a; Reeder et al. 2008, 2011; Rick et al. 2005). Recent stratigraphic research suggests that the age of the human bones found by Orr may be close to around 12,900 cal BP (Erlandson et al. 2008a, 2011a; Johnson et al. 2002; Kennett et al. 2008). If confirmed, this chronology would place seafaring Paleoindians on Santarosae Island by about 13,000 cal BP, essentially contemporary with the Clovis complex in the continental interior.

Recent research at Arlington Springs has produced no additional human remains or diagnostic artifacts, although a few small fragments of chipped-stone debitage were found in Orr's soil block and the paleosol from which the bones appear to have been removed. The absence of diagnostic artifacts or other habitation debris does not allow for detailed reconstructions of the subsistence strategies or lifeways of these early Channel Islanders, but this important locality confirms a terminal Pleistocene occupation by maritime paleocoastal peoples, who appear to have at least occasionally used the island interior.

Radio Point (CA-SRI-512W and CA-SRI-26), Santa Rosa Island

Radio Point is located to the east of Arlington Canyon, and it is one of the areas Orr (1968) argued contained Pleistocene archaeological sites. Two sites in this area have produced evidence of terminal Pleistocene occupations with faunal remains and chipped-stone tools. These are CA-SRI-26, first recorded and investigated by Orr (1968) and later by Erlandson (1994), and CA-SRI-512W, first investigated by Erlandson and Rick (Erlandson et al. 2011a). The larger of the two sites, CA-SRI-512W, is the most well-documented. Currently situated on a raised marine terrace just above a rocky beach, a dark paleosol is exposed in alluvium on the terrace. At the time it was occupied, the site appears to have been about 5–7 km from the coast, however, and our excavations suggest that the site may have been a temporary camp where people prepared stone tools for hunting waterfowl and other foods

(Erlandson et al. 2011a). A suite of six AMS radiocarbon dates on bird bone and charcoal samples from the deposits suggest that the site was occupied between about 12,000 and 11,350 cal BP, with a most likely date of 11,800 to 11,500 cal BP, corresponding with the latter centuries of the Younger Dryas. Excavations and surface collection at the site produced sixty-six small stemmed CIB points, nineteen crescents, a number of biface performs, an abundance of chipped-stone debitage, numerous flake tools, red ochre, and worked bone (Erlandson et al. 2011a). No shellfish were recovered, but bird, fish, and marine mammal bones are all represented, including migratory waterfowl (snow and Canada geese), *Chendytes lawi* (an extinct flightless duck), harbor seal (*Phoca vitulina*), rockfish (*Sebastes* spp.), and perch (Ebiotocidae). These data provide some of the earliest evidence for the hunting of waterfowl in the Americas and document important technologies used by coastal peoples near the close of the Younger Dryas.

Although Orr (1968) speculated that CA-SRI-26 dated to the late Pleistocene, Erlandson's (1994) investigation produced a date of around 8000–7800 cal BP for a buried, red abalone, midden at the site. In 2010, we reexamined eroding exposures at CA-SRI-26, identifying a 40–45 cm thick archaeological component in a paleosol about 2.25 m below the surface (Erlandson et al. 2011b). Surface collections and a small, test pit excavated in intact portions of the paleosol provide preliminary data, producing over 100 chipped-stone artifacts, including several Channel Island Barbed points and an Amol point, a few crescents, more than 200 bird, fish, marine mammal, and rodent bones, and small amounts of marine shell. An AMS radiocarbon date obtained for a California mussel shell provided a date of 11,340–11,220 cal BP that is similar to CA-SRI-512W (Erlandson et al. 2011b). Together evidence from CA-SRI-512W and CA-SRI-26 documents a sophisticated hunting tradition and the presence of at least two hunting camps on the northwest coast of Santa Rosa Island near the end of the Younger Dryas.

SRI Bluffs (CA-SRI-706 and CA-SRI-707), Santa Rosa Island

Two sites that were identified during the 2007–2008 seasons were on the high bluffs overlooking the southwest coast of Santa Rosa Island. They contained evidence for early occupations, including a low-density, shell deposit at one site dated to the terminal Pleistocene. These sites, CA-SRI-706 and CA-SRI-707, have produced chipped-stone crescents and Arena points, respectively. Both sites are located on the rim of the steep southern escarpment, with a commanding view of the shoreline and coastal waters below. Located on a gently sloping terrace overlooking the southwest coast, CA-SRI-706 is a large lithic scatter with chipped-stone tools, cobbles, and debitage of Monterey, Cico, and local cherts. Most of the soil has been scoured off the site surface, leaving behind a caliche hardpan and caliche-encrusted, soil remnants, as well as a sparse deflated scatter of California mussel (*Mytilus californianus*), red abalone (*Haliotis rufescens*), and giant gumboot chiton (*Cryptochiton stelleri*) shells. A few small, soil islands with nonnative grass cover are present on the site, mostly on the northern edge. A few formal tools, including biface fragments and four crescents, similar to artifacts recovered from Cardwell Bluffs just across the San Miguel Passage suggested a paleocoastal age for the site. Younger materials may also be present, but no tool types diagnostic of later time periods were noted.

During fieldwork in 2008, a red abalone shell, still embedded in the caliche encrusted soil and surrounded by a variety of chipped-stone debitage, was identified in the eastern area of the site. This shell was photographed in situ and removed for radiocarbon dating. A well-preserved fragment of the red abalone shell produced an AMS ^{14}C date of 11,500 cal BP (Reeder et al. 2011), which is similar to dates for the Cardwell Bluffs sites on San Miguel Island (Table 4.1). Although no artifacts have been found embedded in the remnant soils at the site, this date and the chipped-stone crescent from the surface suggest a terminal Pleistocene age range for the site.

About 5–7 m south of the embedded abalone shell was a small cluster of about 10–20 thin Monterey chert pebbles or small cobbles that had been tested by knappers, a few flakes, and a crude biface. The directly dated, red abalone shell embedded in the site's deposits suggests that the site's occupants harvested these large, marine mollusks. The California mussels and giant chitons may also date to the same time period, as similar shellfish assemblages are found in terminal Pleistocene sites on San Miguel Island (Erlandson et al. 2011a). The dearth of intact midden at the site currently makes it difficult to infer what the subsistence strategies were for the early peoples who occupied this site.

Located about 2 km to the east, CA-SRI-707 is a large, lithic scatter, which is widely dispersed over a low, caliche knoll that represents the base of an ancient, dune ridge. Chipped-stone tools, cobble cores and hammers, and abundant debitage of Monterey and Cico cherts, metavolcanics, quartzite, and other cherts are scattered across the site. Occasional fragments of mussel, barnacle, and abalone shell are also present on the site's surface, but no signs of an intact midden were noted. As with CA-SRI-706, most of the site's surface soil is badly eroded, with a caliche hardpan and some caliche-encrusted soil remnants left behind. Although the site is large, we found few formal tools.

Table 4.1 Summary of calibrated radiocarbon age ranges and associated artifacts from terminal Pleistocene, Channel Island sites.

Site	Material dated	Calibrated age range (cal BP)	Associated technology	References
CA-SMI-678	Twelve dates on marine shell	12,240–11,190	Chipped-stone crescents and Channel Island barbed points	Erlandson et al. 2011a
CA-SMI-679	Five dates on marine shell and charcoal	12,920–11,430	Chipped-stone crescents and Channel Island barbed points	Erlandson et al. 2011a
CA-SMI-261	Three dates on marine shell and charcoal	12,600–11,240	Expedient chipped-stone tools	Erlandson et al. 1996; Rick et al. 2001
CA-SRI-173	Six dates on human bone collage, charcoal, and mouse bone	~13,000–12,000	Human remains and no tools	Johnson et al. 2002
CA-SRI-26	One date on marine shell	11,340–11,220	Chipped-stone artifacts, including Channel Island barbed points and an Amol point	Erlandson et al. 2011b
CA-SRI-512W	Six dates on charcoal and bird bone	12,010–11,360	Chipped-stone crescents and Channel Island barbed points and a bone tool	Erlandson et al. 2011a
CA-SRI-706	One date on marine shell	11,620–11,240	Chipped-stone crescent and expedient tools	This paper; Reeder et al. 2011

Nonetheless, some of those found are relatively rare and significant: two large Arena points, two crescent fragments, along with several nondiagnostic biface fragments. These artifacts are similar to those from assemblages at the Cardwell Bluffs sites and from CA-SRI-706, suggesting that CA-SRI-707 may also have been occupied during the terminal Pleistocene or early Holocene. But, the site may also contain a younger component. Collectively, CA-SRI-706 and CA-SRI-707 confirm an early human presence on the west end of Santa Rosa Island, including at least one occupation that occurred near the end of the Younger Dryas. The chipped-stone crescents and points also show that paleocoastal peoples were using relatively sophisticated, projectile technologies to hunt or fish on the island.

Daisy Cave (CA-SMI-261), San Miguel Island

Consisting of a cave and rockshelter complex on San Miguel Island's northeast coast, Daisy Cave (CA-SMI-261) has also produced a low-density, shell midden dated to approximately 11,900 ± 200 cal BP, with a denser series of early Holocene midden strata deposited between around 10,200 to 8500 cal BP, and later middle and late Holocene materials (Erlandson 2007; Erlandson et al. 1996; Rick et al. 2001). Daisy Cave contains a rockshelter about 4 × 5 m wide with a shell midden sloping in front of the shelter and an interior fissure about 11 m deep and 1.5 to 3 m wide. Cave of the Chimneys (CA-SMI-603) also has deposits going back to at least 8000 cal BP (Vellanoweth et al. 2003). With relatively steep offshore bathymetry, Daisy Cave remained fairly close to late Pleistocene shorelines and provided excellent shelter from the elements.

Daisy Cave was first excavated by Charles Rozaire (1978) in the 1960s, with later work by Pandora Snethkamp, Dan Guthrie, and Don Morris in the 1980s. Since 1992, teams led by Erlandson have conducted detailed excavations at the site, accompanied by extensive radiocarbon dating and analyses of the recovered materials, including work in the earliest component as well as the later middle and late Holocene materials (Erlandson 2007; Erlandson et al. 1996). Detailed chronological, artifact, and faunal data, along with material from the early site deposits from Daisy Cave have been reported (Connolly et al. 1995; Erlandson 2005; Erlandson and Jew 2009; Erlandson et al. 1996; Rick et al. 2001; Vellanoweth et al. 2003). These studies have produced some of the oldest perishable technologies and shell beads along the Pacific Coast of North America, the earliest fishhooks in the New World, and evidence for relatively intensive marine fishing in near-shore, kelp forests starting around 10,000 to 9500 cal BP (Connolly et al. 1995; Rick et al. 2001).

The terminal Pleistocene component (Stratum G) dates between roughly 12,000 and 11,250 cal BP (see Table 4.1) This low-density midden produced a small assemblage of shellfish remains (red abalone, California mussel, black turban [*Tegula funebralis*], crab, chiton, and so forth), very small amounts of bone, and a few chipped-stone tools and pieces of debitage made from Monterey chert (Erlandson 1993, 2007; Erlandson and Jew 2009; Erlandson et al. 1996) that is now known to have a local source on eastern San Miguel Island (Erlandson et al. 2008b) (Table 4.2). The sample from Stratum G produced about twenty-one pieces of fish bone, including two identifiable bones from a rockfish (*Sebastes* spp.) (Rick et al. 2001). Though the samples are small, Stratum G is currently among the oldest, securely dated, shell middens in the New World, and it confirms the use of watercraft and exploitation of near-shore shellfish as early as 12,000 cal BP.

During the 1960 excavations just outside the rockshelter at Daisy Cave, Rozaire (1978) recovered a finely made, stemmed point now recognized as an Arena. Erlandson and Jew (2009) noted that this point came from deep within the midden sequence at Daisy Cave, suggesting that it was associated with either the early Holocene or terminal Pleistocene strata. More recent analysis of Rozaire's field notes, however, suggests that this barbed point came from the very base of the shell midden, probably from the terminal Pleistocene occupation of Stratum G. This association is consistent with recent discoveries of similar points at the Cardwell Bluffs sites, which are dated between about 12,000 and 11,500 years.

Cardwell Bluffs (CA-SMI-678 and CA-SMI-679), San Miguel Island

From 2005 to 2010, excavations at a large complex of lithic scatters and low-density shell middens located on the bluffs overlooking Cardwell Point near the east end of San Miguel Island produced extensive evidence for terminal Pleistocene and early Holocene occupations. Three discrete sites (CA-SMI-678, -679, and -680) were identified in eroded areas that were probably exposed by historic-era overgrazing. Obscured by vegetation and sediments in places, these sites may ultimately be found to cover a continuous area about 500 m long (north-south) and up to 300 m wide (east-west). The Cardwell Bluffs sites are located on an ancient raised marine terrace about 60–75 m asl, where beach cobbles of Cico and Tuqan Monterey cherts (Erlandson et al. 2008b, 2011a) were brought to the surface by the shrinking and swelling of clay vertisols (see Johnson 1972; Wood and Johnson 1978). This cobble sheet, which appears to have been covered by dune sand

Table 4.2 Summary of major dietary faunal remains identified in terminal Pleistocene, Channel Island sites.

	Habitat	Santa Rosa sites (CA-SRI-512W, CA-SRI-706)[1]	San Miguel sites (CA-SMI-261, CA-SMI-678, CA-SMI-679)[1]
Marine invertebrates			
Black turban (*Chlorostoma funebralis*)	Rocky intertidal, middle intertidal	–	Common at CA-SMI-678 and CA-SMI-679. Present at CA-SMI-261
California mussel (*Mytilus californianus*)	Rocky intertidal, mid-intertidal zone to 24 m.	Small amounts present at CA-SRI-26	Common at CA-SMI-678 and CA-SMI-679. Present at CA-SMI-261
Chiton undif.	Rocky intertidal	–	Common at CA-SMI-678 and CA-SMI-679
Crab undif.	Rocky intertidal	–	–
Giant chiton (*Cryptochiton stelleri*)	Rocky intertidal, soft bottoms, low intertidal to 21m.	–	–
Red abalone (*Haliotis rufescens*)	Rocky intertidal, kelp forest, low intertidal to 40 m	Small amounts embedded in surface at CA-SRI-706	Common at CA-SMI-678 and CA-SMI-679. Present at CA-SMI-261

Table 4.2 *Continued*

	Habitat	Santa Rosa sites (CA-SRI-512W, CA-SRI-706)[1]	San Miguel sites (CA-SMI-261, CA-SMI-678, CA-SMI-679)[1]
Vertebrates			
Rockfish (*Sebastes* sp.)	Rocky reef/kelp forest	Present at CA-SRI-512	Present at CA-SMI-261
Snow and Canada Goose (Anserini)	Migratory waterfowl	Common at CA-SRI-512	—
Albatross? (Diomedeidae)	Migratory seabird	Present at CA-SRI-512	—
Extinct flightless duck (*Chendytes lawi*)	Unknown, resident seabird?	Present at CA-SRI-512	—
Harbor seal (*Phoca vitulina*)	Resident marine mammal	Present at CA-SRI-512	—

[1] All faunal data from San Miguel and Santa Rosa Island sites are from Erlandson et al. (2011a) and Rick et al. 2001.

later in the Holocene, attracted paleocoastal peoples away from the now, drowned shorelines which would have been located between 1–2 km to the north and south. Hundreds of broken bifaces have been collected from the eroded sites' surfaces, ranging from crude pre-forms to finished points, including numerous finely made crescents, Channel Island Barbed points, and small stemmed and serrated points (Erlandson et al. 2011a). All three of these artifact types, relatively rare on the Channel Islands until recently, have been recognized as early time markers (Erlandson et al. 2011a). The finished crescents and stemmed points are often extremely delicate and well-made, in con-trast to early Milling Stone projectile points from the mainland coast (see Rogers 1929).

In several areas where intact soils still exist at CA-SMI-678 and -679, these bifaces and other quarry/workshop debris are asso-ciated with the remnants of low-density, shell middens that have produced calibrated AMS ^{14}C dates ranging between about 12,000 and 11,500 cal BP (Erlandson et al. 2011a). Sampling of these mid-dens accomplished so far has produced no animal bone, but shell-fish assemblages are mostly dominated by large red abalone shells (*Haliotis rufescens*), California mussels (*Mytilus californianus*), giant chitons (*Cryptochiton stelleri*), black turban (*Tegula funebralis*), crab shell (Brachyura), and other cool-water, shellfish taxa (Erlandson et al. 2011a). One small midden feature at CA-SMI-679 contained nu-merous shells of black turban snails (Erlandson et al. 2011a), a rela-tively small species sometimes regarded as a low-ranked resource (Raab 1992). Although the faunal remains from the Cardwell Bluffs sites suggest a heavy emphasis on shellfish collecting by paleocoast-al peoples, the numerous bifaces and points tell a different tale. They suggest that hunting of seabirds and other waterfowl, sea mam-mals, and fishing were also important activities, just as they were at CA-SRI-512W (Erlandson et al. 2011a).

Except for the terminal Pleistocene components at Arlington Springs and Daisy Cave, where sample sizes are very low and diagnostic arti-facts have not yet been recovered, crescents and/or stemmed points have been found at all the terminal Pleistocene sites identified on San Miguel and Santa Rosa islands so far. Shellfish remains are present at most of these early localities, but animal bone is rare, possibly reflect-ing the differential processing and transport of various marine faunal remains from coastlines located a kilometer or more from most of the sites. Intertidal shellfish are smaller and more easily transported than pinnipeds, for instance, and can remain alive for 2–3 days out of the water. The shellfish assemblages associated with the known terminal Pleistocene sites on San Miguel and Santa Rosa islands also contain a suite of shellfish species that thrive in relatively cool waters, which is consistent with paleoecological data that suggest that the Younger Dryas was a period of relatively cold, sea surface temperatures. These terminal Pleistocene shellfish assemblages are different from those recovered from most early Holocene sites from the same islands, which contain more fish bones, fewer diagnostic lithic artifacts, and more expedient chipped-stone technology.

The Early Holocene Record

Beginning about 10,000 cal BP the number of datable site components on the Channel Islands begins to increase dramatically. This may be due in part to population growth, but it is also likely influenced by increased site visibility in recent times, better preservation as shorelines progressively approached the modern coast, and younger sites generally being easier to locate. On San Miguel Island at least twenty-eight sites have produced calibrated ^{14}C dates falling between about 10,200 and 8000 cal BP—with Daisy Cave containing at least four to five discrete occupations dating to this interval and several other sites producing artifacts (crescents, Channel Island Barbed points) diagnostic of the early Holocene. On Santa Rosa Island, at least eighteen sites date to between 10,000 and 8000 cal BP (Reeder et al. 2008), and crescents or Channel Island Barbed points have been found at several others. Although systematic investigation for early sites on the other islands has not been as intensive as on San Miguel or Santa Rosa, CA-SCRI-109 on Santa Cruz Island and Eel Point (CA-SCLI-43) on San Clemente Island contain occupations in excess of 8,000 calendar years (Cassidy et al. 2004; Glassow et al. 2008).

Faunal remains from sites dating to the early Holocene on the Channel Islands suggest a heavy reliance on marine shellfish, especially California mussel and black abalone (Erlandson et al. 2007b; Rick et al. 2005). Fishes and other vertebrate remains are much less common in the excavated sites, except for Daisy Cave where early Holocene deposits have produced roughly 27,000 bones from near-shore, marine fishes, suggesting relatively sophisticated fishing capabilities by this early date (Rick et al. 2001). Although few of these artifacts have been found in association with faunal remains, chipped-stone bifaces, Channel Island Barbed points, and crescents from early sites may indicate the exploitation of marine mammals and birds despite the dearth of these bones in early sites (Erlandson and Braje 2007; Erlandson et al. 2008b). Although it seems logical that the early Holocene peoples who created these sites were descended from the earlier occupants of Arlington Springs, Radio Point, Cardwell Bluffs, Daisy Cave, and

CA-SRI-706, two gaps of more than a millennium currently limit our understanding of the relationships between these paleocoastal peoples.

Discussion

The rapid climatic changes during the Younger Dryas have attracted considerable attention from researchers. Several studies have shown that these changes varied around the world, with some areas, particularly in the southern hemisphere showing limited evidence for cooling (see Ackert et al. 2008; Barrows et al. 2008; Lowell and Kelly 2008). The proposed causes of Younger Dryas cooling are also diverse, ranging from catastrophic floods of glacial meltwater to extraterrestrial impacts (Broecker 2006; Firestone et al. 2007; Haynes 2008; Surovell et al. 2009). Archaeological data have also shown that human lifeways and survival strategies during the Younger Dryas were equally diverse and complex (see Straus et al. 1996).

Although not well-documented due to the effects of postglacial, sea-level rise, this is probably particularly true for coastal areas that were rapidly changing geographically and ecologically after the end of the last glacial. Some scholars have drawn interesting connections to early island colonization and the onset of the Younger Dryas (e.g., Broodbank 2006), but the detailed relationships between climatic events and human colonization remain poorly understood. The early Channel Island sites described above suggest that seafaring Paleoindians first colonized California's Channel Islands at least 13,000 years ago, with seven sites now dated to the general Younger Dryas climatic interval, between about 13,000 and 11,500 cal BP (Reeder et al. 2011). The Arlington Springs human remains appear to date near the onset of the Younger Dryas, followed by a gap of several centuries for which no archaeological sites have been identified on the Channel Islands (see Kennett et al. 2008). Between about 12,000–11,500 cal BP, Daisy Cave, the Radio Point and Cardwell Bluffs sites, and CA-SRI-706 were all occupied, followed by another gap of roughly 1,000 years before the earliest Holocene occupations are known at Daisy Cave, CA-SMI-522, and Seal Cave (CA-SMI-610; Erlandson et al. 2008a, 2011a).

Although tantalizing, the evidence from the earliest of these sites currently raises as many questions as it answers. Arlington Springs, for instance, contains just three human bones and small amounts of tool-making debris, but lacks details of the nature of this person's life and activities. The terminal Pleistocene deposits at Daisy Cave have produced a small assemblage of faunal remains and expedient chipped-stone artifacts, little more than a "postcard from the past" (Erlandson 2007). The Cardwell Bluffs sites contain several, discrete, shell middens associated with extensive collections of bifaces and tool-making debris from an early maritime technology. The stratified Radio Point sites have produced numerous Arena points and crescents associated with the bones of waterfowl, marine mammal, and fish bones, but little or no marine shell. The site, CA-SRI-706, provides a secure early date, but the crescents and other chipped-stone artifacts from the site surface cannot be definitively associated with the dated shell.

Like Broodbank's (2006) assessment of Mediterranean Islands, there appears to be a temporal link between early Channel Island occupations and the Younger Dryas. Unlike the Mediterranean, where humans (and earlier hominids) were present for many millennia prior to island colonization, the colonization of California's Channel Islands may be related to the initial migration of maritime peoples down the Pacific Coast of the Americas. If so, these early seafarers appear to have been an extension of a much earlier development of maritime adaptation than is apparent in the Mediterranean, beginning with voyaging and fishing activity that developed in the islands of Southeast Asia, greater Australia, western Melanesia, and East Asia between about 55,000 and 35,000 years ago (Erlandson 2002, 2010).

The dramatic return to near glacial conditions during the Younger Dryas may have resulted in a variety of changes on the California Coast, including cooler ocean temperatures and changes in sea level, marine productivity, and terrestrial plant communities (Reeder et al. 2011). During the Younger Dryas, the northern islands were still connected in a single land mass, which did not break up until about 10,000 ± 1000 cal BP, splitting first in the east at Anacapa Island and then moving westward (see Kennett et al. 2008; Porcasi et al. 1999). Rising seas reduced the available land by around 50% between the LGM and 10,000 cal BP and also reduced the amount of reef area and kelp forest habitats (Kinlan et al. 2005). This pattern became more pronounced as sea levels continued to rise during the middle Holocene and one that would have greatly affected the resources and habitats available for early human exploitation (Graham et al. 2003; Kennett et al. 2008).

Kelp forests are productive marine habitats, which have long been exploited by Native Americans and other coastal peoples (see Dillehay et al. 2008; Steneck et al. 2002). Kelp forests contain rich communities of fishes, marine mammals, and shellfish that were a focus for Native peoples on the California Channel Islands throughout human occupation (see Rick et al. 2005). Although subsistence remains in the earliest Channel Island sites are limited, the shellfish that have been identified suggest that people collected rocky intertidal species, as well as deeper-water, red abalones found in kelp forests (Erlandson et al. 2011a). By the early Holocene, people were taking a variety of finfish (especially California sheephead and rockfish) and shellfish from kelp forests. Erlandson et al. (2007a) suggested that the peopling of the Americas may have been facilitated by the exploitation of kelp resources, as a more-or-less continuous ring of kelp ecosystems may have extended around the North Pacific Rim after about 16,000 cal BP. Documenting the nature, extent, and evolution of late Pleistocene kelp forests is difficult, especially when trying to compare relatively recent changes between the LGM and the early Holocene, as fossil records are limited and archaeological sites contain only a fraction of the resources available.

Graham et al. (2003) argued that near the end of the LGM (~18,500 years ago), kelp-forest productivity was high, as rocky reef areas were larger than today because of lowered seas. Stable isotope records of Foraminera, along with sedimentary sequences, and faunal data from a core extracted from the Santa Barbara Basin provide evidence for abrupt ocean cooling during the Younger Dryas (Hendy et al. 2002). Upwelling and marine productivity appear to have decreased during the Younger Dryas when compared to the more productive Bølling warm interval, suggesting there was no linear correlation between cool and warm temperatures and marine productivity (Hendy et al. 2004; Pospelova et al. 2006). Because there were larger reef areas during the Younger Dryas compared to the Holocene, the greater productivity of near-shore, kelp forests may have helped offset the lower upwelling and oceanic productivity somewhat, but precisely how these variables affected early peoples occupying the islands is not known.

Whatever the nature of marine productivity across the general Younger Dryas interval, early peoples would have lived on islands that were undergoing dramatic geographic changes, including the reorganization of terrestrial and marine ecosystems. Since initial human populations were likely low and they entered a presumably "virgin" landscape, these environmental developments may not have had as great an effect on early colonists as they would if populations were larger. If pygmy mammoth populations still existed when the first humans arrived (Agenbroad et al. 2005), they would have represented a potentially large "walking larder" and their demise may have led to considerable vegetation changes. If pinniped populations approached or exceeded modern levels, they would have represented an enormous store of meat and calories for early maritime peoples. If kelp forests were considerably more extensive as Kinlan et al. (2005) have suggested, sea otter, fish, and shellfish populations may also have been extremely rich. Finally, if foxes were not part of the endemic Pleistocene fauna of the islands (see Rick et al. 2008), populations of sea birds and other waterfowl (including the flightless duck, *Chendytes lawi*) may have been much larger than they are today.

As sea levels continued to rise, sandy habitats appear to have increased with kelp forests declining from the terminal Pleistocene to the middle/late Holocene (Graham et al. 2003). The scant archaeological data from the terminal Pleistocene on the Channel Islands makes it difficult to test the abundance of resources available using the archaeological record. Recent research at Daisy Cave, Cardwell Bluffs, Radio Point, and CA-SRI-706 is providing important data on the nature of these changes, but without more information, specific interpretations must remain speculative. In particular, the contents of Cardwell Bluffs, which appear to be dominated by the cool-water-loving, red abalone may indicate a cooling of ocean temperatures, perhaps related to the Younger Dryas. Today, red abalones are mostly subtidal in southern California where waters are cooler. Most early Holocene sites on the islands are dominated by black abalone and California mussel, which are both found in the intertidal. Red abalones reappear again in many sites after about 8,000 years ago (Braje et al. 2009). The red abalone at Cardwell Bluffs, along with giant chiton, another cold-water-loving species, may support the argument for the cooling of ocean conditions during the Younger Dryas; but, this is currently speculative, and additional field and lab work are needed to test this hypothesis, including stable isotope analyses of these marine shells.

Further, changes in terrestrial communities were equally complicated, with new data suggesting changes to island regimes, large-scale wildfires and erosion, and a general loss of conifers on the Channel Islands beginning around 13,000 years ago and persisting throughout the Younger Dryas, cold period (see Anderson et al. 2010; Kennett et al. 2008; Reeder et al. 2011). Ocean cores from the Santa Barbara Basin contain evidence for extensive wildfires in the region just before the onset of Younger Dryas (Anderson et al. 2010; Kennett et al. 2008; Pinter and Anderson 2006). The cause of these wildfires continues to be debated, ranging from massive wildfires set by early human colonists (Pinter and Anderson 2006) to an extraterrestrial impact resulting in widespread burning and concomitant erosion and mass wasting (Kennett et al. 2008). Whatever the cause, there appears to be a change in plant communities on the islands at this time. Pollen evidence from land and ocean cores suggest a decrease in conifers and increase in oak woodland, coastal sage scrub, and other nonarboreal, plant communities (see Anderson 2002; Anderson et al. 2010; Heusser 1998; Kennett et al. 2008; Reeder et al. 2011). These changes during the Younger Dryas suggest a dynamic period that would have posed new challenges and opportunities for early Channel Island peoples.

Conclusions

Archaeological data from California's Channel Islands document a human occupation extending back at least 13,000 calendar years. Research at Daisy Cave and at the recently documented Radio Point, Cardwell Bluffs, and CA-SRI-706 sites provides compelling evidence for human occupation between around 12,200 to 11,400 cal BP. These sites, among the oldest along the Pacific Coast of the Americas, indicate the use of watercraft for colonization and exploitation of marine resources by some of the earliest people to occupy North America. The technologies used by these paleocoastal peoples are poorly known, but recent research is helping to fill this gap. Daisy Cave, CA-SRI-706, and the Radio Point and Cardwell Bluffs sites have all produced chipped-stone crescents, Channel Island Barbed points, and other stemmed points and bifaces that date to the terminal Pleistocene and early Holocene (Erlandson et al. 2008a, 2011a; Erlandson and Braje 2007; Glassow et al. 2008; Reeder et al. 2008, 2011; Rick 2008). Because most of these artifacts have been found on eroded site surfaces, their precise chronology remained uncertain until crescents and stemmed points were recovered in situ at CA-SRI-26, CA-SRI-512W, and CA-SMI-678, where they have been dated between 12,200 and 11,400 cal BP (Erlandson et al. 2011a). As for their function, they appear to be part of a maritime, hunting technology, possibly used to hunt birds and marine mammals and to spear fish (Erlandson and Braje 2007; Erlandson et al. 2011a; Glassow et al. 2008).

While these early Channel Island sites are located far from a Beringian entry point into the Americas, the great antiquity and association with island and coastal lifeways lends support to a coastal migration into the Americas (Erlandson et al. 2007a, 2008a). If Dillehay et al. (2008) are correct in interpreting the Monte Verde II site as a southern extension of an early migration down the Pacific Coast, we might expect to find that California's Channel Islands were first explored by maritime peoples as early as 15,000 cal BP. At present, however, we have just a handful of fairly ephemeral sites, providing glimpses of paleocoastal peoples from about 13,000 to 11,500 cal BP, leaving many unanswered questions about the origin and nature of these occupations. Have we identified the oldest sites on the islands? Were the southern Channel Islands also colonized during the terminal Pleistocene; and, if not, why did human settlement there lag behind the northern islands? Were the northern Channel Islands abandoned between roughly 13,000 and 12,000 cal BP (see Kennett et al. 2008) and again between about 11,400 and 10,200 cal BP, or have we simply not found sites of this antiquity? How large were early populations, and what was the nature of their settlement and subsistence strategies? How are these people related to the better documented early Holocene peoples in the region? Finally, how did these paleocoastal people adjust to the rapid and dynamic climatic and environmental conditions of the terminal Pleistocene and early Holocene, particularly the Younger Dryas cold spell?

Paleoclimatic data from the Santa Barbara Channel region are extraordinary, providing an opportunity to model marine and terrestrial environments during this time and the context of these early coastal peoples. Records of marine climate suggest that the Younger Dryas resulted in cool ocean conditions, but reduced upwelling, at least when compared to the productive and warm Bølling (Hendy et al. 2002, 2004; Pospelova et al. 2006). Changes on land are less well known, but there appears to have been a transition from arboreal conifers to a less wooded, oak woodland/grass habitat during the Younger Dryas (Anderson 2002; Heusser 1998; Kennett et al. 2008; Reeder et al. 2011). Sea-level rise may have slowed, but the northern Channel Islands remained connected throughout the Younger Dryas, and reef area and kelp forest habitats were considerably larger than during most of the Holocene (see Graham et al. 2003).

Superimposing a fragmentary and limited archaeological record on top of these environmental records is relatively speculative. What we can say is that there appears to be a correlation between Younger Dryas climate change and the earliest evidence for human occupation of the Channel Islands. The earliest paleocoastal peoples on the islands may have lived in fairly low population densities and they may even have abandoned the islands at times, though caution is necessary as many of the earliest coastal settlements may now be underwater. If populations were low, responses to climatic variability of the Younger Dryas may have been less pronounced, especially because rich, marine habitats would have provided a wealth of resources for colonists. As little as twenty years ago, most scholars probably would have dismissed the possibility of a Paleoindian occupation of the Channel Islands, so the next decade or two should provide important archaeological discoveries on the nature of the earliest New World, coastal adaptations and human responses to terminal Pleistocene, environmental changes. With a number of research projects currently searching for or investigating early sites on the Channel Islands, the future of paleocoastal archaeology looks bright.

Acknowledgments

We thank Ann Huston, Kelly Minas, Don Morris, Mark Senning, and Ian Williams of Channel Islands National Park for supporting our research on San Miguel and Santa Rosa islands. We also thank those colleagues who freely shared their knowledge and data that contributed to our interpretations, including Todd Braje, Michael Glassow, Mike Graham, John Johnson, Doug Kennett, James Kennett, Nicholas Pinter, Leslie Reeder, Tom Rockwell, Pandora Snethkamp, Rene Vellanoweth, and Jack Watts. Our work at Cardwell Bluffs, Radio Point, and SRI Bluffs has been supported by National Science Foundation awards, EAR 0746314 (Erlandson), and BCS 0917677 (Erlandson and Rick). Finally, we thank Metin Eren for inviting us to participate in this volume and anonymous reviewers for constructive comments that significantly improved our chapter.

References

Ackert, R., Jr., R. Becker, B. Singer, M. Kurz, M. Caffee, and D. Mickelson
2008 Patagonian Glacier Response during the Late Glacial-Holocene Transition. *Science* 321:392–395.

Agenbroad, L.
1998 New Pygmy Mammoth (*Mammuthus exilis*) Localities and Radiocarbon Dates from San Miguel, Santa Rosa, and Santa Cruz Islands, California. In *Contributions to the Geology of the Northern Channel Islands, Southern California*, edited by P. Weigand, pp. 169–175. Bakersfield: Pacific Section of the American Association of Petroleum Geologists.

Agenbroad, L., J. Johnson, D. Morris, and T. Stafford, Jr.
2005 Mammoths and Humans as Late Pleistocene Contemporaries on Santa Rosa Island. In *Proceedings of the Sixth California Islands Symposium*, edited by D. Garcelon and C. Schwemm, pp. 3–7. National Park Service Technical Publication CHIS-05-01, Institute for Wildlife Studies, Arcata.

Anderson, R.
2002 *Fire and Vegetation History of Santa Rosa Island, Channel Islands National Park, California*. Final Report for a Cooperative Agreement (1443CA8000-8-0002) between Channel Islands National Park and Northern Arizona University. Channel Islands National Park, Ventura.

Anderson, R., S. Starratt, R. Brunner Jass, and N. Pinter
2010 Fire and Vegetation History on Santa Rosa Island, Channel Islands, and Long-term Environmental Change in Southern California. *Journal of Quaternary Science* 25:782–797.

Arnold, J., M. Walsh, and S. Hollimon
2004 The Archaeology of California. *Journal of Archaeological Research* 12:1–73.

Bailey, G.
2004 World Prehistory from the Margins: The Role of Coastlines in Human Evolution. *Journal of Interdisciplinary Studies in History and Archaeology* 1:39–50.

Bailey, G., N. Flemming, G. King, K. Lambeck, G. Momber, L. Moran, A. Al-Sharekh, and C. Vita-Finzi
   2007 Coastlines, Submerged Landscapes, and Human Evolution: The Red Sea Basin and the Farasan Islands. *Journal of Island and Coastal Archaeology* 2:127–160.

Bard, E., B. Hamelin, and R. Fairbanks
   1990 U-Th Ages Obtained by Mass-spectrometry in Corals from Barbados-sea-Level during the Past 130,000 Years. *Nature* 346:456–458.

Bard, E., B. Hamelin, M. Arnold, L. Montaggioni, G. Cabioch, G. Faure, and F. Rougerie
   1996 Deglacial Sea-level Record from Tahiti Corals and the Timing of Global Meltwater Discharge. *Nature* 382:241–244.

Barrows, T., S. Lehman, L. Fifield, and P. De Deckker
   2008 Absence of Cooling in New Zealand and the adjacent Ocean during the Younger Dryas Chronozone. *Science* 318:86–89.

Binford, L.
   1968 Post-Pleistocene Adaptations. In *New Perspectives in Archaeology*, edited by S. Binford and L. Binford, pp. 313–341. Aldine, Chicago.

Braje, T., J. Erlandson, T. Rick, P. Dayton, and M. Hatch
   2009 Fishing from Past to Present: Long-term Continuity and Resilience of Red Abalone Fisheries on California's Northern Channel Islands. *Ecological Applications* 19:906–919.

Broecker, W.
   2006 Was the Younger Dryas Triggered by a Flood? *Science* 312:1146–1148.

Broodbank, C.
   2006 The Origins and Development of Mediterranean Early Maritime Activity. *Journal of Mediterranean Archaeology* 19:199–230.

Cassidy, J., L. Raab, and N. Kononenko
   2004 Boats, Bones, and Biface Bias: The Early Holocene Mariners of Eel Point, San Clemente Island, California. *American Antiquity* 69:109–130.

Connolly, T., J. Erlandson, and S. Norris
   1995 Early Holocene Basketry and Cordage from Daisy Cave, San Miguel Island, California. *American Antiquity* 60:309–318.

Davis, L.
   2006 Geoarchaeological Insights from Indian Sands, a Late Pleistocene Site on the Southern Northwest Coast, USA. *Geoarchaeology* 21:351–361.

Davis, L., M. Punke, R. Hall, M. Fillmore, and S. Willis
   2004 A Late Pleistocene Occupation on the Southern Coast of Oregon. *Journal of Field Archaeology* 29:7–16.

Davis, T., J. Erlandson, G. Fenenga, and K. Hamm
   2010 Chipped Stone Crescents and the Antiquity of Maritime Settlement on San Nicolas Island. *California Archaeology* 2:185–202.

de France, S.
   2005 Late Pleistocene Marine Birds from Southern Peru: Distinguishing Human Capture from El Niño-induced Windfall. *Journal of Archaeological Science* 32:1131–1146.

de France, S., D. Keefer, J. Richardson, and A. Umire Alvarez
2001 Late Paleoindian Coastal Foragers: Specialized Extractive Behavior at Quebrada Tacahuay, Peru. *Latin American Antiquity* 12:413–426.

des Lauriers, M.
2006 Terminal Pleistocene and Early Holocene Occupations of Isla de Cedros, Baja California, Mexico. *Journal of Island and Coastal Archaeology* 1:255–270.

Dillehay, T., C. Ramirez, M. Pino, M. Collins, J. Rossen, J. Pino-Navarro
2008 Monte Verde: Seaweed, Food Medicine, and the Peopling of South America. *Science* 320:784–786.

Erlandson, J.
1993 Evidence for a Terminal Pleistocene Human Occupation of Daisy Cave, San Miguel Island. *Current Research in the Pleistocene* 10:17–21.

1994 *Early Hunter-gatherers of the California Coast.* Plenum, New York.

2001 The Archaeology of Aquatic Adaptations: Paradigms for a New Millennium. *Journal of Archaeological Research* 9:287–350.

2002 Anatomically Modern Humans, Maritime Voyaging, and the Pleistocene Colonization of the Americas. In *The First Americans: The Pleistocene Colonization of the New World*, edited by N. Jablonski, pp. 59–92. Memoirs of the California Academy of Sciences 27. California Academy of Sciences, San Francisco.

2005 An Eccentric Crescent from Daisy Cave, San Miguel Island, California. *Current Research in the Pleistocene* 22:45–46.

2007 Sea Change: The Paleocoastal Occupations of Daisy Cave. In *Seeking Our Past: An Introduction to North American Archaeology*, edited by S. Neusius and G. Gross, pp. 135–143. Oxford University Press, Oxford.

2010 Neptune's Children: The Origins and Evolution of Seafaring. In *Global Origins and Development of Seafaring*, edited by A. Anderson, J. Barrett, and K. Boyle, pp. 18–27. McDonald Institute for Archaeological Research, Cambridge University, Cambridge.

Erlandson, J., and T. Braje
2007 Early Maritime Technology on California's San Miguel Island: Arena Points from CA-SMI-575-NE. *Current Research in the Pleistocene* 24:85–86.

2008 Five Crescents from Cardwell: Context and Function of Eccentric Crescents from CA-SMI-679, San Miguel Island, California. *Pacific Coast Archaeological Society Quarterly* 40:35–45.

Erlandson, J., and S. Fitzpatrick
2006 Oceans, Islands, and Coasts: Current Perspectives on the Role of the Sea in Human Prehistory. *Journal of Island and Coastal Archaeology* 1:5–32.

Erlandson, J., and N. Jew
2009 An Early Maritime Biface Technology from Daisy Cave, San Miguel Island, California: Reflections on Sample Size, Site Function, and Other Issues. *North American Archaeologist* 30:145–165.

Erlandson, J., D. Kennett, B. Ingram, D. Guthrie, D. Morris, M. Tveskov, G. West, and P. Walker
  1996 An Archaeological and Paleontological Chronology for Daisy Cave (CA-SMI-261), San Miguel Island, California. *Radiocarbon* 38:355–373.
Erlandson, J., M. Graham, B. Bourque, D. Corbett, J. Estes, and R. Steneck
  2007a The Kelp Highway Hypothesis: Marine Ecology, the Coastal Migration Theory, and the Peopling of the Americas. *Journal of Island and Coastal Archaeology* 2:161–174.
Erlandson, J., T. Rick, T. Jones, and J. Porcasi
  2007b One if by Land, Two if by Sea: Who Were the First Californians? In *California Prehistory: Colonization, Culture, and Complexity*, edited by T. Jones and K. Klar, pp. 53–62. AltaMira Press, Walnut Creek.
Erlandson, J., M. Moss, and M. des Lauriers
  2008a Life on the Edge: Early Maritime Cultures of the Pacific Coast of North America. *Quaternary Science Reviews* 27:2232–2245.
Erlandson, J., T. Braje, and T. Rick
  2008b Tuqan Chert: A "Mainland" Monterey Chert Source on San Miguel Island, California. *Pacific Coast Archaeological Society Quarterly* 40:23–34.
Erlandson, J., T. Braje, T. Rick, T. Davis, and J. Southon
  2009 The Archaeology of Seal Cave (CA-SMI-604): A Paleocoastal Shell Midden on San Miguel Island. *Proceedings of the Sixth California Islands Conference*, edited by C. Damiani and D. Garcelon, pp. 33–42. Institute for Wildlife Studies, Arcata.
Erlandson, J., T. Rick, T. Braje, M. Casperson, B. Culleton, B. Fulfrost, T. Garcia, D. Guthrie, N. Jew, D. Kennett, M. Moss, L. Reeder, C. Skinner, J. Watts, and L. Willis
  2011a Paleocoastal Seafaring, Maritime Technologies, and Coastal Foraging on California's Channel Islands. *Science* 331:1181–1185.
Erlandson, J., T. Rick, and N. Jew
  2011b CA-SRI-26: A Terminal Pleistocene Site on Santa Rosa Island, California. *Current Research in the Pleistocene*, in press.
Fairbanks, R.
  1989 A 17,000-year Glacio-eustatic Sea Level Record: Influence of Glacial Melting Rates on the Younger Dryas Event and Deep-ocean Circulation. *Nature* 342:637–642.
Fedje, D., and T. Christensen
  1999 Modeling Paleoshorelines and Locating Early Holocene Coastal Sites in Haida Gwaii. *American Antiquity* 64:635–652.
Fedje, D., and R. Mathewes (editors)
  2005 *Haida Gwaii: Human History and Environment from the Time of Loon to the Time of the Iron People.* University of British Columbia Press, Vancouver.
Fedje, D., Q. Mackie, E. Dixon, and T. Heaton
  2004 Late Wisconsin Environments and Archaeological Visibility on the Northern Northwest Coast. In *Entering America: Northeast Asia and*

Beringia before the Last Glacial Maximum, edited by D. Madsen, pp. 97–138. University of Utah Press, Salt Lake City.

Fedje, D., H. Josenhans, J. Clague, J. Vaughn Barrie, D. Archer, and J. Southon
2005a Hecate Strait Paleoshorelines. In *Haida Gwaii: Human History and Environment from the Time of Loon to the Time of the Iron People*, edited by D. Fedje and R. Mathewes, pp. 21–37. University of British Columbia Press, Vancouver.

Fedje, D., T. Christensen, H. Josenhans, J. Mc Sporran, and J. Strang
2005b Millennial Tides and Shifting Shorelines: Archaeology on a Dynamic Landscape. In *Haida Gwaii: Human History and Environment from the Time of Loon to the Time of the Iron People*, edited by D. Fedje and R. Mathewes, pp. 163–186. University of British Columbia Press, Vancouver.

Firestone, R., A. West, J. Kennett, L. Becker, T. Bunch, Z. Revay, P. Schultz, T. Belgya, D. Kennett, J. Erlandson, O. Dickerson, A. Goodyear, R. Harris, G. Howard, J. Kloosterman, P. Lechler, P. Mayewski, J. Montgomery, R. Poreda, T. Darrah, S. Que Hee, A. Smith, A. Stich, W. Topping, J. Wittke, and W. Wolbach
2007 Evidence for an Extraterrestrial Impact 12,900 Years Ago that Contributed to the Megafaunal Extinctions and the Younger Dryas Cooling. *Proceedings of the National Academy of Sciences* 104:16016–16021.

Fladmark, K.
1979 Routes: Alternate Migration Corridors for Early Man in North America. *American Antiquity* 44:55–69.

Glassow, M., P. Paige, and J. Perry
2008 *The Punta Arena Site and Early and Middle Holocene Cultural Development on Santa Cruz Island, California*. Santa Barbara Museum of Natural History Contributions in Anthropology, Santa Barbara.

Graham, M., P. Dayton, and J. Erlandson
2003 Ice-ages and Ecological Transitions on Temperate Coasts. *Trends in Ecology and Evolution* 18:33–40.

Haynes, C. Vance, Jr.
2008 Younger Dryas "Black Mats" and the Rancholabrean Termination in North America. *Proceedings of the National Academy of Sciences* 105:6520–6525.

Hendy, I., J. Kennett, E. Roark, and B. Ingram
2002 Apparent Synchroneity of Submillennial Scale Climate Events between Greenland and Santa Barbara Basin, California from 30–10 ka. *Quaternary Science Reviews* 21:1167–1184.

Hendy, I., T. Pedersen, J. Kennett, and R. Tada
2004 Intermittent Existence of a Southern California Upwelling Cell during Submillenial Climate Change of the Last 60 Kyr. *Paleoceanography* 19:1–15.

Heusser, L.
1998 Direct Correlation of Millennial-scale Changes in Western North America Vegetation and Climate with Changes in the California Current System over the Past ~60 Kyr. *Paleoceanography* 13:252–262.

Inman, D.

1983 Application of Coastal Dynamics to the Reconstruction of Paleocoastlines in the Vicinity of La Jolla, California. In *Quaternary Coastlines and Marine Archaeology*, edited by P. Masters and N. Flemming, pp. 1–49. Academic Press, New York.

Inman, D., P. Master, and S. Jenkins

2005 Facing the Coastal Challenge: Modeling Coastal Erosion in Southern California. *California and the World Ocean '02*, edited by O. Magoon, pp. 38–52. American Society of Civil Engineers, Reston.

Johnson, D.

1972 *Landscape Evolution on San Miguel Island, California.* Unpublished Ph.D. dissertation, Department of Geography, University of Kansas. UMI, Ann Arbor.

1983 The California Continental Borderland: Landbridges, Watergaps, and Biotic Dispersals. In *Quaternary Coastlines and Marine Archaeology*, edited by P. Masters and N. Flemming, pp. 482–527. Academic Press, New York.

Johnson, J., T. Stafford, Jr., H. Ajie, and D. Morris

2002 Arlington Springs Revisited. In *Proceedings of the Fifth California Islands Symposium*, edited by D. Browne, K. Mitchell, and H. Chaney, pp. 541–545. Santa Barbara Museum of Natural History, Santa Barbara.

Keefer, D., S. de France, M. Moseley, J. Richardson, D. Satterlee, and A. Day-Lewis

1998 Early Maritime Economy and El Nino Events at Quebrada Tacahuay, Peru. *Science* 281:1833–1835.

Kennett, D.

2005 *The Island Chumash: Behavioral Ecology of a Maritime Society.* University of California Press, Berkeley.

Kennett, D., J. Kennett, J. Erlandson, and K. Cannariato

2007 Human Responses to Middle Holocene Climate Change on California's Channel Islands. *Quaternary Science Reviews* 26:351–367.

Kennett, D., J. Kennett, G. West, J. Erlandson, J. Johnson, I. Hendy, A. West, T. Jones, and T. Stafford, Jr.

2008 Wildfire and Abrupt Ecosystem Disruption on California's Northern Channel Islands at the Ållerød-Younger Dryas Boundary (13.0–12.9 ka). *Quaternary Science Reviews* 27–28:2530–2545.

Kinlan, B., M. Graham, and J. Erlandson

2005 Late Quaternary Changes in the Size and Shape of the California Channel Islands: Implications for Marine Subsidies to Terrestrial Communities. In *Proceedings of the Sixth California Islands Symposium*, edited by D. Garcelon and C. Schwemm, pp. 131–142. National Park Service Technical Publication CHIS-05-01, Institute for Wildlife Studies, Arcata.

Klein, R., G. Avery, K. Cruz-Uribe, D. Halkett, J. Parkington, T. Steele, T. Volman, and R. Yates

2004 The Yserfontein 1 Middle Stone Age Site, South Africa, and Early Human Exploitation of Coastal Resources. *Proceedings of the National Academy of Sciences* 101:5708–5715.

Lowell, T., and M. Kelly
2008 Was the Younger Dryas Global? *Science* 321:348–349.

Marean, C., M. Bar-Matthews, J. Bernatchez, E. Fisher, P. Goldberg, A. Herries, Z. Jacobs, A. Jerardino, P. Karkanas, P. Minichillo, P. Nilssen, E. Thompson, I. Watts, and H. Williams
2007 Early Human Use of Marine Resources and Pigment in South Africa during the Middle Pleistocene. *Nature* 449:905–908.

Masters, P., and I. Aiello
2007 Postglacial Evolution of Coastal Environments. In *California Prehistory: Colonization, Culture, and Complexity*, edited by T. Jones and K. Klar, pp. 35–51. AltaMira Press, Walnut Creek.

Nardin, T., R. Osborn, D. Bottjer, and R. Scheidemann
1981 Holocene Sea Level Curves for Santa Monica Shelf, California Continental Borderland. *Science* 213:331–333.

Orr, P.
1968 *Prehistory of Santa Rosa Island*. Santa Barbara Museum of Natural History, Santa Barbara.

Osborn, A.
1977 Strandloopers, Mermaids, and Other Fairy Tales: Ecological Determinants of Marine Resource Utilization—The Peruvian Case. In *For Theory Building in Archaeology*, edited by L. Binford, pp. 157–205. Academic Press, New York.

Pinter, N., and S. Anderson
2006 A Mega-fire Hypothesis for the Latest Pleistocene Paleo-environmental Change on the Northern Channel Islands, California. *Geological Society of America Abstracts with Programs* 38:66–130.

Porcasi, P., J. Porcasi, and C. O'Neill
1999 Early Holocene Coastlines of the California Bight: The Channel Islands as First Visited by Humans. *Pacific Coast Archaeological Society Quarterly* 35:1–24.

Pospelova, V., T. Pedersen, and A. de Vernal
2006 Dinoflagellate Cysts as Indicators of Climatic and Oceanographic Changes during the Past 40 Kyr in the Santa Barbara Basin, Southern California. *Paleoceanography* 21, PA2010:1–16.

Raab, L.
1992 An Optimal Foraging Analysis of Prehistoric Shellfish Collecting on San Clemente Island, California. *Journal of Ethnobiology* 12:63–80.

Raab, L., and A. Yatsko
1992 Ancient Maritime Adaptations on the California Bight: A Perspective from San Clemente Island. In *Essays on the Prehistory of Maritime California*, edited by T. Jones, pp. 173–193. Center for Archaeological Research at Davis Publication 10. University of California, Davis.

Reeder, L., T. Rick, and J. Erlandson
2008 Forty Years Later: What Have We Learned about the Earliest Human Occupations of Santa Rosa Island, California? *North American Archaeologist* 29:37–64.

Reeder, L., J. Erlandson, and T. Rick
2011 Younger Dryas Environments and Human Adaptations on the West Coast of the United States and Baja California. *Quaternary International* 242:463–478.

Richardson, J., III
1998 Looking in the Right Places: Pre-5000 BP Maritime Adaptations in Peru and the Changing Environment. *Revista de Arquelogia Americana* 15:33–56.

Rick, T.
2008 An Arena Point and Crescent from Santa Rosa Island, California. *Current Research in the Pleistocene* 25:140–142.

Rick, T., J. Erlandson, and R. Vellanoweth
2001 Paleocoastal Marine Fishing on the Pacific Coast of the Americas: Perspectives from Daisy Cave, California. *American Antiquity* 66:595–613.

2006 Taphonomy and Site Formation on California's Channel Islands. *Geoarchaeology* 21:567–589.

Rick, T., J. Erlandson, R. Vellanoweth, and T. Braje
2005 From Pleistocene Mariners to Complex Hunter-gatherers: The Archaeology of the California Channel Islands. *Journal of World Prehistory* 19:169–228.

Rick, T., J. Erlandson, R. Vellanoweth, T. Braje, P. Collins, and T. Stafford, Jr.
2008 Origins and Antiquity of the Island Fox (*Urocyon littoralis*) on the California Channel Islands. *Quaternary Research* 71:93–98.

Rogers, D.
1929 *Prehistoric Man of the Santa Barbara Coast*. Santa Barbara Museum of Natural History, Santa Barbara.

Rondeau, M., J. Cassidy, and T. Jones
2007 Colonization Technologies: Fluted Projectile Points and the San Clemente Island Woodworking/Microblade Complex. In *California Prehistory: Colonization, Culture, and Complexity*, edited by T. Jones and K. Klar, pp. 63–70. AltaMira Press, Walnut Creek.

Rozaire, C.
1978 *A Report of the Archaeological Investigations of Three California Channel Islands: Santa Barbara, Anacapa, and San Miguel*. Report on file at the Central Coast Archaeological Information Center, University of California, Santa Barabra.

Sandweiss, D., H. McInnis, R. Burger, A. Cano, B. Ojeda, R. Paredes, M. Sandweiss, and M. Glascock
1998 Quebrada Jaguay: Early South American Maritime Adaptations. *Science* 281:1830–1833.

Schoenherr, A., C. Feldmeth, and M. Emerson
1999 *Natural History of the Islands of California*. University of California Press, Berkeley.

Steneck, R., M. Graham, B. Bourque, D. Corbett, J. Erlandson, J. Estes, and
M. Tegner
    2002 Kelp Forest Ecosystems: Biodiversity, Stability, Resilience, and Future.
    Environmental Conservation 29:436–459.

Stothert, K., D. Piperno, and T. Andres
    2003 Terminal Pleistocene/Early Holocene Human Adaptation in Coastal
    Ecuador: The Las Vegas Evidence. *Quaternary International* 109/110:23–43.

Straus, L., B. Eriksen, J. Erlandson, and D. Yesner (editors)
    1996 *Humans at the End of the Ice Age: The Archaeology of the Pleistocene-
    Holocene Transition.* Plenum, New York.

Surovell, T., V. Holliday, J. Gringerich, C. Ketron, C. Vance Haynes,
Jr., I. Hilman, D. Wagner, E. Johnson, and P. Claeys
    2009 An Independent Evaluation of the Younger Dryas Extraterrestrial
    Impact Hypothesis. *Proceedings of the National Academy of Sciences*
    106:18155–18158.

Vellanoweth, R., M. Lambright, J. Erlandson, and T. Rick
    2003 Early New World Maritime Technologies: Sea Grass Cordage, Shell
    Beads, and a Bone Tool from Cave of the Chimneys, San Miguel Island,
    California. *Journal of Archaeological Science* 30:1161–1173.

Wood, W., and D. Johnson
    1978 A Survey of Disturbance Processes in Archaeological Site Formation.
    Advances in Archaeological Method and Theory 1:315–381. Academic Press,
    New York.

Yesner, D.
    1980 Maritime Hunter-gatherers: Ecology and Prehistory. *Current Anthro-
    pology* 21:727–750.

    1987 Life in the Garden of Eden: Causes and Consequences of the
    Adoption of Marine Diets by Human Societies. In *Food and Evolution,*
    edited by M. Harris and E. Ross, pp. 285–310. Temple University Press,
    Philadelphia.

5

EVALUATING THE EFFECT OF THE YOUNGER DRYAS ON HUMAN POPULATION HISTORIES IN THE SOUTHEASTERN UNITED STATES

Scott C. Meeks and David G. Anderson

Introduction

The Pleistocene/Holocene transition was a period of tremendous environmental dynamism coincident with the Younger Dryas event. Representing one of the largest abrupt climate changes that has occurred within the past 100,000 years, the onset of the Younger Dryas (~12,900 cal BP) occurred too rapidly to be explained by normal, orbital-forcing events, occurring within a few decades. It has been suggested that the forcing mechanism driving this abrupt cooling event was freshwater influx into the North Atlantic resulting from catastrophic outbursts of the glacial lakes Agassiz and Ojibway into the Saint Lawrence drainage system and/or the diversion of Laurentide ice-sheet melt water from the Mississippi River into the Saint Lawrence system (Broecker and Denton 1990; Broecker et al. 1990; Leverington et al. 2000; Overpeck et al. 1989; but see Firestone et al. 2007 for a more controversial interpretation). The net effect of these outbursts of freshwater into the North Atlantic was a reduction in sea surface salinity, which altered the thermohaline conveyor belt; effectively slowing ocean circulation of warmer waters (heat) to the north and bringing cold conditions. This disruption in oceanic, thermohaline circulation

Hunter-Gatherer Behavior: Human Response during The Younger Dryas, edited by Metin I. Eren, 111–138. © Left Coast Press. All rights reserved.

resulted in significantly lower temperatures in both Europe and Greenland during the Younger Dryas compared to later Holocene temperatures. After a 1,300-year period of climatic cooling, the Younger Dryas terminated abruptly, occurring within a few decades as evidenced by a 7° C rise in temperature approximately 11,600 cal BP (Alley 2000; Alley et al. 1993). Although the Younger Dryas event is generally associated with the North Atlantic region, paleoclimate and paleovegetation proxy records from the northern and parts of the southern hemispheres provide evidence indicating that this event was largely a global phenomena (e.g., Abell and Plug 2000; Cwynar and Spear 2001; Denniston et al. 2001; Shuman et al. 2002; Thompson 2000; Van't Veer et al. 2000; Yu and Eicher 1998).

The fossil pollen records of the southeastern United States that encompass the Younger Dryas interval, although few in number, indicate that vegetation shifts, in some cases abrupt and characterized by oscillations, were occurring across the region during the Pleistocene/Holocene transition and that these shifts in vegetation were synchronic with the Younger Dryas event. However, both the magnitudes and signatures of these vegetation shifts were not uniform across the region, suggesting that a variety of factors, such as amplified seasonality, ocean and atmospheric circulation patterns, and temperature/moisture-balance gradients, were influencing the responses of local vegetation to climate change during the Younger Dryas in the southeastern United States.

The majority of pollen sites in the lower Southeast extending back to the Younger Dryas exhibit cooler, moisture conditions. Sandy Run Creek, Georgia (LaMoreaux et al. 2009), records cool, moist conditions associated with the Younger Dryas through an increased occurrence of mesic tress and an increase in riparian populations of alder. The Younger Dryas at White Pond, South Carolina (Watts 1980), and Clear Pond, South Carolina (Hussey 1993), is marked by increases in beech suggesting cool, moist conditions. In the southern Appalachians of northern Georgia, Pigeon Marsh (Watts 1975) also records a prominent spike in beech pollen, indicating cooler, moisture conditions during the Younger Dryas. In the upper middle Atlantic Coastal Plain, the pollen record at Rockyhock Bay, North Carolina (Whitehead 1981) exhibits higher percentages of hemlock, beech, and white pine during the Younger Dryas, also suggesting cooler, moisture conditions.

Pollen records, however, suggest there was some variation within the region. For example, other sites in the eastern and lower Southeast indicate that climate during the Younger Dryas was warmer and wetter. In the central Appalachians of Virginia, the pollen record at Browns Pond (Kneller and Peteet 1999) exhibits marked increases in hemlock and declines in fir during the Younger Dryas, indicating warmer, wetter conditions. At Cahaba Pond in northeastern Alabama, a rise in pine at the terminus of the Younger Dryas indicates wetter conditions (cf. Delcourt 1983). Pollen records from Florida, including Camel Lake (Watts et al. 1992), Lake Tulane (Grimm et al. 2006), and Sheelar Lake (Watts and Hansen 1994), exhibit prominent spikes in pine pollen, suggesting increased moisture availability and warmer temperatures during the Younger Dryas. Yet, a pollen record from the Tampa Bay area in Florida (Willard et al. 2007) is marked by a dominance of oak and herbs, indicating cooler, drier conditions during the Younger Dryas.

Fossil-pollen sites in the interior and western regions of the southeastern United States with records during the window of time associated with the Younger Dryas are few in number. In the northern interior of the southeastern United States, the pollen record at Jackson Pond, Kentucky (Wilkins et al. 1991), contains several pronounced reciprocal oscillations in abundances of spruce and oak, reflecting shifts between boreal/deciduous, forest ecotones associated with cool/wet and cool/dry conditions, respectively. To the north of Jackson Pond, sites such as Smoot Lake Bog, Ohio, Stotzel-Leis, Ohio, and Pretty Lake, Indiana, indicate the east-west expansion of pine into the interior Midwest during the Younger Dryas, suggesting the establishment of cooler, drier conditions (Shuman et al. 2002). However, the expansion of warm-tolerant elm in the pollen record from Chatsworth Bog, Illinois (Shuman et al. 2002), coupled with a low occurrence of spruce, fir, and birch, indicate warmer, wetter conditions.

Along the western margins of the Southeast, the pollen record from Hood Lake, Arkansas (Delcourt and Delcourt 1989), records a dominance of herbs (primarily grass and ragweed) and oak, indicating cooler, drier temperatures and open woodland during the Younger Dryas. Similar cooler, drier conditions are expressed in paleoecological records to the north in the Ozark Highlands of Missouri. The pollen record at Cupola Pond (Smith 1984) in southeastern Missouri records cool, drier conditions associated with the Younger Dryas through an increased occurrence of oak, indicating an open oak woodland with patches of prairie. A carbon isotope record from a buried, soil sequence at the Big Eddy site (Dorale et al. 2010) in southwestern Missouri, indicates an expansion of C_4 grasses during the Younger Dryas, suggesting the development of grasslands related to cooler, drier conditions.

Although the fossil-pollen record for the southeastern United States is coarse-grained and often conflicting in terms of inferred, climate conditions occurring across the region during the Younger Dryas, it does provide evidence that the Younger Dryas event was influencing biotic communities in the Southeast. This is important, as climate change during the Younger Dryas has been attributed a causal role in Paleoindian culture change across the southeastern United States. With the onset of the Younger Dryas, the widespread Clovis tradition fragmented, and more geographically circumscribed cultural traditions emerged (Anderson 1996a, 2001; Anderson and Faught 2000). Based on the numbers of sites and artifacts reported, human populations appear to have been quite low at the beginning of the Younger Dryas, while at its end, large numbers of people were apparently present across the region (Anderson 1990, 1996b; Daniel and Goodyear 2006; Driskell et al. 2012; Goodyear 2006; MacAvoy 1992; Meeks 2001). In this chapter, we employ two proxy methods, frequency analysis of hafted bifaces and summed probability analysis of ^{14}C dates, to estimate and characterize human, population histories in the southeastern United States. By using these proxy records, we hope to further evaluate what, if any, impact the Younger Dryas may have had on the population histories of Paleoindian and initial early Archaic peoples in the region.

The Chronology of Paleoindian and Initial Early Archaic Hafted Bifaces in the Southeast

Of paramount importance in considering possible cultural responses of human populations to the Younger Dryas is accurate temporal control for the various Paleoindian hafted, biface forms and associated assemblages found throughout the southeastern United States. Although large numbers of Paleoindian, hafted bifaces have been found across the region, the vast majority come from contexts that lack stratigraphic integrity and/or ^{14}C dates in clear association with diagnostic, cultural material. As a consequence, "dating" of many Paleoindian, hafted bifaces in the region has been inferential, based on cross-dating with similar forms found from other regions.

In attempt to provide chronological control of Paleoindian and initial early Archaic, hafted, biface forms, we amassed a suite of 39 ^{14}C dates from the southeastern United States and adjacent regions associated with Paleoindian and initial early Archaic, hafted bifaces (Table 5.1). The ^{14}C dates used in our analysis were selected based on creditable associations with archaeological materials and with standard deviations equal to or less than 250 years (30 of the 39 dates used in the analysis have standard deviations equal to or less than 100). The uncalibrated ^{14}C dates in our database were calibrated in the CALIB 6.0.1 program using the Intcal09 curve (Stuiver and Reimer 1993). Following the calibration of the ^{14}C dates, CALIB 6.0.1 was used to sum the probabilities to produced probability distributions for each of the Paleoindian and initial early Archaic, hafted biface forms (Figure 5.1). For illustration

Table 5.1 ¹⁴C-dates from the Southeastern United States and adjacent regions associated with Paleoindian and early Archaic diagnostics.

Site	Association	Lab number	¹⁴C yr bp	s.d.	Reference
Sloth Hole	Clovis-?	SL-2850	11,050	50	Hemmings 2004
Paleo Crossing	Gainey	AA-8250A, D, E (Average)	10,980	75	Brose 1994
Shawnee-Minisink	Gainey	Beta-101935, Beta-127162 (Average)	10,910	40	Waters and Stafford 2007
Shawnee-Minisink	Gainey	Beta-203865, UCIAMS-24865 (Average)	10,930	15	Waters and Stafford 2007
Shawnee-Minisink	Gainey	UCIAMS-24866	11,020	30	Waters and Stafford 2007
Big Eddy	Gainey	AA-26654	10,710	85	Hajic et al. 1998
Dust Cave	Quad/Beaver Lake	Beta-133790	10,310	60	Sherwood et al. 2004
Dust Cave	Quad/Beaver Lake	Beta-65181	10,310	230	Sherwood et al. 2004
Dust Cave	Quad/Beaver Lake	Beta-81609	10,340	130	Sherwood et al. 2004
Dust Cave	Quad/Beaver Lake	Beta-40680	10,345	80	Sherwood et al. 2004
Dust Cave	Quad/Beaver Lake	Beta-65179	10,390	80	Sherwood et al. 2004
Dust Cave	Quad/Beaver Lake	Beta-81613	10,490	60	Sherwood et al. 2004
Dust Cave	Quad/Beaver Lake	Beta-81599	10,500	60	Sherwood et al. 2004

(Continued)

Table 5.1 *Continued*

Site	Association	Lab number	^{14}C yr bp	s.d.	Reference
Dust Cave	Dalton	Beta-133788	9950	50	Sherwood et al. 2004
Dust Cave	Dalton	Beta-147132	10,010	40	Sherwood et al. 2004
Dust Cave	Dalton	Beta-81602	10,070	70	Sherwood et al. 2004
Dust Cave	Dalton	Beta-133791	10,100	50	Sherwood et al. 2004
Dust Cave	Dalton	Beta-147135	10,140	40	Sherwood et al. 2004
Dust Cave	Dalton	Beta-41063	10,330	120	Sherwood et al. 2004
Olive Branch	Dalton	AA-4805	9975	125	Gramly 2002
Big Eddy	Dalton	AA-26653	10,185	75	Hajic et al. 1998
Big Eddy	Dalton	AA-27480	10,340	100	Hajic et al. 1998
Big Eddy	Dalton	AA-27487	10,400	75	Hajic et al. 1998
Big Eddy	Dalton	AA-29022	10,430	70	Hajic et al. 1998
Dust Cave	Early Side Notched	Beta-81602	10,070	60	Sherwood et al. 2004
Page-Ladson	Early Side Notched	Beta-058858	9930	60	Webb and Dunbar 2006
Page-Ladson	Early Side Notched	Beta-103888	9950	70	Webb and Dunbar 2006
Page-Ladson	Early Side Notched	Beta-058857	10,000	80	Webb and Dunbar 2006
Page-Ladson	Early Side Notched	Beta-21750	10,016	124	Webb and Dunbar 2006

Table 5.1 *Continued*

Site	Association	Lab number	¹⁴C yr bp	s.d.	Reference
8LE2105	Early Side Notched	Beta-81467, Beta-81468 (Average)	9870	38	Faught et al. 2003
8LE2105	Early Side Notched	Beta-81469	10,090	70	Faught et al. 2003
Warm Mineral Springs	Early Side Notched	I-7205, I-7209, I-7216, I-7217, I-7218 (Average)	9967	58	Webb and Dunbar 2006
James Farnsley	Early Side Notched	Beta-152586	9680	170	Stafford and Cantin 2009
James Farnsley	Early Side Notched	ISGS-4897	9700	100	Stafford and Cantin 2009
James Farnsley	Early Side Notched	Beta-13574	10,020	100	Stafford and Cantin 2009
James Farnsley	Early Side Notched	ISGS-4797	10,050	100	Stafford and Cantin 2009
James Farnsley	Early Side Notched	ISGS-4835	10,090	120	Stafford and Cantin 2009
James Farnsley	Early Side Notched	ISGS-4898	10,100	100	Stafford and Cantin 2009

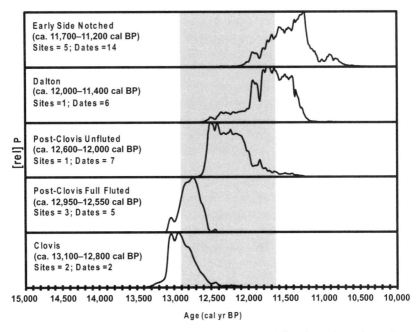

Figure 5.1 Summed probability plots of calibrated ¹⁴C-dates for Paleoindian and early Archaic hafted bifaces. Shaded gray area denotes the Younger Dryas chronozone. Black solid vertical lines denote calibrated median dates of individual age determinations.

purposes, the probabilities for each of the hafted biface forms analyzed were renormalized so that the maximum probability equaled one. We assumed that the greatest, summed-probability distribution for each of the hafted, biface forms was reflective of their approximate age range. This is, admittedly, a tenuous task as the use of ¹⁴C dates is hampered by a host of problems, including old wood effects, dates with large statistical errors, plateaus and wiggles in the calibration curve, taphonomic processes that are time-dependent, variation in the comprehensiveness of ¹⁴C dates reported for individual sites and regions, and the fact that the ¹⁴C record is more a reflection of archaeological investigations and less a record of the totality of human occupation in a region (e.g., Erlandson et al. 2001; Guilderson et al. 2005; Rick 1987; Surovell and Brantingham 2007). Despite these problems, the position taken here is that the ¹⁴C database used in our study provides an approximation of both the duration of the various Paleoindian and initial early Archaic hafted, biface forms in the southeastern United States and when these forms occurred in relation to the Younger Dryas.

Clovis (~ 13,100–12,750 cal BP)

Despite ample archaeological evidence for extensive Clovis occupation across the southeastern United States, there are few sites from the region with ^{14}C dates in direct association with Clovis-aged materials. The earliest ^{14}C dates reported in association with Clovis materials in the southeastern United States were obtained from Stratum IV at the Johnson site in central Tennessee (Broster and Barker 1992; Broster et al. 1991; Broster and Norton 1996). Two of these ^{14}C dates (12,660 ± 970 BP [16,516–13,834 cal BP; p = 1.00] and 11,700 ± 980 BP [15,226–12,515 cal BP; p = 0.98]) have large standard deviations and are too inexact to provide accurate chronological information. A third ^{14}C date of 11,980 ± 110 BP (13,731–12,733 cal BP; p = 1.00) was obtained from a basin-shaped hearth in association with a Clovis preform. However, this date is problematic as it dates approximately 600 calendar years older than most accepted dates for Clovis-age materials in North America. The earliest accepted ^{14}C date for Clovis-age material in the southeastern United States was obtained from Sloth Hole, Florida (Hemmings 2004). An ivory foreshaft that produced a ^{14}C date of 11,050 ± 50 BP (13,081–12,865 cal BP; p = 1.00) is presumed to be associated with a Clovis occupation of the site. A ^{14}C date of 10,920 ± 250 BP (13,088–12,613 cal BP; p = 1.00) was obtained from a hearth associated with the Clovis occupation at Cactus Hill in Virginia (Feathers et al. 2006; McAvoy and McAvoy 1997). Taken together, the summed probability distribution of the Clovis ^{14}C dates from Sloth Hole and Cactus Hill indicates a temporal span from 13,100 to 12,750 cal BP (about a 350-calendar-year duration) in the southeastern United States. Importantly, this temporal span places the development of Clovis during the late Ållerød and terminating within the first century or so of the onset of the Younger Dryas. This approximately 350-year interval spanning the later Ållerød and early Younger Dryas for Clovis in the southeastern United States closely follows a recent assessment of the extant Clovis ^{14}C record of North America (Waters and Stafford 2007).

Post-Clovis Fluted (~12,950–12,550 cal BP)

Post-Clovis fluted hafted bifaces in the southeastern United States encompass a variety of constricted, haft forms, including Cumberland, Barnes, and Redstone. Currently, there are no dates associated with these post-Clovis fluted, hafted bifaces in the southeastern United States. These various southeast, post-Clovis, fluted forms are morphologically similar to Gainey hafted bifaces from the Midwest, which have been dated at several sites in proximity to the

Southeast. The pooled average of three ^{14}C dates obtained from a post mold at the Paleo Crossing site in Ohio produced a date of 10,980 ± 75 BP (12,950–12,711 cal BP; p = 1.00) (Brose 1994). Excavation of two hearths associated with the Gainey occupation at Shawnee-Minisink in Pennsylvania produced dates ranging between 11,020 ± 30 BP (12,968–12,768 cal BP; p = 0.95) and 10,896 ± 22 BP (12,825–12,671 cal BP; p = 1.00) (Waters and Stafford 2007). The Big Eddy site in Missouri produced a ^{14}C date of 10,710 ± 85 BP (12,685–12,561 cal BP; p = 1.00) on charcoal in close association with a Gainey hafted biface (Hajic et al. 1998; Lopinot et al. 2000). Assuming that the summed probability of the Gainey dates from these three midwestern sites is applicable to the morphologically similar post-Clovis, fluted, hafted bifaces in the Southeast; the development of post-Clovis, fluted forms across the region can be tentatively placed from 12,950 to 12,550 cal BP. This temporal span places the development of post-Clovis fluted, hafted bifaces in the Southeast during the first four centuries of the Younger Dryas.

Post-Clovis Unfluted (~12,600–12,000 cal BP)

Post-Clovis, unfluted, hafted bifaces in the Southeast encompasses a series of lanceolate, waisted forms, including Beaver Lake, Quad, Coldwater, Hinds, Arkabutla, Suwannee, and Simpson. Presently, the only ^{14}C dates associated with post-Clovis, unfluted hafted bifaces in the southeastern United States are from Dust Cave in northwestern Alabama (Sherwood et al. 2004). A suite of seven ^{14}C dates obtained from the lowest cultural zone (Zone U) associated with a relatively discrete Quad/Beaver Lake occupation produced dates ranging between 10,500 ± 60 BP (12,562–12,390 cal BP; p = 1.00) and 10,300 ± 60 BP (12,166–11,989 cal BP; p = 0.73). The summed probability distribution of the Quad and Beaver Lake ^{14}C dates indicates a temporal span from approximately 12,600 to 12,000 cal BP (a ~600-calendar-year duration). This temporal span places the development of Quad and Beaver Lake, hafted bifaces and presumably other morphologically similar post-Clovis, unfluted forms across the southeastern United States well within the Younger Dryas.

Dalton and Dalton Variants (~12,000–11,400 cal BP)

Dalton hafted bifaces and Dalton variants (e.g., Colbert, Greenbrier, Hardaway, and San Patrice) are common across much of the Southeast, being rare only in Florida. Although Dalton occupations are prevalent across the region, the dating of Dalton in the southeastern United States has been problematic (Ellis et al. 1998; Goodyear 1982). Stratigraphic evidence from Dust Cave, Alabama, and the Hester site in Mississippi indicate that Dalton occupations occur in archaeological contexts overlying Quad and Beaver Lake occupations, indicating that Dalton post-dates various post-Clovis, unfluted forms (at least in the case of Quad and Beaver Lake forms) in the Southeast (McGahey 1996; Sherwood et al. 2004). Six ^{14}C dates obtained from a probable Dalton occupation (Zone T) at the site produced dates ranging between 10,330 ± 120 BP (12,410–11,974 cal BP; p = 0.99) and 9950 ± 50 BP (11,405–11,254 cal BP; p = 0.87) (Sherwood et al. 2004). The summed probability distribution of these ^{14}C dates indicates a temporal span from approximately 12,000 to 11,400 cal BP (~600-calendar-year duration). This temporal span places the development of Dalton near the terminus of the Younger Dryas and extending into the onset of the early Holocene. However, ^{14}C dates from sites from the central Mississippi Valley and Ozark Highlands (the Dalton Heartland) indicate that Dalton in this region developed several centuries earlier compared to the lower Southeast. At the Big Eddy site, a suite of ^{14}C dates obtained from a late Paleoindian occupation associated with Dalton, San Patrice, and Wilson hafted bifaces produced dates ranging between 10,430 ± 70 BP (12,359–12,210 cal BP; p = 0.53) and 10,185 ± 75 BP (12,042–11,751 cal BP; p = 0.99). Two ^{14}C dates (10,530 ± 650 BP [12,970–11,382 cal BP; p = 0.97]) and 10,200 ± 330 BP [12,236–11,393 cal BP; p = 0.86]) from the lower occupations at Rodgers Rockshelter in Missouri provide some support for the early development of Dalton in the region, although their large standard deviations are too inexact to provide accurate chronological information (Ahler 1976). Excavations at the Olive Branch in Illinois produced a ^{14}C date of 9975 ± 125 BP (11,630–11,248 cal BP; p = 0.94) near the base of the cultural deposits in association with the Dalton occupation (Gramly 2002). This date likely represents a terminal date for Dalton in the region and overlaps with several of the later Dalton dates from Dust Cave. Importantly, the early ^{14}C dates from the Dalton heartland indicate that Dalton in this region immediately followed post-Clovis, fluted forms (i.e., Clovis-Gainey-Dalton sequence [Lopinot et al. 2000]), a sequence that is different from that witnessed in the lower Southeast.

Early Side Notched (~11,700–11,200 cal BP)

Initial early Archaic occupations across the southeastern United States are recognized by the development of a series of regional side-notched, hafted bifaces, including Bolen, Early Side Notched (formerly Big Sandy), Taylor, and Kessel, and Cache River. In Florida, a Bolen occupation at the Page-Ladson site yielded four ^{14}C dates ranging between 10,016 ± 124 BP (11,719–11,301 cal BP; p = 0.95) and 9930 ± 60 BP (11,404–11,240 cal BP; p = 0.93). Two additional Bolen sites in Florida, Warm Mineral Springs and 8LE2105, produced similar date ranges. Four ^{14}C dates in association with a Bolen burial at Warm Mineral Springs produced a pooled average of 9967 ± 58 BP (11,409–11,266 cal BP; p = 0.65) (Webb and Dunbar 2006), and two Bolen hearths at 8LE2105 produced ^{14}C dates ranging between 10,090 ± 70 BP (11,823–11,594 cal BP; p = 0.65) and 9870 ± 38 BP (11,285–11,226 cal BP; p = 0.94) (Faught et al. 2003). In northern Alabama, the Early Side Notched occupation at Dust Cave, stratigraphically positioned above the late Paleoindian occupations, produced a ^{14}C date of 10,070 ± 60 BP (11,760–11,593 cal BP; p = 0.53). Further north in southern Indiana, excavations at the James Farnsley site identified an Early Side Notched occupation with ^{14}C dates ranging between 10,100 ± 100 BP (11,831–11,596 cal BP; p = 0.57) and 9680 ± 170 BP (10,846–10,768 cal BP; p = 1.00) (Stafford and Cantin 2009). Taken together, the summed probability distribution of the ^{14}C dates for Early Side Notched indicates a temporal span from 11,700 to 11,200 cal BP (about a 500-calendar-year duration). This temporal span places the development of Early Side Notched, hafted bifaces at the terminus of the Younger Dryas, suggesting that the development of these side-notched bifaces was largely coincident with the onset of the early Holocene.

In sum, the ^{14}C record associated with Paleoindian and initial early Archaic, hafted bifaces in the southeastern United States and adjacent regions, although admittedly fraught with problems, provides an *approximation* of both the duration of the various hafted, biface forms and when these forms occurred relative the to Younger Dryas. Importantly, the summed probability analysis of the calibrated ^{14}C record illustrates that Clovis developed during the late Ållerød and continued to within the first century or so of the Younger Dryas, eventually being replaced by various post-Clovis, fluted forms across the region. During the middle part of the Younger Dryas, post-Clovis, fluted forms appear to have given way to a series of geographically discrete post-Clovis, unfluted forms that in turn developed into Dalton and Dalton variants during the later part of the Younger Dryas, at least in the lower Southeast. In the Dalton heartland, it appears that Dalton occurred several centuries earlier compared to the lower Southeast and immediately followed post-Clovis, fluted forms in this region. Early Side Notched, hafted bifaces, although overlapping temporally with the terminus of the Younger Dryas, appear to be largely a post-Younger Dryas manifestation with the greatest probability associated with the first few centuries of the early Holocene.

Estimating Population Histories in the Southeast during the Younger Dryas

Having established a chronological framework for the various forms of Paleoindian and initial early Archaic, hafted biface forms across the southeastern United States, we now consider what affect, if any, the Younger Dryas may have had on human population histories across the region. To examine this question we employed two proxy methods to estimate and characterize human population histories in the Southeast: summed probability analysis of ^{14}C dates and frequency analysis of Paleoindian and initial early Archaic, hafted bifaces.

The first approach that we employed to explore population histories during the late Pleistocene and early Holocene in the southeastern United States was the dates-as-data approach; a technique that uses changes in the summed probability distribution of a group of ^{14}C dates as a proxy for inferring population history (e.g., Blackwell and Buck 2003; Buchanan et al. 2008; Gamble et al. 2005; Hunt and Lipo 2006; Nunn et al. 2007; Shennan and Edinborough 2007; Surovell et al. 2005). In all, we collected 226 ^{14}C dates between 13,000 and 7000 BP from fifty-six archaeological sites across the Southeast that were associated with cultural material, although not necessarily in clear association with diagnostic materials. To account for the potential that multiple dates associated with a single occupation from a given site might bias the results, we averaged the conventional ^{14}C dates that were from the same context (e.g., stratum, feature, or dated specimen) *and* were statistically the same to produce a pooled, mean date using the CALIB 6.0.1 program. This resulted in a final tally of 140 ^{14}C dates from fifty-six sites in the database (Table 5.2).

The conventional ^{14}C dates in the database were calibrated in the CALIB 6.0.1 program using the Intcal09 curve (Stuiver and Reimer 1993). Following the calibration of the dates, CALIB 6.0.1 was used to sum the probabilities to produce a single probability distribution. During our analysis, we assumed that the major peaks and troughs in the summed, probability distribution reflected fluctuations in population size and/or level of occupational intensity. Although many of the potential biases inherent in ^{14}C dates that we noted earlier also apply to our summed probability analysis, we suggest that the radiocarbon database used in our analysis is robust enough to obviate these concerns, and that it allows general trends in population histories

Table 5.2 Absolute frequencies of ^{14}C-dates between 13,000 and 7000 yr bp by state.

State	Number of sites	Number of dates	Number of dates (w/averaging)
Alabama	4	43	17
Arkansas	1	5	3
Delaware	2	2	2
Florida	9	50	25
Georgia	2	4	4
Kentucky	11	35	24
Louisiana	0	0	0
Maryland	0	0	0
Mississippi	3	4	3
North Carolina	2	6	5
South Carolina	1	1	1
Tennessee	12	44	32
Virginia	4	6	6
West Virginia	5	26	18
Total	56	226	140

across the southeastern United States during the late Pleistocene and early Holocene to be investigated. Figure 5.2 illustrates the summed probability distribution of the calibrated ^{14}C dates over the period of 16,000 to 7000 cal BP. Several peaks and troughs are depicted in the summed probability distribution spanning the late Pleistocene and early Holocene, which we interpret as population events related to fluctuations in population size and/or level of occupational intensity. Our focus here is the period from 15,000 to 11,200 cal BP, which we have divided into five population events.

Frequency analysis of Paleoindian and initial early Archaic, hafted bifaces was based on data contained in the Paleoindian Database of the Americas (PIDBA, http://pidba.utk.edu; accessed 02/23/2010). A total of 9,003 hafted bifaces could be assigned to one of five forms: Clovis, post-Clovis fluted, post-Clovis unfluted, Dalton, and Early Side Notched (Table 5.3). The underlying assumption of this hafted bifaces-as-data approach is that diachronic shifts in hafted-biface frequencies reflect broad demographic trends and/or the amount of activity within a region during a particular time span (i.e., more hafted bifaces equates with more people). Inferring temporal, demographic trends using

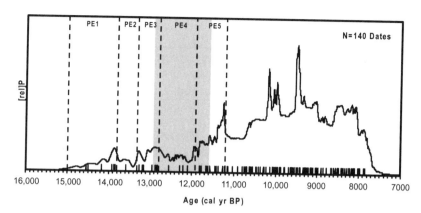

Figure 5.2 Summed probability plot of calibrated ¹⁴C-dates dating between 16,000 and 7000 cal yr BP. Shaded gray area denotes the Younger Dryas chronozone. Black solid vertical lines denote calibrated median dates of individual age determinations. Black dashed lines denote population events (PE1 = colonization; PE2 = contraction; PE3 = demic expansion; PE4 = contraction; PE5 = main demic expansion).

the number of hafted bifaces must be scrutinized, however, because the frequency of hafted bifaces is a problematic gauge with respect to population size. A larger number of hafted bifaces for a particular time period might indicate that there was a larger population or that more activity (i.e., increased land-use) transpired during that period. Alternatively, it might indicate that a steady or even a diminishing population was more dispersed across the landscape and may be reflective of settlement reorganization. What is more, the PIDBA has several inherent biases related to surface visibility and farming practices, intensity of archaeological investigations, misidentification or inaccurate dating of hafted, biface forms, varying durations of hafted, biface forms, and uneven sampling at both the state and county levels (see Anderson and Faught 1998).

As Table 5.3 and Figure 5.3 clearly illustrate, the PIDBA data are uneven in terms of counts for various hafted, biface forms and the level of state and county reporting. In order to account for varying durations of time associated with the various hafted, biface forms, coupled with the uneven recording of various forms in each state, the PIDBA data were normalized by dividing the total number of hafted bifaces per 1,000 km² for a given form by its estimated duration. The results of this data normalization are provided in Table 5.4 and presented graphically in Figure 5.4. Although normalization of the PIDBA data cannot rectify all the potential biases noted above, the use of a large number of hafted

Table 5.3 Absolute frequencies of Paleoindian and early Archaic hafted bifaces by state in the PIDBA.

State	Clovis	Post-Clovis fluted	Post-Clovis unfluted	Dalton	Early Side Notched	Total
Alabama	398	341	337	12	0	1088
Arkansas	97	24	2	2	0	125
Delaware	22	0	0	6	0	28
Florida	159	17	462	0	0	638
Georgia	345	37	229	828	0	1439
Kentucky	5	66	11	19	0	101
Louisiana	0	0	0	0	0	0
Maryland	19	0	0	3	0	22
Mississippi	81	20	270	519	632	1522
North Carolina	174	65	2	50	0	291
South Carolina	214	43	83	311	424	1075
Tennessee	671	544	637	772	0	2624
Virginia	0	49	0	0	0	49
West Virginia	1	0	0	0	0	1
Total	2186	1206	2033	2522	1056	9003

bifaces covering the southeastern United States provides baseline data for exploring broad demographic trends in the archaeological record. In the ensuing discussion, the demographic trends are examined only with respect to the Southeast as a whole with no reference made to the specific states owing to incomplete reporting. While such an approach undoubtedly masks subregional variation, the goal of our analysis is to examine demographic trends at the regional level.

Building on the combined results of the PIDBA and summed probability analyses, several events related to human population histories in the southeastern United States appear to be reflected in the two datasets (Figures 5.2 and 5.4). Population Event 1, depicted in the summed probability distribution, is a marked by a slow rise in population across the southeastern United States between around 15,000 and 13,800 cal BP. Predating Clovis by several centuries, this population event may reflect

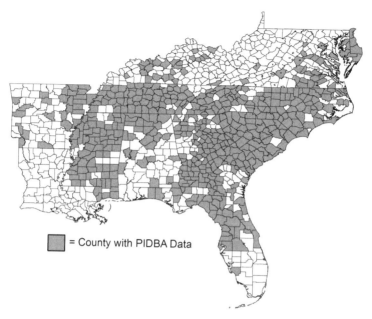

Figure 5.3 Distribution of counties in the southeastern United States containing PIDBA data used in the frequency analysis of Paleoindian and early Archaic hafted bifaces.

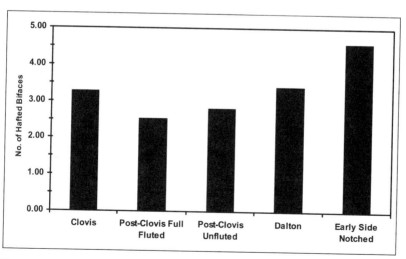

Figure 5.4 Normalized PIDBA data illustrating the number of hafted bifaces (per 1,000 km²/duration) for Paleoindian and early Archaic hafted bifaces in the southeastern United States.

Table 5.4 Normalization of hafted biface data contained in the PIDBA database.

Type	Number hafted bifaces	Counties used in analysis	Area (km²)	Hafted bifaces per 1,000 km²	Duration (yrs)	Hafted bifaces (per 1,000 km²/duration)
Clovis	2186	359	190,885	11.45	350	3.27
Post-Clovis full fluted	1206	232	119,313	10.11	400	2.53
Post-Clovis unfluted	2033	220	120,805	16.83	600	2.80
Dalton	2522	249	123,354	20.45	600	3.41
Early Side Notched	1056	73	45,979	22.97	500	4.59

initial colonization of the region by pre-Clovis peoples. This inferred colonization event has some support in the archaeological record, as several pre-Clovis sites have been reported for the Southeast and adjacent regions including Cactus Hill, Virginia (McAvoy and McAvoy 1997), Little Salt Spring (Clausen et al. 1979) and Page-Ladson (Webb and Dunbar 2006) in Florida, Topper, South Carolina (Goodyear 2000, 2005), and Meadowcroft Rockshelter, Pennsylvania (Adovasio et al. 1990). Whether such a pre-Clovis colonization event formed the basis for subsequent Clovis populations or represents a failed migration (or series of failed migrations) is unclear (Anderson and Gillam 2000). However, the apparent 600-year gap in the summed probability distribution, denoted as Population Event 2 in Figure 5.2, between this colonization event and the first demic expansion event (Population Event 3) supports the idea of a failed migration.

Population Event 3 is an approximately 400-year period spanning the interval from around 13,200 to 12,800 cal BP. Occurring during the later part of the Ållerød and extending into the onset of the Younger Dryas, this population event represents the first unequivocal evidence for widespread human occupation across the southeastern United States and falls within the time frame for Clovis settlement of the region. Both the large number of Clovis hafted bifaces reported for the Southeast (e.g., Anderson and Faught 1998; Anderson and Gillam 2000; Anderson et al. 2005, 2010) and the presence of several sites with dense assemblages, including Belle Mina in Alabama (Ensor 1992), Carson-Conn-Short in Tennessee (Broster and Norton 1996; Broster et al. 1996), Adams in Kentucky (Sanders 1990) and Topper in South Carolina (Miller 2007), support the idea that considerable human populations were present in the region.

Following the Clovis, demic expansion, there is a marked decline in the summed probability distribution that we interpret as a drop in human population across the southeastern United States. Spanning the period from around 12,800 to 11,900 cal BP, this population event (Population Event 4) occurs during the early and middle Younger Dryas and represents the contraction of both post-Clovis fluted and post-Clovis unfluted populations in the region. Trends in the normalized PIDBA data provide support for this interpretation, as there is a decrease in the number of post-Clovis fluted forms relative to Clovis. Following the decline in post-Clovis, full fluted forms, there is a slight rise in the number of post-Clovis unfluted, hafted bifaces relative to the preceding post-Clovis fluted, hafted bifaces. We interpret this as a period of population stasis and continued low population levels throughout the region. It is also during this time span that the archaeological record reflects the fragmentation of the regional Clovis culture and the subsequent development of geographically circumscribed subregional, cultural traditions in the southeastern United States (Anderson 2001; Anderson and Faught 2000). That these subregional traditions are limited in spatial scale and are located in resource rich environments suggests the possibility that post-Clovis populations during this roughly 900-year interval had a strong sense of place, concentrating their occupations in advantageous locations in relation to key resources that they may have relied on to mitigate the impact of changes in biota during the Younger Dryas.

Between about 11,900 and 11,200 cal BP there is a marked rise in the summed probability distribution that we interpret as a substantial increase in human population across the Southeast. Occurring during the later part of the Younger Dryas and extending into the early Holocene, this main demic expansion (Population Event 5) coincides with the development of Dalton and Early Side Notched, hafted biface forms across the region. The PIDBA data supports this interpretation, as there is a noticeable rise in the number of hafted bifaces of both forms indicating denser populations on the landscape. This population increase is further supported by a substantial rise in the number of Dalton and Early Side Notched sites across the Southeast (Anderson 1996b; Driskell et al. 2012; Meeks 2001; Walthall 1998). It appears that, at least by Dalton times, peoples in the southeastern United States were becoming less tethered to the landscape, a trend that seems more pronounced with Early Side Notched forms during the onset of the Holocene.

Conclusion

The data presented herein are a first approximation at evaluating the possible effect that the Younger Dryas may have had on the population histories of Paleoindian and initial early Archaic peoples in the southeastern United States. Given the potential biases inherent in both the ^{14}C record and the PIDBA data employed in our analyses and the limitations of what such data can tell us about the past, it is impossible to account for other possible factors (e.g., changes in settlement, subsistence, technology, and social interaction) that undoubtedly influenced the population patterns noted. Recognizing these problems, the population trends inferred from our analyses do suggest decreased populations and increased circumscription on the landscape during the early and middle Younger Dryas relative to preceding the Clovis period, which in turn was followed by an apparent rapid increase in populations and expanded land-use during the terminal Younger Dryas and the onset of the early Holocene. That such patterns are coincident with both the onset and terminus of the Younger Dryas is suggestive of at least some connection between climate and culture change. However, correlation does not equal causation. Until we have a better understanding of climate change across the southeastern United States, how climate change may have fostered changes in both flora and fauna resources on the landscape, and how people may have adapted to these changes in biota, we cannot implicate the Younger Dryas as the primary casual mechanism in our reconstruction of Paleoindian and early Archaic population histories.

References

Abell, P., and I. Plug
2000 The Pleistocene/Holocene Transition in South Africa: Evidence for the Younger Dryas Event. *Global and Planetary Change* 26:173–179.
Adovasio, J., J. Donahue, and R. Stuckenrath
1990 The Meadowcroft Rockshelter Radiocarbon Chronology 1975–1990. *American Antiquity* 55:348–354.
Ahler, S.
1976 Sedimentary Processes at Rodgers Shelter. In *Prehistoric Man and His Environments: A Case Study in the Ozark Highland*, edited by W. Wood and R. McMillan, pp. 123–139. Academic Press, New York.
Alley, R.
2000 The Younger Dryas Cold Interval as Viewed from Central Greenland. *Quaternary Science Reviews* 19:213–226.
Alley, R., D. Meese, C. Shuman, A. Gow, K. Taylor, P. Grootes, J. White, M. Ram, E. Waddington, P. Mayewski, and G. Zielinski
1993 Abrupt Increase in Greenland Snow Accumulation at the End of the Younger Dryas Event. *Nature* 362:527–529.
Anderson, D.
1990 A North American Paleoindian Projectile Point Database. *Current Research in the Pleistocene* 7:67–69.
1996a Models of Paleoindian and Early Archaic Settlement in the Lower Southeast. In *The Paleoindian and Early Archaic Southeast*, edited by D. Anderson and K. Sassaman, pp. 28–57. The University of Alabama Press, Tuscaloosa.
1996b Modeling Regional Settlement in the Archaic Period Southeast. In *Archaeology of the Mid Holocene Southeast*, edited by K. Sassaman and D. Anderson, pp. 157–176. University Presses of Florida, Gainesville.
2001 Climate and Culture Change in Prehistoric and Early Historic Eastern North America. *Archaeology of Eastern North America* 29:143–186.
Anderson, D., and M. Faught
1998 The Distribution of Fluted Paleoindian Projectile Points: Update 1998. *Archaeology of Eastern North America* 26:163–188.
2000 Paleoindian Artifact Distributions: Evidence and Implications. *Antiquity* 74:507–513.

Anderson, D., and J. Gillam
2000 Paleoindian Colonization of the Americas: Implications from an Examination of Physiography, Demography, and Artifact Distribution. *American Antiquity* 65:43–66.

Anderson, D., D. Miller, S. Yerka, and M. Faught
2005 Paleoindian Database of the Americas: 2005 Status Report. *Current Research in the Pleistocene* 22:91–92.

Anderson, D., D. Miller, S. Yerka, J. Gillam, E. Johanson, D. Anderson, A. Goodyear, and A. Smallwood
2010 PIDBA (Paleoindian Database of the Americas) 2010: Current Status and Findings. *Archaeology of Eastern North America* 38:63–90.

Blackwell, P., and C. Buck
2003 The Late Glacial Human Reoccupation of North-Western Europe: New Approaches to Space-time Modeling. *Antiquity* 77:232–240.

Broecker, W., G. Bond, and M. Klas
1990 A Salt Oscillator in the Glacial North Atlantic? The Concept. *Paleoceanography* 5:469–477.

Broecker, W., and G. Denton
1990 The Role of Ocean-Atmosphere System Reorganizations in Glacial Cycles. *Quaternary Science Reviews* 9:305–341.

Brose, D.
1994 Archaeological Investigations at the Paleo Crossing Site: A Paleoindian Occupation in Medina County, Ohio. In *The First Discovery of America: Archaeological Evidence of the Early Inhabitants of the Ohio Area*, edited by W. Dancey, pp. 61–76. Ohio Archaeological Council, Columbus.

Broster, J., and G. Barker
1992 Second Report of Investigations at the Johnson Site (40Dv400): The 1991 Field Season. *Tennessee Anthropologist* 17:120–130.

Broster, J., D. Johnson, and M. Norton
1991 The Johnson Site: A Dated Clovis-Cumberland Occupation in Tennessee. *Current Research in the Pleistocene* 8:8–10.

Broster, J., and M. Norton
1996 Recent Paleoindian Research in Tennessee. In *The Paleoindian and Early Archaic Southeast*, edited by D. Anderson and K. Sassaman, pp. 288–297. University of Alabama Press, Tuscaloosa.

Broster, J., M. Norton, D. Stanford, C. Vance Haynes, Jr., and M. Broster
1996 Stratified Fluted Point Deposits in the Western Valley of Tennessee. In *Proceedings of the 14th Annual Mid-South Archaeological Conference*, edited by R. Walling, C. Wharey, and C. Stanley, pp. 1–11. Panamerican Consultants, Special Publications 1, Tuscaloosa.

Buchanan, B., M. Collard, and K. Edinborough
2008 Paleoindian Demography and the Extraterrestrial Impact Hypothesis. *Proceedings of the National Academy of Sciences of the United States* 105:11651–11654.

Clausen, C., A. Cohen, C. Emeliani, J. Holman, and J. Stipp
1979 Little Salt Spring, Florida: A Unique Underwater Site. *Science* 203:609–614.

Cwynar, L., and R. Spear
2001 Late Glacial Climate Change in the White Mountains of New Hamsphire. *Quaternary Science Reviews* 20:1265–1274.

Daniel, I., and A. Goodyear
2006 An Update on the North Carolina Paleoindian Point Survey. *Current Research in the Pleistocene* 23:88–90.

Delcourt, H.
1983 A 12,000 Year Record of Forest History from Cahaba Pond, St. Clair County, Alabama. *Ecology* 64:874–887.

Delcourt, P., and H. Delcourt
1989 Final Report of Palynological and Plant-microfossil Analysis, Hood Lake, Pointsett County, Arkansas. In *Cultural Resource Investigations in the L'Anguille River Basin*, edited by D. Anderson, pp. 16–29. Garrow and Associates, Inc. Submitted to the U.S. Army Corps of Engineers, Memphis District.

Denniston, R., L. Gonzalez, Y. Asmerom, V. Polyak, M. Reagan, and M. Saltzman
2001 A High-resolution Speleothem Record of Climatic Variability at the Ållerød-Younger Dryas Transition in Missouri, Central United States. *Palaeogeography, Palaeoclimatology, Palaeoecology* 176:147–155.

Dorale, J., L. Wozniak, E. Bettis, III, S. Carpenter, R. Mandel, E. Hajic, N. Lopinot, and J. Ray
2010 Isotopic Evidence for Younger Dryas Aridity in the North American Midcontinent. *Geology* 38:519–522.

Driskell, B., S. Meeks, and S. Sherwood
2012 The Transition from Paleoindian to Archaic in the Middle Tennessee Valley. In *On the Brink: Transformations in Human Organization and Adaptation at the Pleistocene-Holocene Boundary in North America*, edited by C. Bousman and B. Vierra, pp. 306–332. Texas A&M Press, College Station.

Ellis, C., A. Goodyear, D. Morse, and K. Tankersley
1998 Archaeology of the Pleistocene-Holocene Transition in Eastern North America. *Quaternary International* 49–50:151–166.

Ensor, H.
1992 The Clovis Assemblage from the Belle Mina Paleo-Indian Locality, Middle Tennessee Valley, Limestone County, Alabama. Paper presented at the annual meeting of the Alabama Archaeological Society, Montgomery.

Erlandson, J., T. Rick, D. Kennett, and P. Walker
2001 Dates, Demography, and Disease: Cultural Contacts and Possible Evidence for Old World Epidemics among the Protohistoric Island Chumash. *Pacific Coast Archaeological Society Quarterly* 37:11–26.

Faught, M., M. Hornum, R. Goodwin, B. Carter, and S. Webb
   2003 Earliest-Holocene Tool Assemblages from Northern Florida with Stratigraphically Controlled Radiocarbon Estimates (Sites 8LE2105 and 8JE591). *Current Research in the Pleistocene* 20:16–18.
Feathers, J., E. Rhodes, S. Huot, and J. McAvoy
   2006 Luminescence Dating of Sand Deposits Related to Late Pleistocene Human Occupation at the Cactus Hill Site, Virginia, USA. *Geochronology* 1:167–187.
Firestone, R., A. West, J. Kennett, L. Becker, T. Bunch, Z. Revay, P. Schultz, T. Belgya, D. Kennett, J. Erlandson, O. Dickerson, A. Goodyear, R. Harris, G. Howard, J. Kloosterman, P. Lechler, P. Mayewski, J. Montgomery, R. Poreda, T. Darrah, S. Que Hee, A. Smith, A. Stich, W. Topping, J. Wittke, and W. Wolbach
   2007 Evidence for an Extraterrestrial Impact 12,900 Years Ago that Contributed to the Megafaunal Extinctions and the Younger Dryas Cooling. *Proceedings of the National Academy of Sciences* 104:16016–16021.
Gamble, C., W. Davies, P. Pettitt, L. Hazelwood, and M. Richards
   2005 The Archaeological and Genetic Foundations of the European Population during the Late Glacial: Implications for 'Agricultural Thinking'. *Cambridge Archaeological Journal* 15:193–223.
Goodyear, A.
   1982 The Chronological Position of the Dalton Horizon in the Southeastern United States. *American Antiquity* 47:382–395.
   2000 The Topper Site 2000: Results of the 2000 Allendale Paleoindian Expedition. *Legacy* 5:18–25. Newsletter of the South Carolina Institute of Archaeology and Anthropology, University of South Carolina, Columbia.
   2005 Evidence of Pre-Clovis Sites in the Eastern United States. In *Paleoamerican Origins: Beyond Clovis*, edited by R. Bonnichsen, B. Lepper, D. Stanford, and M. Waters, pp. 103–112. Texas A&M University Press, College Station.
   2006 Recognizing the Redstone Fluted Point in the South Carolina Paleoindian Point Database. *Current Research in the Pleistocene* 23:100–103.
Gramly, R.
   2002 *Olive Branch: A Very Early Archaic Site on the Mississippi River*. Persimmon Press, North Andover.
Grimm, E., W. Watts, G. Jacobson, Jr., B. Hansen, H. Almquist, and A. Dieffenbacher-Krall
   2006 Evidence for Warm Wet Heinrich Events in Florida. *Quaternary Science Reviews* 25:2197–2211.
Guilderson, T., P. Reimer, and T. Brown
   2005 The Boon and Bane of Radiocarbon Dating. *Science* 307:362–364.
Hajic, E., R. Mandel, J. Ray, and N. Lopinot
   1998 Geomorphology and Geoarchaeology. In *The 1997 Excavations at the Big Eddy Site (23CE426) in Southwest Missouri*, edited by N. Lopinot, J. Ray, and M. Conner, pp. 26–35. Special Publication No. 2: Center for Archaeological Research, Southwest Missouri State University, Springfield.

Hemmings, C.
2004 *The Organic Clovis: A Single Continent-wide Cultural Adaptation.* Unpublished Ph.D. dissertation, Department of Anthropology, University of Florida, Gainsville.

Hunt, T., and C. Lipo
2006 Late Colonization of Easter Island. *Science* 311:1603–1606.

Hussey, T.
1993 A 20,000-year History of Vegetation and Climate at Clear Pond, Northeastern South Carolina. Unpublished MS thesis, University of Maine, Orono.

Kneller, M., and D. Peteet
1999 Late-glacial to Early Holocene Climate Changes from a Central Appalachian Pollen and Macrofossil Record. *Quaternary Research* 51:133–147.

Koldehoff, B., and J. Walthall
2009 Dalton and the Early Holocene Midcontinent: Setting the Stage. In *Archaic Societies: Diversity and Complexity across the Midcontinent*, edited by T. Emerson, D. McElrath, and A. Fortier, pp. 137–151. State University of New York Press, Albany.

LaMoreaux, H., G. Brook, and J. Knox
2009 Late Pleistocene and Holocene Environments of the Southeastern United States from the Stratigraphy and Pollen Content of a Peat Deposit on the Georgia Coastal Plain. *Palaeogeography, Palaeoclimatology, Palaeoecology* 280:300–312.

Leverington, D., J. Mann, and J. Teller
2000 Changes in the Bathymetry and Volume of Glacial Lake Agassiz between 11,000 and 9,300 ^{14}C yr BP. *Quaternary Research* 54:174–181.

Lopinot, N., J. Ray, and M. Conner
2000 *The 1999 Excavations at the Big Eddy Site (23CE426).* Center for Archaeological Research, Southwest Missouri State University Special Publication No. 3, Springfield.

McAvoy, J.
1992 *Nottoway River Survey Part I: Clovis Settlement Patterns: The 30 Year Study of a Late Ice Age Hunting Culture on the Southern Interior Coastal Plain of Virginia.* Archeological Society of Virginia Special Publication Number 28, Richmond.

McAvoy, J., and L. McAvoy
1997 *Archaeological Investigations of Site 44SX202, Cactus Hill, Sussex County, Virginia.* Virginia Department of Historic Resources, Research Report Series No. 8. Richmond.

McGahey, S.
1996 Paleoindian and Early Archaic Data from Mississippi. In *The Paleoindian and Early Archaic Southeast*, edited by D. Anderson and K. Sassaman, pp. 354–384. University of Alabama, Tuscaloosa.

Meeks, S.
2001 Wandering around Dust Cave: An Overview of Late Paleoindian and Early Archaic Settlement Patterns in the Middle Tennessee River Valley. Paper presented in a symposium at the 58th Annual Meeting of the Southeastern Archaeological Conference, Knoxville, Tennessee.

Miller, D.
2007 Site Formation Processes in an Upland Paleoindian Site: The 2005–2007 Topper Firebreak Excavations. Master's thesis, Department of Anthropology, University of Tennessee, Knoxville.

Nunn, P., R. Hunter-Anderson, M. Carson, F. Thomas, S. Ulm, and M. Rowland
2007 Times of Plenty, Times of Less: Last-millennium Societal Disruption in the Pacific Basin. *Human Ecology* 35:385–401.

Overpeck, J., L. Peterson, N. Kipp, J. Imbrie, and D. Rind
1989 Climate Change in the Circum-North Atlantic Region during the Last Deglaciation. *Nature* 338:553–557.

Rick, J.
1987 Dates as Data: An Examination of the Peruvian Preceramic Radiocarbon Record. *American Antiquity* 52:55–73.

Sanders, T.
1990 *Adams: The Manufacturing of Flaked Stone Tools at a Paleoindian Site in Western Kentucky.* Persimmon, Buffalo.

Shennan, S., and K. Edinborough
2007 Prehistoric Population History: From the Late Glacial to the Late Neolithic in Central and Northern Europe. *Journal of Archaeological Science* 34:1339–1345.

Sherwood, S., B. Driskell, A. Randall, and S. Meeks
2004 Chronology and Stratigraphy at Dust Cave, Alabama. *American Antiquity* 69:533–554.

Shuman, B., T. Webb, III, P. Bartlein, and J. Williams
2002 The Anatomy of a Climatic Oscillation: Vegetation Change in Eastern North America during the Younger Dryas Chronozone. *Quaternary Science Reviews* 21:1777–1791.

Smith, E.
1984 Late-Quaternary Vegetation History at Cupola Pond, Ozark National Scenic Riverways, Southeastern Missouri. Unpublished MS thesis, The University of Tennessee, Knoxville.

Stafford, C., and M. Cantin
2009 Archaic Period Chronology in the Hill County of Indiana. In *Archaic Societies: Diversity and Complexity across the Midcontinent*, edited by T. Emerson, D. McElrath, and A. Fortier, pp. 287–313. State University of New York Press, Albany.

Stuiver, M., and P. Reimer
1993 Extended ¹⁴C Database and Revised CALIB 3.0 ¹⁴C Age Calibration Program. *Radiocarbon* 35:215–230.

Surovell, T., and P. Brantingham
2007 A Note on the Use of Temporal Frequency Distributions in Studies of Prehistoric Demography. *Journal of Archaeological Science* 34:1868–1877.

Surovell, T., N. Waguespack, and P. Brantingham
2005 Global Archaeological Evidence for Proboscidean Overkill. *Proceedings of the National Academy of Sciences of the United States* 102:6231–6236.

Thompson, L.
2000 Ice Core Evidence for Climate Change in the Tropics: Implications for Our Future. *Quaternary Science Reviews* 19:19–37.

Van't Veer, R., G. Islebe, and H. Hooghiemstra
2000 Climatic Change during the Younger Dryas Chron in Northern South America: A Test of the Evidence. *Quaternary Science Reviews* 19:1821–1835.

Walthall, J.
1998 Rockshelters and Hunter-gatherer Adaptation to the Pleistocene/Holocene Transition. *American Antiquity* 63:223–238.

Waters, M., and T. Stafford, Jr.
2007 Redefining the Age of Clovis: Implications for the Peopling of the Americas. *Science* 315:1122–1126.

Watts, W.
1975 Vegetation Record of the Last 20,000 Years from a Small Marsh on Lookout Mountain, Northwestern Georgia. *Geological Society of America Bulletin* 86:289–291.

1980 Late-Quaternary Vegetation History at White Pond on the Inner Coastal Plain of South Carolina. *Quaternary Research* 13:187–199.

Watts, W., and B. Hansen
1994 Pre-Holocene and Holocene Pollen Records of Vegetation History from the Florida Peninsula and Their Climatic Implications. *Palaeogeography, Palaeoclimatology, Palaeoecology* 109:163–176.

Watts, W., B. Hansen, and E. Grimm
1992 Camel Lake: A 40,000 yr Record of Vegetational and Forest History from Northwest Florida. *Ecology* 73:1056–1066.

Webb, S., and J. Dunbar
2006 Carbon Dates. In *First Floridians and Last Mastodons: The Page-Ladson Site in the Aucilla River*, edited by S. Webb, pp. 83–101. Springer, New York.

Whitehead, D.
1981 Late-Pleistocene Vegetational Changes in Northeastern North Carolina. *Ecological Monographs* 51:451–471.

Wilkins, G., P. Delcourt, H. Delcourt, F. Harrison, and M. Turner
    1991 Paleoecology of Central Kentucky since the Last Glacial Maximum. *Quaternary Research* 36:224–239.
Willard, D., C. Bernhardt, G. Brooks, T. Cronin, T. Edgar, and R. Larson
    2007 Deglacial Climate Variability in Central Florida, USA. *Palaeogeography, Palaeoclimatology, Palaeoecology* 251:366–382.
Yu, Z., and U. Eicher
    1998 Abrupt Climate Oscillations during the Last Deglaciation in Central North America. *Science* 282:2235–2238.

6

HUNTER-GATHERER ADAPTATIONS OF THE CENTRAL PLAINS AND ROCKY MOUNTAINS OF WESTERN NORTH AMERICA

Jason M. LaBelle

Introduction

Remarkable discoveries during the 1920s and 1930s at the Clovis and Folsom type sites of eastern New Mexico produced the first widely accepted evidence for the Pleistocene colonization of North America by pedestrian hunter-gatherers (Boldurian 1990; Boldurian and Cotter 1999; Hester 1972; Howard 1935; Meltzer 2006). These locales demonstrated deep human antiquity in the New World and cemented an unquestionable relationship between ancient hunters and their favored prey. Paleoindians were, by popular definition, big game hunters of mammoth and bison. A seminal publication, H. Marie Wormington's (1957) title—*Ancient Man in North America*—Figures 1, 3, and 5—highlighted Folsom points lodged in the rib cage of extinct bison, powerfully branding an iconographic standard that lives with us to this day (Roberts 1940; Sellards 1952). Yet, this monotypic interpretation of specialized and highly mobile hunters certainly downplays the complexity of human adaptations at play during the late Pleistocene, specifically during the Last Glacial Maximum, subsequent deglaciation, and the Younger Dryas.

Hunter-Gatherer Behavior: Human Response during The Younger Dryas, edited by Metin I. Eren, 139–164. © Left Coast Press. All rights reserved.

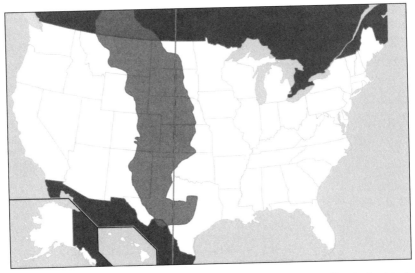

Figure 6.1   The Great Plains of North America. The 100th meridian is depicted, which is the approximate dividing line between the modern distribution of short and tall grass prairies. The majority of information presented in this chapter relates to the Central Plains and the State of Colorado.

This chapter describes the variation seen in human occupation within the Central Plains and Rocky Mountains of the western United States at the end of the Pleistocene (Figure 6.1). I argue that human settlement systems changed dramatically during the Younger Dryas chronozone, where regional reorganization by Folsom groups (and others) followed hundreds if not thousands of years of colonization efforts by Clovis and perhaps earlier populations. The late Pleistocene marked a time of humans settling into the landscape, detailed natural resource mapping, and in some ways, the beginnings of social intensification. This process is the by-product of thousands of years of population growth and the slow in-filling of a landscape previously devoid of people. This shift in cultural form is best understood by first outlining the changing climate during the Younger Dryas.

Northern Colorado during the Younger Dryas

The glacial record of northern Colorado has been well studied in past decades (Benedict 1973; Doerner 2007; Elias 1983; Elias and Nelson 1989; Madole 1986; Menounos and Reasoner 1997), in part because of its proximity to major urban and academic research centers. The local mountain range, referred to as the Front Range, forms the Continental Divide along the midcontinent and separates the watersheds that drain into the Pacific and Atlantic Oceans. Elevations range from 1,300 m along its eastern shortgrass steppes to over 4,300 m in the alpine country to the west. Horizontal distances between these two extremes are quite short, in many cases less than 40 km, thereby providing prehistoric foragers quick access to a number of diverse habitats within a relatively short foraging distance (Benedict 1992).

The last large glacial advance during the Pleistocene is regionally referred to as the Pinedale, where the Last Glacial Maximum occurred between approximately 23,500 and 19,000 BP (28,250 to 22,800 cal BP) (Benson et al. 2004; Doerner 2007; Madole 1986). The Pinedale advance was a mountain glaciation only, as at no time did these glaciers reach the foothills or grasslands located at much lower elevations to the east. The glaciation would not have presented much difficulty to humans in the lower elevations; however, crossing the mountains might have been a challenging task for humans and animals alike during the late Pleistocene. During the late glacial period, mean July temperatures may have been 10–11° C colder, with January winters 26–30° C colder than present-day temperatures, according to paleo-beetle assemblages collected from lake sediments in the Colorado high country (Elias 1985, 1986, 1996; Elias and Toolin 1989).

Subsequent deglaciation is thought to have begun by approximately 14,000–13,000 BP (17,100 to 15,700 cal BP) (Benson et al. 2004; Doerner 2007) or during pre-Clovis times in the Central Plains and Rocky Mountains. Massive outwash from these glaciated valleys created large, braided channels on major drainages like the South Platte River of eastern Colorado, forming the Kersey Terrace (Haynes et al. 1998; Holliday 1987; McFaul et al. 1994) and subsequently burying many late Pleistocene and early Holocene sites in alluvial fill (e.g., Borresen 2002; Brunswig 2007a, 2007b; Slessman 2004; Wheat 1979; Zier et al. 1993). Rapid warming characterized this late Pleistocene period, where summer temperatures were perhaps only 3–4° C cooler than modern day conditions (Elias 1996).

Following this warming, a small reglaciation occurred, locally referred to as the Satanta Peak advance (Doerner 2007; Menounos and Reasoner 1997). It was relatively small in comparison to the earlier Pinedale event. Temperatures are estimated to be only 0.4–0.9° C cooler than the preceding period, or perhaps 4–5° C cooler than today (Short and Elias 1987). Glacial advance was not extensive, but it would have continued to make some, if not all of the alpine tundra inhabitable for anything but specialized, short term functions. The Satanta Peak advance is thought to correspond to the Younger Dryas, which was a cooling event, and quite possibly a dry event, based on geoarchaeological work on the Southern Plains (Haynes 1991, 1995; Holliday 2000a, 2000b). Despite the regional evidence for glacial readvance, the degree to which the Younger Dryas would have affected peoples living in the Great Plains and Rocky Mountains is arguable.

Meltzer and Holliday (2010) recently summarized available pollen and stratigraphic evidence bracketing the Younger Dryas chronozone within the Plains and Rocky Mountains. Paleoclimatic records suggest widespread cooling, although the effect varied depending on location across North America, and climate change was most "apparent...alongside the North Atlantic, and at higher elevations," (Meltzer and Holliday 2010:26). Based on the available Younger Dryas climate data, the authors conclude (Meltzer and Holliday 2010:30) that it "will be difficult to demonstrate that a particular change in the archaeological record was a direct response to climatic or environmental change at a specific archaeological moment and location." After the conclusion of the Younger Dryas, local conditions appear to have changed quickly. Summer and winter temperatures rose, tree lines moved uphill, and modern climatic regimes were in place by perhaps as early as 9000 BP (10,100 cal BP) (Doerner 2007). Many late Paleoindian groups (noted by the emergence of diverse projectile point styles) appear in the Plains and Rockies during this early Holocene period (Bradley 1993).

Human Responses to Late Pleistocene Environmental Change

Human groups adapted to changing resource distributions and environmental conditions, subtlety shifting their subsistence and settlement patterns during the late Pleistocene. At the same time, human communities also began to change shape, with increasing population size, expansion into new areas, and bands splitting into daughter groups, perhaps forming new cultural identities over time (Hayden 1982; Meltzer 2002:39–42). I believe that these changes to the social landscape were just as important (if not more so) for humans to adapt to as the changing environment.

Human responses to the late Pleistocene are best observed in three distinct periods: the initial colonization by earliest settlers (Goebel et al. 2008; Haynes 1993), followed by the well-known Clovis peoples (Hester 1972; Stanford 1999), and finally by Folsom groups (Meltzer 2006; Roberts 1935). Each period left a characteristic settlement footprint in the region, which allows us to place the effects of the Younger Dryas into the larger context of late Pleistocene climate change.

Pleistocene Colonization

The region is well known for Paleoindian archaeology (for a detailed review, see LaBelle 2005), having yielded a number of type sites over the last eighty years, as well as large caches of bifaces (Holen and Muñiz 2005; Stanford and Jodry 1988), animal kill and processing sites (Fulgham and Stanford 1982; Stanford 1984), and camp sites dating to the late Pleistocene and early Holocene (Borresen 2002; Slessman 2004; Wheat 1979). Despite this large body of research, the region has not yielded any widely accepted human occupations dating before approximately 11,000 BP (the earliest accepted dates are from the Clovis period Dent site, averaging 10,990 +/– 25 BP [12,900 cal BP] Waters and Stafford 2007: Table S1).

Several sites have been put forth as evidence for pre-Clovis (or before 11,000 BP) human occupation, such as Kanorado (Mandel et al. 2004, 2005), Lamb Spring (Rancier et al. 1982; Stanford et al. 1981), Selby (Graham 1981; Stanford 1979), Dutton (Graham 1981; Stanford 1979), and La Sena (Holen 2006; Holen and May 2002), among others. These sites contain Pleistocene megafauna, often with spirally fractured bone. While some researchers argue that the spirally fractured bone represents human agency related to food acquisition or for materials for bone tool production (Holen 2006; Stanford 1979), most Paleoindian archaeologists remain skeptical given the lack of associated lithics (chipped-stone tools or debitage) or features (hearths or storage pits) associated with these faunal assemblages (Haynes 2002).

Despite years of research, it seems clear that the initial peopling of the Americas left a small material footprint and conclusive evidence is lacking for this early presence in the Central Plains and Rocky Mountains. If sites such as Kanorado or La Sena are in fact legitimate pre-Clovis manifestations, they demonstrate that these early human populations were perhaps very mobile and spent little time at these sites, leaving little to no material remains (lithics and features) at kill and camp locales. Population size must have been small to leave such a minimal presence.

Based on this evidence, I mildly question the relevance of the Central Plains and Rocky Mountains to understanding the pathways to colonization of the New World. The region may have been one of the last places to be colonized if initial migration routes followed resource-rich, ocean coastlines (Fladmark 1979). This is quite contrary to possibly being one of the first places to be colonized if humans entered the New World via the midcontinental ice free corridor, if that was even a viable migration route (Anderson and Gillam 2000; Mandryk 1990; Wilson and Burns 1999). Given the renewed interest in coastal migration as a possible entrant for migrations into the Americas (Bradley and Stanford 2004; Dixon 1999), it seems the days of looking toward the Great Plains for answers related to earliest colonization may be waning. The Great Plains might instead turn out to be a historical irony, a region where many Paleoindian complexes were first documented and where preservation can be spectacular, but a region far removed from the earliest cultural history of the continent.

Clovis Arrives

By contrast, the archaeological record of the subsequent Clovis period is one of ubiquitous presence but of generally low frequency in the Central Plains and Rocky Mountains (Brunswig 2003; Hofman and Hesse 1996; Hofman and Wyckoff 1991; Holen 2001). Clovis occupations conservatively date between 11,050–10,800 BP (12,900 to 12,700 cal BP) (Taylor et al. 1996; Waters and Stafford 2007), which places Clovis occupations distinctly at the time of transition into the Younger Dryas period.

Three distinct types of Clovis sites are present in the region. Small lithic scatters (such as the Klein II site, Zier et al. 1993) are the most common, usually containing but a single Clovis point (Bever and Meltzer 2007; Holen 2001). Often these are mixed with later components, making the association between the lithic scatter and the Clovis point difficult to determine. Some archaeologists argue that these small but ubiquitous scatters are remnants of larger sites, victims of differential erosion and exposure and active surface collection by local artifact collectors (LaBelle 2003). However, given the sheer volume of these sites, evidence suggests that many of them do indeed reflect short term (hours, days?) and low intensity (number of activities) events (LaBelle 2005), if the small assemblage size and spatial extent is an accurate proxy measure for occupation length.

The second site type is that of tool caches, often containing large bifaces manufactured from raw material sources located up to several hundred kilometers distant (Hofman 1999; Holen and Muñiz 2005; Kilby 2008). The Drake cache is one such example that is stored on the empty grasslands of northeastern Colorado away from significant landmarks or waterways (Stanford and Jodry 1988). These sites could represent insurance caches, related to initial (or at least early) peopling of the region, meant to stockpile raw materials in areas of unknown lithic resources. Others caches suggest grave offerings, such as the Anzick child burials in southern Montana (Jones and Bonnichsen 1994; Owsley and Hunt 2001; Wilke et al. 1991).

The final Clovis site type contains mammoth faunal remains, which are often interpreted as kill sites. The Dent mammoth site is perhaps the best example from the Central Plains and Rocky Mountains. Fifteen mammoths were found associated with three stone tools, including two Clovis points and a bifacial knife. Recent reanalysis by Brunswig (2007a) and others (Fisher and Fox 2007; Saunders 2007; Scott Cummings and Albert 2007) suggests the site may represent one or two Clovis ambush kills and/or perhaps scavenging events. Yet, rather than the norm, these mammoth kills are unquestionably the rarest of all Clovis sites in the region. Is this simply a sampling issue?

Of late there has been considerable debate regarding the favored prey species of Clovis peoples. Some continue to argue Clovis as mammoth hunters (Haynes 2002; Surovell and Waguespack 2008), while others question the nature of this widely held association (Grayson and Meltzer 2002, 2003), not quite willing to discard the idea of mammoth predation altogether. Fourteen sites, mostly from the American West, have been agreed upon as to possessing definitive human evidence for megafauna predation, specifically mammoths and mastodons (Grayson and Meltzer 2002, 2003; Surovell and Waguespack 2008). However, the degree of human involvement in these select fourteen sites is arguably low. Most contain but a few scattered tools and flakes per site (yet, many of the tools used in the kill/scavenge/butchery at the sites could have been recovered by Clovis groups after the fact). This is not to say all Clovis groups in western North America failed to leave sizable trash deposits. The Gault site (Collins 1998; Collins and Hester 1998), as well as Murray Springs (Haynes and Huckell 2007) and Blackwater Draw (Boldurian and Cotter 1999; Hester 1972), represent areas that were repeatedly reoccupied or intensively used for longer periods. However, as it relates to the Central Plains and Rocky Mountains, most of the Clovis record appears related to transitory use as expressed by a rather ephemeral record of isolates, small sites, and caches. Mammoth hunting was perhaps a rare event based on sites such as Dent and the Union Pacific Mammoth (Irwin et al. 1962). This pattern of minimal site investment (in terms of the quantity of flakes/tools discarded and overall spatial footprint) is remarkably different than the following Folsom period.

Folsom Settles In

Coinciding with the Younger Dryas, the Folsom record presents a decidedly different story (Taylor et al. 1996). Characteristically, the Folsom record is dominated by small sites, again mostly isolated finds and small lithic scatters (Andrews et al. 2008; Hofman and Ingbar 1988;

Kornfeld 1988; LeTourneau 2000). Midsize sites (as defined by the tool-assemblage size and an increasing, spatial footprint) are also present. Examples of midsize sites include the Folsom type site (Meltzer 2006), as well as Johnson (Galloway and Agogino 1961) and Fowler-Parrish sites (Agogino and Parrish 1971), each containing between ten and thirty points and preforms. Another distinct site type, that of the spatially large residential base, emerged in the region during the Younger Dryas likely reoccupied during cold-weather seasons.

Compare the seemingly paltry Clovis record of points found at mammoth kills to that of the Lindenmeier Folsom site in northern Colorado (Haynes and Agogino 1960; Roberts 1935, 1936; Wilmsen 1974; Wilmsen and Roberts 1978), where over 600 projectile points have been recovered to date from perhaps as little as half of the total suspected buried site (Ambler 1999; Cotter 1978; Gantt 2002; Newton and LaBelle 2008; Wilmsen and Roberts 1978). Contrary to recent arguments (Bamforth 2007), Lindenmeier cannot simply be explained away as a sampling phenomenon, where previous archaeological excavation has simply exposed a large habitation site. Large scale collecting over the past eighty years by amateur and professional archaeologists alike, during periods of drought and otherwise (Seebach 2006), has failed to discover many sites similar to Lindenmeier in size and in complexity (LaBelle 2005). Furthermore, Lindenmeier is not located on top of a major lithic quarry, further emphasizing the fact that most of the toolstone had to be carried in from elsewhere. Along with the appearance of large residential bases (Lindenmeier and others such as Agate Basin, Barger Gulch, and Mountaineer), there are four additional characteristics that sets the Folsom complex apart from previous cultural adaptations.

Regional Packing

First, Folsom coincides with the emergence of distinct regional, style zones within North America based on the proliferation of new projectile point styles. Geographically, Folsom is found between the Canadian Prairie Provinces and Northern Mexico, throughout the Great Plains, Rocky Mountains, and the now Desert Southwest (Amick 1994a; Andrews et al. 2008; LeTourneau 2000; Munson 1990). Compare this spatial distribution to the earlier Clovis form (Anderson and Faught 1998, 2000), which is found nearly coast to coast in North America (albeit showing slight regional variations, part of which might be temporally related stylistic variability).

Most archaeologists view Folsom hunters as participating in a highly mobile hunting system, with individual bands foraging far and wide in the pursuit of *Bison antiquus* (Ahler and Geib 2000; Hofman 2002; Hofman and Todd 2001; Jodry 1999a; Kelly and Todd 1988; Stanford 1999). The geographic distribution of the complex (in terms of the locations of all known sites and isolated projectile points and preforms) might represent the hunters themselves, with their mobility propelling a technological system across many different physiographic regions. Whereas some exchange may have occurred (Hayden 1982), many argue that Folsom groups commonly maintained high residential mobility based on the recovery of distant raw materials (exotics) from bison kills and camps (Amick 1994a; Bement 1999a, 1999b; Hofman 1991, 1992; Hofman et al. 1990, 1991; Jodry 1999a; Jodry and Stanford 1992; MacDonald 1998, 1999).

However over the last twenty years, archaeologists have begun to detect subtle regional differences among Folsom sites. For instance, distinct patterns of raw material use have been identified for the southern High Plains (Bement 1999a; Hofman 1992, 1994), the Southwest (Amick 1996, 2000), and in Colorado (Stiger 2006; Surovell and Waguespack 2007). In some cases, these patterns demonstrate reliance on distant raw material sources (southern High Plains) where in other regions, the tools are made from mostly local sources (Foothills and southern Rocky Mountains; Black 2000). The interrelationships between these regions are currently under debate, but in my mind there is clearly not one "pan-Folsom" adaptation (cf. Meltzer 1993 for a discussion of Clovis adaptation) in terms of mobility and perhaps in subsistence either (Andrews et al. 2008; Bamforth 2002).

Folsom sites in the region are often clustered in the mountains basins of Colorado, such as the San Luis Valley (Jodry 1999b), the Gunnison Basin (Stiger 2006), and Middle Park near the Colorado River (Kornfeld and Frison 2000; Naze 1986). Based on climatic reconstructions (Balakrishnan et al. 2005; Kornfeld et al. 1999; Mayer et al. 2005; Reasoner and Jodry 2000), these must have been cold and dry locations as compared to adjacent regions on the Central Plains. So why risk exploiting such areas? Folsom people were likely using these basins logistically, venturing from base camps for specialized activities, and returning to centralized locations as needed (Binford 1980, 1982, 1983). Perhaps the draw was the ease of mapping onto game corridors in such bounded systems—there was no need for large mobility in areas where game was predictable and abundant. Likewise, abiotic resources such as toolstone were plentiful. For example, the Mountaineer site is sitting in a very rich area of quartzite toolstone (Stiger 2001, 2006); Barger Gulch is in an area of Troublesome Formation chert (Surovell and Waguespack 2007; Surovell et al. 2003); and the Hell Gap site of southern Wyoming is found near Madison Formation chert and Spanish Diggings quartzite (Larson et al. 2009).

In some areas, Folsom groups may have been spatially separated from one another during the Younger Dryas, as mountain passes would have been treacherous places filled with glacial ice. Extensive survey work and collector documentation in the Colorado Front Range by Brunswig (2005) and Benedict (2000) has recovered only a handful of Folsom points from the alpine tundra, demonstrating that Folsom was not using the high country as extensively as late Paleoindian groups did some 500–2,000 radiocarbon years later (Brunswig 2007b; Pitblado 2003, 2007). Perhaps Folsom groups could not easily traverse the high country due to ice and snow-blocked passes (Benedict 1992). The mountain resources would have been of poor quality and low abundance, or instead, Folsom groups had already settled into a handful of core areas within the entire Folsom range.

See and Be Seen

A second specific land-use behavior emerges within the Central Plains and Rocky Mountains, where the very largest Folsom sites utilize viewsheds that allow one to "See and Be Seen." For example, the Mountaineer site is situated in the Gunnison Basin, a large valley surrounded by high mountains (Stiger 2006). The ability to see big game (bison, elk, bighorn sheep, deer, and pronghorn) from great distances probably played a role in the site's use as a camp and an overlook. For at Mountaineer, the camp towers some 200–250 m over the surrounding landscape, providing excellent views of game movement along the creeks and rivers surrounding the site. During winter, game such as bison would have appeared as brown dots against the overwhelming background of brilliant white snow, providing a way to easily view and track game from great distances (Stiger, personal communication 2002). The viewshed at the Lindenmeier site is equally impressive, with wide views along the hogback foothills of the Front Range, where Folsom groups could easily map distant peaks, hills, and drainages. Standing at Lindenmeier today, you can easily see the general location of other known Folsom sites located within the Colorado Piedmont.

But perhaps an equally salient feature is that human groups foraging out on that same landscape, Folsom people or otherwise, would have also been able to see people camping on top of this prominent site, with smoke wafting to the sky and welcoming travelers into this base camp. Camping at Lindenmeier, as compared to the myriad of possible camping spots in the area, would allow people to see where you were camping from considerable distances away. Lindenmeier inhabitants were not hiding themselves from others on this empty human landscape; quite the reverse, they were probably initiating contact and this was a deliberate choice. There are excellent sites for winter encampments within 5 km of Lindenmeier, and these areas contain extensive evidence for sites from other later cultural periods (LaBelle et al. 2007; LaBelle and Bush 2007). However, one can neither see or be seen from these more sheltered locales, suggesting that the Lindenmeier viewshed was perhaps of great importance to those Folsom foragers returning home to their main camp.

Furthermore, the Lindenmeier site occupies an important ecological and physiographic boundary. The site is located on the edge between the Great Plains and the foothills of the Rocky Mountains, and between the lowlands of the Colorado Piedmont and the rolling valleys of the Wyoming High Plains (Trimble 1980). Springs are abundant along this ecological boundary, providing bountiful resources within a short foraging radius of the site. The site can be seen for distances of well over 50 km to the south, as red cliffs tower above the site and distinctive white Oligocene sediments underlay the Folsom deposits. After long consideration, I no longer think it is a coincidence that the largest Folsom site (in terms of the sheer number of tools) is also located nearly halfway between the northern and southern limits of Folsom (southern Canada and northern Mexico respectively) and between the eastern and western boundaries (far eastern Utah and eastern Nebraska/Kansas). Being in the center of the Folsom world, places like Lindenmeier (and Mountaineer, Barger Gulch, others) could have served as lighthouses, places to facilitate interaction and communication over vast empty territories.

Landscape Architecture

Another common Folsom characteristic is the mapping of space as suggested by the construction of a formal, landscape-settlement architecture, indicating that Folsom groups made strategic decisions about where to camp over and over again. Not only did Folsom often reoccupy older Clovis sites (Hester 1975a, 1975b; Hester and Grady 1977), but many of the largest Folsom sites also represent places occupied more than once during the Folsom period (Lindenmeier, Agate Basin, Cooper, Reddin; see Andrews et al. 2008).

At this time, it is not known whether these formal places were reoccupied by related kin groups, or simply by those sharing a looser connection under the Folsom projectile point complex. For example at Lindenmeier, Wilmsen and Roberts (1978: Map 1) documented stylistically distinguishable Folsom occupations, separated from one another by approximately 100 m (Area I versus Area II). The groups were differentiated by variation in edge flaking, retouch, and fluting style (Wilmsen and Roberts 1978:145). These are characteristics stylistically encoded during manufacture, perhaps culturally transferred between human generations, and not related to technological systems of projectile point use and resharpening. It still remains to be shown whether these Folsom substyles occurred in chronological succession, one after another, or whether they were simultaneous, representing two foraging groups coming together (i.e., aggregation) at Lindenmeier (Andrews et al. 2008; Hofman 1994).

An interesting point for comparison is the 1935 excavation of the site, where two crews simultaneously worked the site: one field crew from the Colorado Museum of Natural History (Cotter 1978) and the other crew from the Smithsonian Institution (Wilmsen and Robert 1978). Here were two culturally related groups (mostly Western Americans), coming together, at the same time (summer 1935), at the same place (Lindenmeier), and for the same purpose (uncovering the secrets of "Folsom Man"), but for some reason deciding to set up their camps around 100 m apart. Ethnographic comparisons of aggregated camps also show a general pattern of diffuse site structure rather than tightly clustered camps (Andrews et al. 2008), perhaps suggesting cross-cultural patterns related to the layout of rendezvous camps.

In addition to mapping on to the same location, Folsom marks the beginning of a formal physical architecture. Stiger (2006) has documented the traces of at least one if not two (or more) house structures at Mountaineer. The structures were identified through patterns in the distribution of bone and lithic debris, as well as features, and concentrations of burnt daub, some of which contain impressions of poles used for roof support. Surovell and Waguespack (2007) also documented hearth activity areas at the Barger Gulch, in Middle Park, Colorado. Here, clusters of bone and lithic debris, some of which are burned, might suggest an additional Folsom structure of the same general size as the Mountaineer example. To the north, it has also been suggested that Folsom houses are present at the Hanson (Frison and Bradley 1980) and Agate Basin (Frison 1982a) sites of Wyoming. The presence of Folsom houses might indicate an adaptation to colder, Younger Dryas settings or to investment in certain locales, which were occupied for longer periods than earlier Clovis groups.

At Lindenmeier, Frank Roberts attempted to discover Folsom houses in the 1930s, but he was not able to do so, perhaps given his excavation methodology and the then lack of comparative data on prehistoric hunter-gatherer site structure. Yet the number and layout of the site's artifact concentrations, coupled with low-density scatters in between clusters, is quite reminiscent of Barger Gulch and Mountaineer, suggesting that Lindenmeier too may actually contain structures. Indeed, the presence of decorative bone and beads in various states of manufacture (Wilmsen and Roberts 1978:126–134) suggests nonsubsistence activities that would be expected from houses occupied in cold season, winter settings (Frison 1982b; Hill 1994, 2001).

Formation of Distinct Stylistic Groups

One final characteristic of the late Pleistocene is the formation of stylistic groups that manifest in projectile point forms. Specifically, Agate Basin, Goshen, and Midland (or unfluted Folsom) points appear during the Folsom period, each distinctive in their design and production (Bradley 1991, 1993; Frison and Stanford 1982; Holliday 2000a; Taylor 2006). It remains unresolved whether these represent different groups of people, a change in technology, or a little of both. We still don't know. But regardless of the source of stylistic variation, the adaptations of Folsom, Goshen, and Agate Basin are more like each other than that of the old story of fluted point evolution—that is of Clovis begetting Folsom, with no overlap between cultural complexes. The three forms appear on the ground at the same time, at several sites in the Northwestern Plains, such as Hell Gap (Irwin-Williams et al. 1973; Larson et al. 2009) and Jim Pitts (Sellet 2001). Does this represent simultaneous occupation of the site or mixing of closely timed occupations? The emergence of stylistic diversity through time suggests increasing definition of the group identity (Meltzer 2002), first beginning during the Younger Dryas.

Conclusion

In summary, the archaeology of the Central Plains and Rocky Mountains contains abundant evidence of Paleoindian subsistence and behavior during the late Pleistocene, adjusting to several periods of major climatic change. Whereas the initial colonization seemingly left little material imprint on the record, the succeeding Clovis period deposited a cultural record of isolates, small sites and a few mammoth bone beds. The Clovis landscape was probably an empty one, with small transitory populations moving through the region, and not settling into the place.

However, the succeeding Younger Dryas chronozone coincides with several significant shifts in hunter-gatherer behavior and land use during the latest Pleistocene. Rather than being widely mobile specialized hunters, I argue that Folsom behavior represents a dramatic shift from earlier occupations. Folsom groups were settling in, mapping the natural and cultural landscapes in detail, and starting to intensify their use of place. Paleoindian behavior appears tied to local and predictable resources, perhaps constricted by the Younger Dryas in regards to animal populations and annual migration patterns. At least some Folsom groups appear to have used seasonal (winter or cold-weather?) residences to establish places of aggregation, used to facilitate interaction within (and perhaps across) cultural group identities on a still sparsely populated human landscape. The Lindenmeier site gives strong evidence for Folsom groups behaving in ways quite different than far ranging bison hunting specialists and as such is emblematic of increasing behavioral complexity. Whereas the timing of these changes coincides with the Younger Dryas, it remains to be proven to what degree climate change (versus population growth for example) was the ultimate cause for these marked cultural changes.

References

Agogino, G., and A. Parrish
1971 The Fowler-Parrish Site: A Folsom Campsite in Eastern Colorado. *Plains Anthropologist* 1652:111–114.

Ahler, S., and P. Geib
2000 Why Flute? Folsom Point Design and Adaptation. *Journal of Archaeological Science* 24:799–820.

Ambler, B.
1999 Folsom Chipped Stone Artifacts from the Lindenmeier Site, Colorado: The Coffin Collection. Master's thesis, Department of Anthropology, Colorado State University, Fort Collins.

Amick, D.
1994a Folsom Diet Breadth and Land Use in the American Southwest. Unpublished Ph.D. dissertation, Department of Anthropology, University of New Mexico, Albuquerque.

1996 Regional Patterns of Folsom Mobility and Land Use in the American Southwest. *World Archaeology* 27:411–426.

2000 Regional Approaches with Unbounded Systems: The Record of Folsom Land Use in New Mexico and West Texas. In *The Archaeology of Regional Interaction: Religion, Warfare, and Exchange across the American Southwest and Beyond*, edited by M. Hegmon, pp. 119–147. University Press of Colorado, Boulder.

Anderson, D., and M. Faught
1998 The Distribution of Fluted Paleoindian Projectile Points: Update 1998. *Archaeology of Eastern North America* 26:163–187.

Anderson, D., and M. Faught
2000 Palaeoindian Artifact Distributions: Evidence and Implications. *Antiquity* 74:507–513.

Anderson, D., and J. Gillam

2000 Paleoindian Colonization of the Americas: Implications from an Examination of Physiography, Demography, and Artifact Distribution. *American Antiquity* 65:43–66.

Andrews, B., J. LaBelle, and J. Seebach

2008 Spatial Variability in the Folsom Archaeological Record: A Multi-scalar Approach. *American Antiquity* 73:464–490.

Balakrishnan, M., C. Yapp, D. Meltzer, and J. Theler

2005 Paleoenvironment of the Folsom Archaeological Site, New Mexico, USA, Approximately 10,500 ¹⁴C yr B.P. as Inferred from the Stable Isotope Composition of Fossil Land Snail Shells. *Quaternary Research* 63:31–44.

Bamforth, D.

2002 High-tech Foragers? Folsom and Later Paleoindian Technology on the Great Plains. *Journal of World Prehistory* 16:55–98.

2007 *The Allen Site: A Paleoindian Camp in Southwestern Nebraska.* University of New Mexico Press, Albuquerque.

Bement, L.

1999a *Bison Hunting at Cooper Site: Where Lightning Bolts Drew Thundering Herds.* University of Oklahoma Press, Norman.

1999b View from a Kill: The Cooper Site Folsom Lithic Assemblages. In *Folsom Lithic Technology: Explorations in Structure and Variation,* edited by D. Amick, pp. 111–121. Archaeological Series No. 12, International Monographs in Prehistory, Ann Arbor, Michigan.

Benedict, J.

1973 Chronology of Cirque Glaciation, Colorado Front Range. *Quaternary Research* 3:584–599.

1992 Footprints in the Snow: High-altitude Cultural Ecology of the Colorado Front Range, U.S.A. *Arctic and Alpine Research* 24:1–16.

2000 Excavations at the Fourth of July Mine Site. In *This Land of Shining Mountains: Archeological Studies in Colorado's Indian Peaks Wilderness Area,* edited by E. Cassells, pp. 159–188. Research Report No. 8, Center for Mountain Archaeology, Ward, Colorado.

Benson, L., R. Madole, W. Phillips, G. Landis, T. Thomas, and P. Kubik

2004 The Probable Importance of Snow and Sediment Shielding on Cosmogenic Ages of North-Central Colorado Pinedale and Pre-Pinedale Moraines. *Quaternary Science Reviews* 23:193–206.

Bever, M., and D. Meltzer

2007 Exploring Cariation in Paleoindian Life Ways: The Third Revised Edition of the Texas Clovis Fluted Point Survey. *Bulletin of the Texas Archeological Society* 78:65–99.

Binford, L.

1980 Willow Smoke and Dogs' Tails: Hunter-gatherer Settlement Systems and Archaeological Site Formation. *American Antiquity* 45:4–20.

Binford, L.
1982 The Archaeology of Place. *Journal of Anthropological Archaeology* 1:5–31.
1983 Long-term Land-use Patterning: Some Implications for Archaeology. In *Working at Archaeology*, by L. Binford, pp. 379–386. Academic Press, New York.

Black, K.
2000 Lithic Sources in the Rocky Mountains of Colorado. In *Intermountain Archaeology*, edited by D. Madsen and M. Metcalf, pp. 132–147. University of Utah Anthropological Papers No. 122, Salt Lake City.

Boldurian, A.
1990 Lithic Technology at the Mitchell Locality of Blackwater Draw: A Stratified Folsom Site in Eastern New Mexico. *Plains Anthropologist* 35(130), Memoir 24.

Boldurian, A., and J. Cotter
1999 *Clovis Revisted: New Perspectives on Paleoindian Adaptations from Blackwater Draw, New Mexico*. University of Pennsylvania Press, Philadelphia.

Borresen, J.
2002 A Faunal Analysis of the Frazier Site, an Agate Basin-age Bison Kill-butchery Site in Northeastern Colorado. Master's thesis, University of Tennessee, Knoxville.

Bradley, B.
1991 Lithic Technology. In *Prehistoric Hunters of the High Plains*, by G. C. Frison, pp. 369–395. Academic Press, San Diego.
1993 Paleo-Indian Flaked Stone Technology in the North American High Plains. In *From Kostenki to Clovis: Upper Paleolithic-Paleo-Indian Adaptations*, edited by O. Soffer and N. Praslov, pp. 251–262. Plenum Press, New York.

Bradley, B., and D. Stanford
2003 Clovis-age Artifacts from Rocky Mountain National Park and Vicinity, North Central Colorado. *Current Research in the Pleistocene* 20:7–9.
2004 The North Atlantic Ice-edge Corridor: A Possible Palaeolithic Route to the New World. *World Archaeology* 36:459–478.
2005 *Prehistoric, Protohistoric, and Early Historic Native American Archeology of Rocky Mountain National Park*. Final Report of System Wide Archeological Inventory Program Investigations by the University of Northern Colorado (1998–2002). Department of Anthropology, University of Northern Colorado, Greeley.

Brunswig, R.
2003 Clovis-age Artifacts from Rocky Mountain National Park and Vicinity, North Central Colorado. *Current Research in the Pleistocene* 20:7–9.
2005 *Prehistoric, Protohistoric, and Early Historic Native American Archeology of Rocky Mountain National Park: Final Report of Systemwide Archeological*

Inventory Program Investigations by the University of Northern Colorado (1998–2002). Department of Anthropology, University of Northern Colorado, Greeley.

2007a New Interpretations of the Dent Mammoth Site: A Synthesis of Recent Multidisciplinary Evidence. In *Frontiers in Colorado Paleoindian Archaeology: From the Dent Site to the Rocky Mountains,* edited by R. H. Brunswig and B. L. Pitblado, pp. 87–121. University Press of Colorado, Boulder.

2007b Paleoindian Cultural Landscapes and Archaeology of North-central Colorado's Rockies. In *Frontiers in Colorado Paleoindian Archaeology: From the Dent Site to the Rocky Mountains,* edited by R. Brunswig and B. Pitblado, pp. 261–310. University Press of Colorado, Boulder.

Collins, M.

1998 Interpreting the Clovis Artifacts from the Gault Site. *TARL Research Notes* 6:5–12, Texas Archeological Research Laboratory, University of Texas, Austin.

Collins, M., and T. Hester

1998 Introduction to the Gault Site. *TARL Research Notes* 6:4, Texas Archeological Research Laboratory, University of Texas, Austin.

Cotter, J.

1978 A Report of Field Work of the Colorado Museum of Natural History at the Lindenmeier Folsom Campsite, 1935. In *Lindenmeier, 1934–1974: Concluding Report on Investigation,* by E. N. Wilmsen and F. H. H. Roberts, Jr., pp. 181–184. Smithsonian Contributions to Anthropology, No. 24. Smithsonian Institution Press, Washington, D.C.

Dixon, E.

1999 *Bones, Boats, and Bison: Archaeology and the First Colonization of Western North America.* University of New Mexico Press, Albuquerque.

Doerner, J.

2007 Late Quaternary Prehistoric Environments of the Colorado Front Range. In *Frontiers in Colorado Paleoindian Archaeology: From the Dent Site to the Rocky Mountains,* edited by R. Brunswig and B. Pitblado, pp. 11–38. University Press of Colorado, Boulder.

Elias, S.

1983 Paleoenvironmental Interpretations of Holocene Inset Fossil Assemblages from the La Poudre Pass Site, Northern Colorado Front Range. *Palaeogeography, Palaeoclimatology, Palaeoecology* 41:87–102.

1985 Paleoenvironmental Interpretation of Holocene Insect Fossil Assemblages from Four High-Altitude Sites in the Front Range, Colorado, U.S.A. *Arctic and Alpine Research* 17:31–48.

1986 Fossil Insect Evidence for Late Pleistocene Paleoenvironments of the Lamb Spring Site, Colorado. *Geoarchaeology* 1:381–386.

1996 Late Pleistocene and Holocene Seasonal Temperatures Reconstructed from Fossil Beetle Assemblages in the Rocky Mountains. *Quaternary Research* 46:311–318.

Elias, S., and A. Nelson
1989 Fossil Invertebrate Evidence for Late Wisconsin Environments at the Lamb Spring Site, Colorado. *Plains Anthropologist* 34:309–326.

Elias, S., and L. Toolin
1989 Accelerator Dating of a Mixed Assemblage of Late Pleistocene Insect Fossils from the Lamb Spring Site, Colorado. *Quaternary Research* 33:122–126.

Fisher, D., and D. Fox
2007 Season of Death of the Dent Mammoths: Distinguishing Single from Multiple Mortality Events. In *Frontiers in Colorado Paleoindian Archaeology: From the Dent Site to the Rocky Mountains*, edited by R. Brunswig and B. Pitblado, pp. 123–153. University Press of Colorado, Boulder.

Fladmark, K.
1979 Routes: Alternative Migration Corridors for Early Man in North America. *American Antiquity* 44:55–69.

Frison, G.
1982a Folsom Components. In *The Agate Basin Site: A Record of the Paleoindian Occupation of the Northwestern High Plains*, edited by G. C. Frison and D. J. Stanford, pp. 37–76. Academic Press, New York.

1982b Paleo-Indian Winter Subsistence Strategies on the High Plains. In *Plains Indian Studies: A Collection of Essays in Honor of John C. Ewers and Waldo R. Wedel*, edited by D. Ubelaker and H. Viola, pp. 193–201. Smithsonian Contributions to Anthropology No. 30, Smithsonian Institution Press, Washington, D.C.

Frison, G., and B. Bradley
1980 *Folsom Tools and Technology at the Hanson Site, Wyoming*. University of New Mexico Press, Albuquerque.

Frison, G., and D. Stanford (editors)
1982 *The Agate Basin Site: A Record of the Paleoindian Occupation of the Northwestern High Plains*. Academic Press, New York.

Fulgham, T., and D. Stanford
1982 The Frasca Site: A Preliminary Report. *Southwestern Lore* 48:1–9.

Galloway, E., and G. Agogino
1961 The Johnson Site: A Folsom Campsite. *Plains Anthropologist* 6:205–208.

Gantt, E.
2002 The Claude C. and A. Lynn Coffin Lindenmeier Collection: An Innovative Method for Analysis of Privately Held Artifact Collections and New Information on a Folsom Campsite in Northern Colorado. Master's thesis, Department of Anthropology, Colorado State University, Fort Collins.

Goebel, T., M. Waters, and D. O'Rourke
2008 The Late Pleistocene Dispersal of Modern Humans in the Americas. *Science* 319:1497–1502.

Graham, R.

1981 Preliminary Report on Late Pleistocene Vertebrates from the Selby and Dutton Archaeological/Paleontological Sites, Yuma County, Colorado. *Contributions to Geology* 20:33–56. University of Wyoming, Laramie.

Grayson, D., and D. Meltzer

2002 Clovis Hunting and Large Mammal Extinction: A Critical Review of the Evidence. *Journal of World Prehistory* 16:313–359.

Grayson, D., and D. Meltzer

2003 A Requiem for North American Overkill. *Journal of Archaeological Science* 30:585–593.

Hayden, B.

1982 Interaction Parameters and the Demise of Paleo-Indian Craftsmanship. *Plains Anthropologist* 27:109–124.

Haynes, C. Vance, Jr.

1991 Geoarchaeological and Paleohydrological Evidence for a Clovis-age Drought in North America and its Bearing on Extinction. *Quaternary Research* 35:438–450.

1993 Clovis-Folsom Geochronology and Climatic Change. In *From Kostenki to Clovis: Upper Paleolithic-Paleo-Indian Adaptations*, edited by O. Soffer and N. Praslov, pp. 219–236. Plenum Press, New York.

1995 Geochronology of Paleoenvironmental Change, Clovis Type Site, Blackwater Draw, New Mexico. *Geoarchaeology* 10:317–388.

Haynes, C. Vance, Jr., and G. Agogino

1960 Geological Significance of a New Radiocarbon Date from the Lindenmeier Site. *Proceedings of the Denver Museum of Natural History* No. 9, Denver.

Haynes, C. Vance, Jr., and B. Huckell (editors)

2007 *Murray Springs: A Clovis Site with Multiple Activity Areas in the San Pedro Valley, Arizona*. Anthropological Papers No. 7, Department of Anthropology, University of Arizona, Tucson.

Haynes, C. Vance, Jr., M. McFaul, R. Brunswig, and K. Hopkins

1998 Kersey-Kuner Terrace Investigations at the Dent and Bernhardt Sites, Colorado. *Geoarchaeology* 13:201–218.

Haynes, G.

2002 *The Early Settlement of North America*. Cambridge University Press, Cambridge.

Hester, J.

1972 *Blackwater Locality No. 1: A Stratified, Early Man Site in Eastern New Mexico*. Fort Burgwin Research Center, Southern Methodist University, Ranchos de Taos, New Mexico.

1975a Paleoarchaeology of the Llano Estacado. In *Late Pleistocene Environments of the Southern High Plains*, edited by F. Wendorf and J. Hester, pp. 247–256. No. 9, Fort Burgwin Research Center, Southern Methodist University, Ranchos de Taos, New Mexico.

Hester, J.
1975b The Sites. In *Late Pleistocene Environments of the Southern High Plains*, edited by F. Wendorf and J. Hester, pp. 13–32. No. 9, Fort Burgwin Research Center, Southern Methodist University, Ranchos de Taos, New Mexico.

Hester, J., and J. Grady
1977 Paleoindian Social Patterns on the Llano Estacado. In *Paleoindian Lifeways*, edited by E. Johnson, pp. 78–96. The Museum Journal No. 17, Lubbock, Texas.

Hill, M.
1994 Subsistence Strategies by Folsom Hunters at Agate Basin, Wyoming: A Taphonomic Analysis of the Bison and Pronghorn Assemblages. Master's thesis, Department of Anthropology, University of Wyoming, Laramie.

2001 Paleoindian Diet and Subsistence Behavior on the Northwestern Great Plains of North America. Unpublished Ph.D. dissertation, Department of Anthropology, University of Wisconsin-Madison.

Hofman, J.
1991 Folsom Land Use: Projectile Point Variability as a Key to Mobility. In *Raw Material Economies among Prehistoric Hunter-gatherers*, edited by A. Monet-White and S. Holen, pp. 335–355. Publications in Anthropology No. 19, University of Kansas, Lawrence.

1992 Recognition and Interpretation of Folsom Technological Variability on the Southern Plains. In *Ice Age Hunters of the Rockies*, edited by D. Stanford and J. Day, pp. 193–224. University Press of Colorado, Niwot.

1994 Paleoindian Aggregations on the Great Plains. *Journal of Anthropological Archaeology* 13:341–370.

1999 Unbounded Hunters: Folsom Bison Hunting on the Southern Plains circa 10,500 BP, the Lithic Evidence. In *Le Bison: Gibier et Moyen de Subsistance des Hommes du Paleolithique aux Paleoindiens des Grandes Plaines*, edited by J. Jaubert, J. Burgal, F. David, and J. Enloe, pp. 383–415. Editions APCDA, Antibes.

2002 High Points in Folsom Archaeology. In *Folsom Technology and Lifeways*, edited by J. Clark and M. Collins, pp. 399–412. Special Publication No. 4, Lithic Technology. Department of Anthropology, University of Tulsa.

Hofman, J., D. Amick, and R. Rose
1990 Shifting Sands: A Folsom-midland Assemblage from a Campsite in Western Texas. *Plains Anthropologist* 35:221–253.

Hofman, J., and I. Hesse
1996 The Occurrence of Clovis Points in Kansas. *Current Research in the Pleistocene* 13:23–25.

Hofman, J., and E. Ingbar
1988 A Folsom Hunting Overlook in Eastern Wyoming. *Plains Anthropologist* 33:337–350.

Hofman, J., and L. Todd

2001 Tyranny in the Archaeological Record of Specialized Hunters. In *People and Wildlife in Northern North America: Essays in Honor of R. Dale Guthrie*, edited by S. Gerlach and M. Murray, pp. 200–215. BAR International Series 944.

Hofman, J., L. Todd, and M. Collins

1991 Identification of Central Texas Edwards Chert at the Folsom and Lindenmeier Sites. *Plains Anthropologist* 36:297–308.

Hofman, J., and D. Wyckoff

1991 Clovis Occupation in Oklahoma. *Current Research in the Pleistocene* 8:29–31.

Holen, S.

2001 Clovis Mobility and Lithic Procurement on the Central Great Plains of North America. Unpublished Ph.D. dissertation, Department of Anthropology, University of Kansas, Lawrence.

2006 Taphonomy of Two Last Glacial Maximum Mammoth Sites in the Central Great Plains of North America: A Preliminary Report on La Sena and Lovewell. *Quaternary International* 142:30–43.

Holen, S., and D. May

2002 The La Sena and Shaffert Mammoth Sites: History of Investigations, 1987–1998. In *Medicine Creek: Seventy Years of Archaeological Investigations*, edited by D. Roper, pp. 20–36. The University of Alabama Press, Tuscaloosa.

Holen, S., and M. Muñiz

2005 A Flattop Chalcedony Clovis Biface Cache from Northeast Colorado. *Current Research in the Pleistocene* 22:49–50.

Holliday, V.

1987 Geoarchaeology and Late Quaternary Geomorphology of the Middle South Platte River, Northeastern Colorado. *Geoarchaeology* 2:317–329.

2000a The Evolution of Paleoindian Geochronology and Typology on the Great Plains. *Geoarchaeology* 15:227–290.

2000b Folsom Frought and Episodic Drying on the Southern High Plains from 10,900–10,200 ^{14}C yr B.P. *Quaternary Research* 53:1–12.

Howard, E.

1935 Evidence of Early Man in North America. *The Museum Journal* 24(2–3).

Irwin, C., H. Irwin, and G. Agogino

1962 Ice-age Man vs. Mammoth in Wyoming. *National Geographic* 121:828–837.

Irwin-Williams, C., H. Irwin, G. Agogino, and C. Vance Haynes

1973 Hell Gap: Paleo-Indian Occupation on the High Plains. *Plains Anthropologist* 18:40–53.

Jodry, M.

1999a Folsom Technological Organization and Socioeconomic Strategies: Views from Stewart's Cattle Guard and the Upper Rio Grande Basin,

Colorado. Unpublished Ph.D. dissertation, Department of Anthropology, American University, Washington, D.C.

1999b Paleoindian Stage. In *Colorado Prehistory: A Context for the Rio Grande Basin*, edited by M. Martorano, T. Hoefer, M. Jodry, V. Spero, and M. Taylor, pp. 45–114. Colorado Council of Professional Archaeologists, Denver.

Jodry, M., and D. Stanford
1992 Stewart's Cattle Guard Site: An Analysis of Bison Remains in a Folsom Kill-butchery Campsite. In *Ice Age Hunters of the Rockies*, edited by D. Stanford and J. Day, pp. 101–168. University Press of Colorado, Niwot.

Jones, S., and R. Bonnichsen
1994 The Anzick Clovis Burial. *Current Research in the Pleistocene* 11:42–43.

Kelly, R., and L. Todd
1988 Coming into the Country: Early Paleoindian Hunting and Mobility. *American Antiquity* 53:231–244.

Kilby, D.
2008 An Investigation of Clovis Caches: Content, Function, and Technological Organization. Unpublished Ph.D. dissertation, Department of Anthropology, The University of New Mexico, Albuquerque.

Kornfeld, M.
1988 The Rocky Folsm Site: A Small Folsom Assemblage from the Northwestern Plains. *North American Archaeologist* 9:197–222.

Kornfeld, M., and G. Frison
2000 Paleoindian Occupation of the High Country: The Case of Middle Park, Colorado. *Plains Anthropologist* 45:129–153.

Kornfeld, M., G. Frison, M. Larson, J. Miller, and J. Saysette
1999 Paleoindian Bison Procurement and Paleoenvironments in Middle Park of Colorado. *Geoarchaeology* 14:655–674.

LaBelle, J.
2003 Coffee Cans and Folsom Points: Why We Cannot Continue to Ignore the Artifact Collectors. In *Archaeological Ethics*, edited by L. Zimmerman, K. Vitelli, and J. Hollowell-Zimmer, pp. 115–127. AltaMira Press, Walnut Creek, California.

2005 Hunter-Gatherer Foraging Variability during the Early Holocene of the Central High Plains of North America. Unpublished Ph.D. dissertation, Department of Anthropology, Southern Methodist University, Dallas, Texas.

LaBelle, J., B. Andrews, and C. Newton
2007 *Class II Archaeological Survey of the Red Mountain Ranch Open Space, Larimer County, Colorado*. Laboratory of Public Archaeology, Department of Anthropology, Colorado State University, Fort Collins, Colorado.

LaBelle, J., and J. Bush
2007 *Class II Archaeological Survey of the Red Mountain Open Space, Larimer County, Colorado*. Laboratory of Public Archaeology, Department of Anthropology, Colorado State University, Fort Collins, Colorado.

Larson, M., M. Kornfeld, and G. Frison (editors)

2009 *Hell Gap: A Stratified Paleoindian Campsite at the Edge of the Rockies*. The University of Utah Press, Salt Lake City.

LeTourneau, P.

2000 Folsom Toolstone Procurement in the Southwest and Southern Plains. Unpublished Ph.D. dissertation, Department of Anthropology, University of New Mexico, Albuquerque.

MacDonald, D.

1998 Subsistence, Sex, and Cultural Transmission in Folsom Culture. *Journal of Anthropological Archaeology* 17:217–239.

1999 Modeling Folsom Mobility, Mating Strategies, and Technological Organization in the Northern Plains. *Plains Anthropologist* 44:141–161.

Madole, R.

1986 Lake Devlin and Pinedale Glacial History, Front Range, Colorado. *Quaternary Research* 25:43–54.

Mandel, R., J. Hofman, S. Holen, and J. Blackmar

2004 Buried Paleo-Indian Landscapes and Sites on the High Plains of Northwestern Kansas. In *Field Trips in the Southern Rocky Mountains, USA*, edited by E. Nelson and E. Erslev, pp. 69–88. Field Guide 5, Geological Society of America, Boulder.

Mandel, R., S. Holen, and J. Hofman

2005 Geoarchaeology of Clovis and Possible Pre-Clovis Cultural Deposits at the Kanorado Locality, Northwestern Kansas. *Current Research in the Pleistocene* 22:56–57.

Mandryk, C.

1990 Could Humans Survive the Ice-Free Corridor? Late-Glacial Vegetation and Climate in West Central Alberta. In *Megafauna and Man: Discovery of America's Heartland*, edited by L. Agenbroad, J. Mead, and L. Nelson, pp. 67–79. The Mammoth Site of Hot Springs, South Dakota.

Mayer, J., T. Surovell, N. Waguespack, M. Kornfeld, R. Reider, and G. Frison

2005 Paleoindian Environmental Change and Landscape Response in Barger Gulch, Middle Park, Colorado. *Geoarchaeology* 20:599–625.

McFaul, M., K. Traugh, G. Smith, W. Doering, and C. Zier

1994 Geoarchaeologic Analysis of South Platte River Terraces: Kersey, Colorado. *Geoarchaeology* 9:345–374.

Meltzer, D.

1993 Is there a Clovis Adaptation? In *From Kostenki to Clovis: Upper Paleolithic-Paleo-Indian Adaptations*, edited by O. Soffer and N. Praslov, pp. 293–310. Plenum Press, New York.

2002 What Do You Do When No One's Been There Before? Thoughts on the Exploration and Colonization of New Lands. In *The First Americans: The Pleistocene Colonization of the New World*, edited by N. Jablonski, pp. 27–58. No. 27, Memoirs of the California Academy of Sciences, San Francisco.

2006 *Folsom: New Archaeological Investigations of a Classic Paleoindian Bison Kill*. University of California Press, Berkeley.

Meltzer, D., and V. Holliday
2010 Would North American Paleoindians Have Noticed Younger Dryas Age Climate Changes? *Journal of World Prehistory* 23:1–41.

Menounos, B., and M. Reasoner
1997 Evidence for Cirque Glaciation in the Colorado Front Range during the Younger Dryas Chronozone. *Quaternary Research* 48:38–47.

Munson, P.
1990 Folsom Fluted Projectile Points East of the Great Plains and Their Biogeographic Correlates. *North American Archaeologist* 11:255–272.

Naze, B.
1986 The Folsom Occupation of Middle Park, Colorado. *Southwestern Lore* 52:1–32.

Newton, C., and J. LaBelle
2008 Shopping Locally: A Foraging Scale Analysis of the Lindenmeier Folsom Tool Stone Sources. Poster presentation at the Plains Anthropological Conference, Laramie, Wyoming, October 2008.

Owsley, D., and D. Hunt
2001 Clovis and Early Archaic Period Crania from the Anzick Site (24PA506), Park County, Montana. *Plains Anthropologist* 46:115–121.

Pitblado, B.
2003 *Late Paleoindian Occupation of the Southern Rocky Mountains.* University Press of Colorado, Niwot.

2007 Angostura, Jimmy Allen, foothills-mountain: Clarifying Terminology for Late Paleoindian Southern Rocky Mountain Spear Points. In *Frontiers in Colorado Paleoindian Archaeology: From the Dent Site to the Rocky Mountains*, edited by R. Brunswig and B. Pitblado, pp. 311–337. University Press of Colorado, Boulder.

Rancier, J., G. Haynes, and D. Stanford
1982 1981 Investigations of Lamb Spring. *Southwestern Lore* 48:1–17.

Reasoner, M., and M. Jodry
2000 Rapid Response of Alpine Timberline Vegetation to the Younger Dryas Climate Oscillation in the Colorado Rocky Mountains, USA. *Geology* 28:51–54.

Roberts, F., Jr.
1935 *A Folsom Complex: Preliminary Report on Investigations at the Lindenmeier Site in Northern Colorado.* Smithsonian Miscellaneous Collections 94(4).

1936 *Additional Information on the Folsom Complex: Report on the Second Season's Investigations at the Lindenmeier Site in Northern Colorado.* Smithsonian Miscellaneous Collections 95(10).

1940 *Developments in the Problem of the North American Paleo-Indian.* Smithsonian Miscellaneous Collections 100:51–116.

Saunders, J.
2007 Processing Marks on Remains of *Mammuthus columbi* from the Dent Site, Colorado, in light of those from Clovis, New Mexico: Fresh-carcass Butchery Versus Scavenging? In *Frontiers in Colorado Paleoindian Archaeology: From the*

Dent Site to the Rocky Mountains, edited by R. Brunswig and B. Pitblado, pp. 155–184. University Press of Colorado, Boulder.

Scott Cummings, L., and R. Albert

2007 Phytolith and Starch Analysis of Dent Site Mammoth Teeth Calculus: New Evidence for Late Pleistocene Mammoth Diets and Environments. In *Frontiers in Colorado Paleoindian Archaeology: From the Dent Site to the Rocky Mountains*, edited by R. Brunswig and B. Pitblado, pp. 185–192. University Press of Colorado, Boulder.

Seebach, J.

2006 Drought or Development? Patterns of Paleoindian Site Discovery on the Great Plains of North America. *Plains Anthropologist* 51:71–88.

Sellards, E.

1952 *Early Man in America*. University of Texas Press, Austin.

Sellet, F.

2001 A Changing Perspective on Paleoindian Chronology and Typology: A View from the Northwestern Plains. *Arctic Anthropology* 38:48–63.

Short, S., and S. Elias

1987 New Pollen and Beetle Analyses at the Mary Jane Site, Colorado: Evidence for Late Glacial Tundra Conditions. *Geological Society of America Bulletin* 98:540–548.

Slessman, S.

2004 The Frazier Site: An Agate Basin Occupation and Lithic Assemblage on the Kersey Terrace, Northeastern Colorado. Master's thesis, Department of Anthropology, Colorado State University, Fort Collins.

Stanford, D.

1979 The Selby and Dutton Sites: Evidence for a Possible Pre-Clovis Occupation of the High Plains. In *Pre-Llano Cultures of the Americas: Paradoxes and Possibilities*, edited by R. Humphrey and D. Stanford, pp. 101–123. The Anthropological Society of Washington, Washington, D.C.

1984 *The Jones-Miller Site: A Study of Hell Gap Bison Procurement and Processing*. National Geographic Society Research Reports (for 1975):615–635.

1999 Paleoindian Archaeology and Late Pleistocene Environments in the Plains and Southwestern United States. In *Ice Age People of North America*, edited by R. Bonnichsen and K. Turnmire, pp. 281–339. Oregon State University Press, Corvallis.

Stanford, D., and M. Jodry

1988 The Drake Clovis Cache. *Current Research in the Pleistocene* 5:21–22.

Stanford, D., W. Wedel, and G. Scott

1981 Archaeological Investigations of the Lamb Spring Site. *Southwestern Lore* 47:14–27.

Stiger, M.

2001 *Hunter-gatherer Archaeology of the Colorado High Country*. University Press of Colorado, Boulder.

2006 A Folsom Structure in the Colorado Mountains. *American Antiquity* 71:321–351.

Surovell, T., and N. Waguespack
2007 Folsom Hearth-centered Use of Space at Barger Gulch, Locality B. In *Frontiers in Colorado Paleoindian Archaeology: From the Dent Site to the Rocky Mountains*, edited by R. Brunswig and B. Pitblado, pp. 219–259. University Press of Colorado, Boulder.
2008 How Many Elephant Kills are 14? Clovis Mammoth and Mastodon Kills in Context. *Quaternary International* 191:82–97.

Surovell, T., N. Waguespack, M. Kornfeld, and G. Frison
2003 *The First Five Seasons at Barger Gulch, Locality B, Middle Park, Colorado.* Technical Report No. 26, George C. Frison Institute of Archaeology and Anthropology, University of Wyoming, Laramie.

Taylor, J.
2006 *Projectile Points of the High Plains.* Sheridan Books, Chelsea, Michigan.

Taylor, R., C. Vance Haynes, Jr., and M. Stuiver
1996 Clovis and Folsom Age Estimates: Stratigraphic Context and Radiocarbon Calibration. *Antiquity* 70:515–525.

Trimble, D.
1980 *The Geologic Story of the Great Plains.* Bulletin 1493, United States Geological Survey.

Waters, M., and T. Stafford, Jr.
2007 Redefining the Age of Clovis: Implications for the Peopling of the Americas. *Science* 315:1122–1126.

Wheat, J.
1979 The Jurgens Site. *Plains Anthropologist* 24(84, Pt. 2), Memoir No. 15.

Wilke, P., J. Flenniken, and T. Ozbun
1991 Clovis Technology at the Anzick Site, Montana. *Journal of California and Great Basin Anthropology* 13:242–272.

Wilmsen, E.
1974 *Lindenmeier: A Pleistocene Hunting Society.* Harper and Row, New York.

Wilmsen, E., and F. Roberts, Jr.
1978 *Lindenmeier, 1934–1974, Concluding Report on Investigations* (1984 printing). Smithsonian Contributions to Anthropology No. 24, Washington, D.C.

Wilson, M., and J. Burns
1999 Searching for the Earliest Canadians: Wide Corridors, Narrow Doorways, and Small Windows. In *Ice Age Peoples of North America: Environments, Origins, and Adaptations of the First Americans*, edited by R. Bonnichsen and K. Turnmire, pp. 213–248. Center for the Study of the First Americans, Oregon State University, Corvallis.

Wormington, H.
1957 *Ancient Man in North America* (4th edition). Denver Museum of Natural History Popular Series 4, Denver.

Zier, C., D. Jepson, M. McFaul, and W. Doering
1993 Archeology and Geomorphology of the Clovis-age Klein Site near Kersey, Colorado. *Plains Anthropologist* 38:203–210.

7

Coping with the Younger Dryas in the Heart of Europe

Michael Jochim

Introduction

The Younger Dryas in Europe has long been recognized as a period of significant environmental and cultural changes. In northern Europe, in particular, the rapid cooling at the onset of this episode is seen to have led to a southward retreat of forests after their initial spread following the glacial maximum. The re-expansion of open, tundra vegetation was accompanied by a reappearance of reindeer-based, hunting economies, such as the Ahrensburgian. Some regions, such as the northern Netherlands, may even have been abandoned due to the rigorous conditions (Stapert 2000). Although debates about the causes of this climatic reversal continue (e.g., Firestone et al. 2007), its effects in many regions appear to have been profound.

In central Europe, on the other hand, the environmental changes of the Younger Dryas are much less dramatic and, as a result, their influence on hunter-gatherer behavior may have been less, or at least more subtle. An examination of the paleoenvironmental and archaeological records of southern Germany and parts of Switzerland will explore the nature of these changes and their impact on cultural behavior.

Hunter-Gatherer Behavior: Human Response during The Younger Dryas, edited by Metin I. Eren, 165–178. © Left Coast Press. All rights reserved.

The Paleoenvironmental Record

During the Younger Dryas, Europe was characterized by a profound temperature gradient from north to south (Coope et al. 1998). It has recently been estimated, for example, that the mean annual temperature for much of Denmark during this period was below –8° C, whereas in southern Germany it was above –1° C (Isarin and Renssen 1999). Due largely to this steep gradient, the vegetational history of southern Germany differed significantly from that of areas farther north.

Most of the lowlands of southern Germany and northern Switzerland were covered by the Alpine ice sheet during the Last Glacial Maximum. Not long thereafter, however, the glaciers began to retreat, so that these areas became completely ice free between 16,000 and 14,000 BP. In the process, a series of lakes was created as meltwater filled numerous basins, a development that would have a profound effect on human use of the landscape. Over the course of the late glacial period, from 14,000 to 10,000 BP, the area witnessed a series of alternating warmer and colder episodes. Pioneer grasses, shrubs, and bushes gradually moved in, creating an open steppe-tundra during the Dryas I period. Juniper, birch, and then pine appeared and spread during the succeeding Bølling-Ållerød period of 13,000–11,000 bp, so that by the end of this phase, a rather uniform forest of pine and birch covered most of the region (Frenzel 1983); although, the progressive development of increasingly dense forests was interrupted for a time by the Laacher See volcanic eruption late in the Ållerød (Rösch 1990). This eruption constitutes a useful marker horizon.

The Younger Dryas itself (11,000–10,000 BP; 12,900–11,500 cal BP) was a complex period. Palynological studies in southern Germany, Switzerland, and eastern France suggest that summer temperatures decreased from the earlier Ållerød somewhere between 1–8° C, with a 2–3° C depression most likely (Lang 2006). Although palynological and oxygen isotope investigations of late glacial sediment cores from the Gerzensee in south-central Switzerland document well the cooling event in the oxygen isotope curve, they show little change in overall arboreal pollen (Eicher and Siegenthaler 1976). Similarly, analysis of sediments, pollen, and geochemicals in Lake Steisslingen, southern Germany, shows the Younger Dryas to have only slight characteristics as a cooling event with no drastic deforestation. Higher erosion of littoral sediments indicates lake-level lowering and thus a dry climate (Esterhues et al. 2002). Studies in the Durchenbergried of southwestern Germany show the Younger Dryas to be characterized by a slight opening of the forest and strong erosion. It was initially a very humid period, with higher lake levels, but later became very dry with lower levels. More generally,

Magny (2004) documented low lake levels during this period in France, Switzerland, and southern Germany. In the later Younger Dryas, pine forests became denser again (Rösch 1990), but in the Black Forest, the tree line did decline from at least 1,100 m asl above sea level in the Ållerød to at least 750 m asl in the Younger Dryas (Lang 2006).

Taken together, these and other studies indicate that, despite a decrease in temperatures, varying with altitude and other factors, vegetational communities were not drastically disrupted. The tree line descended somewhat, forests became more open, at least in places, and the proportions of pine and birch varied. In addition, it seems that the climatic deterioration had a less-marked impact upon the local vegetation around lakes than on the broader regional vegetation, with greater tree cover persisting at the lakes (Peyrona 2005). Lake levels fluctuated, but lower water levels predominated and erosion was at times quite marked.

As forests moved in, the character of the animal communities changed. Among large mammals, reindeer and horse decreased in abundance, to be replaced by aurochs, red deer, and elk, and somewhat later, roe deer and wild boar as well. Smaller woodland mammals such as beaver, marten, fox, and squirrel also became numerous. The succession of birds and fish is less well known, but the new landscape certainly contained a diverse array of game birds and waterfowl and the rivers and lakes a variety of different species of fish and shellfish.

Archaeological Framework

The relative continuity of the vegetation cover in this region during the Younger Dryas is reflected by a relative continuity in the archaeological record as well. In the traditional chronological scheme of the area's culture history, the reindeer and horse economies of the upper Paleolithic Magdalenian develops into the forest-adapted late Paleolithic culture during the Ållerød period, which persisted through the Younger Dryas.

Over fifty-eight Magdalenian sites, mostly dating to the period of 13,000–12,000 BP, have been discovered in southern Germany (Figure 7.1) (Eriksen 1991). Some of these, however, seem to indicate that Magdalenian occupation continued into the early Ållerød period as well (Fisher 2000; Weniger 1982). These sites have provided abundant lithic collections, faunal remains, features, and art objects, allowing for a detailed and convincing reconstruction of subsistence and settlement behavior and perhaps the clearest delineation of an ordered seasonal round for Paleolithic Europe (Weniger 1982). Group aggregations occurred in fall to focus on communal reindeer hunts in lowland areas and near game migration routes, which often lasted into

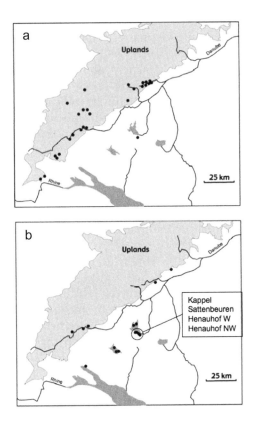

Figure 7.1 Major sites of the a) Magdalenian and b) late Paleolithic in southwest Germany.

winter. The warm seasons, by contrast, witnessed population dispersal into the hills, where subsistence was more diverse.

The late Paleolithic of southern Germany, however, is much less rich. Most sites are surface lithic assemblages, often mixed with materials of other periods. A number of caves with organic remains were excavated early in the last century and are poorly known (Lais 1929; Mieg 1904; Reinerth 1956). Until recently, excavated—definite—late Paleolithic sites were limited to three caves, one rockshelter, and three open-air sites (Hahn and Scheer 1983; Jochim 1998; Kind 1995; Taute 1972, 1978). The caves and the rockshelter have very small lithic assemblages (ca. 100 or fewer artifacts) and only one contains (very fragmentary) faunal remains. The open-air sites are all situated on the former shores of the Federsee. Two of these, Henauhof NW, level 6 and

Henauhof West, also have very small lithic assemblages (97 and 143 artifacts respectively), but both also contain identifiable faunal remains and have been interpreted as a residential base and a more special-purpose, hunting camp respectively (Jochim 1995). The third open-air site, Sattenbeuren, has a larger lithic assemblage (959 artifacts in 109 square meters) but no faunal remains (Kind 1995). None of these sites has produced radiocarbon dates, but stratigraphic and/or faunal indications suggest that many of them date to the Younger Dryas.

Since 1992, my colleague Lynn Fisher, graduate students Susan Harris and Harry Starr, and I have carried out a program of surface survey and test excavations in southern Germany with the support of the National Science Foundation (SBR-9412537), University Research Expeditions Program, the National Geographic Society, the Wenner-Gren Foundation, University of California Santa Barbara, and the State Office of Historic Monuments of Baden-Württemberg (Jochim et al. 1998). The aim of the survey and tests was to broaden our knowledge of Paleolithic, Mesolithic, and Neolithic site distributions beyond the narrow areas of previously concentrated research. To date we have found more than 500 new surface sites and have carried out test excavations at fifteen locations. A number of the surface sites have produced late Paleolithic materials, so that we are beginning to be able to map the distribution of sites of this period in a more comprehensive way. It is now clear, for example, that both the Federsee and another formerly large lake, the Pfrunger Ried, were areas of concentrated settlement during this period.

In 2002, a new site, Kappel, was discovered on the old Federsee shores. A ridge system of gravel and sand about 50 m offshore, previously invisible in a grassy meadow, "emerged" when the water table dropped and the surrounding peat compacted. A few nondiagnostic lithic artifacts were found in mole hills on the ridge surface. Because this land was slated for development, the State Office of Historic Monuments of Baden-Württemberg, recognizing the potential archaeological and geological importance of the location, purchased the parcel. They also provided financial assistance that allowed me to carry out excavations at the site in 2003 and 2004, and together with Claus-Joachim Kind, to continue our field work in 2006 and 2007.

After using air photos and coring to define the limits of the ridge, we excavated a series of test units and larger blocks on the ridge, on its flanks, and in the peat some distance away. Artifacts were piece-plotted and samples of deposits were screened. A total of 235 m^2 was excavated in this manner. In addition, the State Office of Historic Monuments of Baden-Württemberg arranged for a backhoe to dig three long trenches crossing the ridge at various points in order to investigate the geological history of the ridge system. This ridge system is a puzzle in terms of the processes underlying its formation, and three different geologists, including Josef Merkt, a specialist in limnological studies, have examined the profiles. The gravel and sand appear to have been deposited by run-off from a stream during erosional episodes of the Younger Dryas and subsequently reworked by wave action. This ridge sits on top of lake sediments that contain materials of the Laacher See eruption, and thus postdates the late Allerød period.

Analysis of the archaeological finds is ongoing. Our excavations recovered more than 3,000 lithic artifacts and approximately 150 bone fragments. The vast majority are attributable to the late Paleolithic, but some artifacts characteristic of the early Mesolithic and the late Neolithic occur as well; with little deposition accumulating on the ridge since its formation, these later artifacts cannot be stratigraphically separated from the late Paleolithic materials. The density of lithic finds on the ridge is about three times that of the large site of Sattenbeuren. Among the retouched tools, burins, backed points, and scrapers are most abundant. A locally available brown chert dominates the assemblage, but a significant amount of red and green radiolarite was also found. The red radiolarite is also locally available in the morainic gravels of the region, but the green radiolarite appears to derive from southern Bavaria, approximately 60 km away.

The vast majority of the artifacts occur on the top of the ridge, with densities falling sharply toward the edges. On the ridgetop they show a narrow vertical distribution of 15-cm thickness, except in areas where rodent burrows occur. But on the flanks of the ridge, they are more widely distributed throughout the vertical extent of the gravels and sands. Bones occur both in the gravel and sand of the ridge and in the peat along the flanks. The condition of the bones is variable; it is quite good in the gravel/sand and in portions of the peat where wood is also well preserved, but very fragmentary in other areas of peat, apparently due to drying with a drop in water table. Large mammal, bird, and fish occur, as well as several human teeth.

Subsistence and Settlement

The late Paleolithic lasted approximately 1,500 years. The entire period is characterized by a widespread pine-birch forest with some spatial and temporal variations in density and composition. Any open areas of shrubs, herbs, and grasses would have existed only at the higher elevations. The diversity of plant species represented in pollen records is low and included none of obvious value as important human foods. It is likely that the overwhelming majority of human foods were animals, just as they had been in the preceding steppe-tundra of the Magdalenian. In these new forests, the late Paleolithic hunters would have been familiar with all of the major prey, as all were present during the preceding Magdalenian as well. What *was* new was the gradually changing habitat in which these prey were found, the slowly differing relative proportions of each, and the changing behavior of each in the new landscape. In terms of optimal foraging theory, all of the large herbivores had already been in the optimal diet. The herds of reindeer and horse, which had presumably been previously highly ranked in terms of pursuit efficiency, were decreasing in abundance with reforestation. Animals favored by the vegetational changes, on the other hand, would have included red deer, aurochs, and moose. Increasingly during the course of the late Paleolithic, these prey would have been the major food packages on the landscape. These animals, however, are more solitary than the gregarious reindeer and horse, and likely to have been more dispersed throughout the environment. Together with the decreasing visibility in the closed forests and the increasing difficulty in travel, these changes had profound effects on hunting techniques, costs, and efficiency.

The dominant hunting technique changed. In the preceding Magdalenian, seasonal movements of reindeer and horse may have been relatively pronounced and fairly predictable, so that the hunters could focus on intercepting herds in fall and spring at particular points on the landscape. The late glacial prey was more dispersed throughout the forests, especially in the lowlands, their movements were shorter and less predictable, and prey visibility diminished as well. As a result, an intercept strategy was increasingly less likely to be productive. Walking through the forest to encounter prey probably became more important as a hunting technique. Overall, the costs of hunting must have increased, leading to a broadening of the diet to include smaller mammals and more fish and birds.

Fish and waterfowl appear to have played a very small role in Magdalenian subsistence. In the small, warm-weather site of Felsställe, for example, there were only sixteen bones of fish and waterfowl among the total of 2,418 in the Magdalenian levels (Kind 1987). The one known lakeshore site of Schussenquelle reflects this economic orientation. Although much of the faunal collection has been lost since its primary excavation in 1866, it is clear that reindeer were the focus of activities. Very few fish and waterfowl were found. A recent reanalysis of this site concludes that the location was chosen for its hunting potential; the narrow ridge of land between lakes channeled animal movements, allowing easier intercept hunting (Schuler 1994). It should be noted that two other Magdalenian, lakeshore sites discovered in Switzerland, Monruz, and Hauterive-Champreveyres, show a similar pattern (Leesch 1997; Morel and Müller 1997). Although both are situated directly on the shore of Lake Neuchatel, both are dominated by big game, with very few fish and birds.

In the late Paleolithic level of the site of Henauhof NW on the Federsee, fish and birds show a somewhat greater importance (Jochim 1998). It is also clear that the number of fish bones increased significantly from the Magdalenian to the late Paleolithic in both the rockshelter site of Zigeunerfels and the cave of Dietfurt, both on the Danube River, although detailed faunal analyses are not available (Torke 1981). Certainly, in all late Paleolithic sites with faunal assemblages, large game, especially red deer, made up the majority of identified finds, but a growing emphasis on fish, birds, and small mammals appears to reflect the changing ecology of hunting in the late glacial forests.

These changes also affected settlement patterns. With the decline in herd species and the loss of predictable intercept points, group aggregation for cooperative hunting would have become less profitable, and group size appears to have remained small for much of the year. The generally dispersed distribution of prey would have encouraged a dispersal of human populations. Local areas could rather rapidly have been depleted of the larger herbivores, prompting relatively frequent movements. The overlapping distribution of most resources in the lowlands for much of the year would have encouraged an organization around residential mobility rather than logistic mobility (Binford 1980)—so that most sites appear to be residential camps with a variety of activities represented.

In contrast to the preceding Magdalenian, when most sites are caves and rockshelters in valleys flanked by limestone hills, the vast majority of late Paleolithic sites are open-air in the lowlands (Figure 7.2). Moreover, most of these sites are located on the shores of the newly formed lakes; although, our surveys carried out extensive investigations away from water as well. While several of the lakes have scattered traces of Magdalenian artifacts along their shores, true concentrations that reflect occupation are rare. Only one true Magdalenian "site," Schussenquelle, is known just south of the Federsee on a small pond. And this location, as previously mentioned, appears to have been selected to intercept reindeer moving between the two bodies of water (Schuler 1994). On the Federsee shores, only four of the known surface sites have identifiable

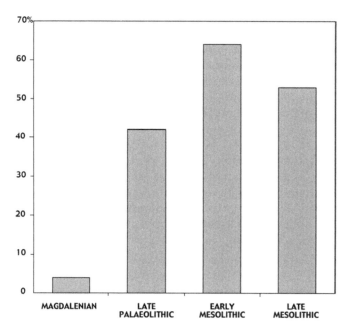

Figure 7.2 Percentage of sites on lakeshores in southwest Germany through time. Total number of sites: Aurignacian/Gravettian, 12; Magdalenian, 27; late Paleolithic, 19; early Mesolithic, 110; late Mesolithic, 15.

Magdalenian artifacts, while thirteen are clearly late Paleolithic sites. Similarly, the Pfrunger Ried surveys discovered only four surface sites on the former shore with Magdalenian artifacts, whereas fourteen late Paleolithic occupation sites were found. In Switzerland a similar pattern is seen. Most Magdalenian sites are caves and rockshelters. Around the shore of the Wauwiler Moos, a former lake in south-central Switzerland, a large number of surface sites have been found (Nielsen 1992). Six of these have a few possible Magdalenian artifacts, whereas forty-five are recognizable late Paleolithic sites. This clear preference for lakeshores may reflect the habits of game that concentrated the animals in such areas, the growing importance of fish and waterfowl in subsistence, and/or the denser and more varied vegetation near the lakes.

Not only is there a shift of occupation to lakeshores, but many of the densest late Paleolithic sites are situated in locations that maximize shoreline access. Such locations include islands, peninsulas, and narrow spits of land jutting into the lakes. They may have provided proximity to water and lacustrine resources as well as wide viewsheds in the newly forested landscape. It is interesting to note that among the modern Chipewyan of Canada, island sites are preferred in summer for a variety of reasons, including isolation from bears, malevolent spirits, and forest fires, as well as the presence of wind for insect dispersal (Irimoto 1980:90).

Technology was affected in various ways as well. If hunting became less reliable and emphasized opportunistic encounters, then it would have been advantageous if weapons were easy to repair. Bleed (1986:739) refers to this characteristic as "maintainability" and suggests that such implements will tend to be lightweight and portable with a modular design that allows easy removal of parts for replacement. Repair of such tools should be ongoing, rather than concentrated during periods of "gearing up." One of the hallmarks of late Paleolithic technology is its simplicity in relation to that of the Magdalenian, with fewer well-defined tool types, generally smaller artifacts, and a relative lack of complex bone harpoons that could not be easily repaired (although one large harpoon was discovered at the site of Kappel).

Large combination tools with multiple working edges also decrease in number. Such tools, for example, burin-scrapers, would have served a variety of functional needs in periods of stress, and constitute over 17% of the retouched nonmicrolithic tools in a sample of early Magdalenian sites studied by Fisher (2000). They seem to have been particularly useful as part of the anticipatory toolkit in intercept hunting and exploitation of the migrating reindeer. In her sample of late Paleolithic sites, on the other hand, such tools make up only 6% of the nonmicrolithic, tool assemblages. Two other of the late Paleolithic sites, Sattenbeuren and Kappel, have assemblages that consist of only 3% and 1% of combination tools respectively.

Late Paleolithic hunting technology appears to have centered on generalized stone-tipped arrows and simple butchering knives, usable in a variety of situations. In the archaeological record, the evidence of tool manufacture and repair is widespread, occurring at most sites, and is characterized by diverse core types with little preshaping and relatively more flakes than more-carefully made blades, in contrast to the earlier Magdalenian (Fisher 2000).

Other aspects of technology may have changed in accordance with the new emphasis on lakeshore settlement. The location of large sites on islands in both the Federsee and Pfrunger Ried imply the development of watercraft, although no remains of such have been found. The discovery of a large harpoon point at Kappel, very different from those found in Magdalenian sites, suggests that fishing technology underwent development as well.

Conclusions

A consideration of the changing ecology of hunting, consequently, together with the existing archaeological record, suggests a number of characteristics of late Paleolithic sites, all representing significant changes from the preceding Magdalenian. These include:

1. Relatively uniformly small site sizes, indicating small groups;
2. Relatively numerous sites, reflecting high mobility;
3. Relatively small assemblages, indicating brief stays;
4. Relatively few constructed features and concentrated middens, also reflecting brief stays;
5. Relatively diverse faunas, suggesting subsistence diversification;
6. A concentration of sites near lakes, rather than migration routes, indicating the diversification of subsistence to include more fish and waterfowl;
7. Relatively diverse lithic assemblages, reflecting the varied activities of residential bases at most sites;
8. Utilization primarily of locally available stone raw material, reflecting the ongoing lithic reduction characteristic of most sites; and
9. The development of fishing technology, including watercraft and new forms of harpoon, as a consequence of the subsistence changes.

References

Binford, L.
 1980 Willow Smoke and Dogs' Tails: Hunter-gatherer Settlement Systems and Archaeological Site Formation. *American Antiquity* 43:330–361.
Bleed, P.
 1986 The Optimal Design of Hunting Weapons: Maintainability or Reliability. *American Antiquity* 51:737–747.
Coope, G., G. Lemdahl, J. Lowe, and A. Walking
 1998 Temperature Gradients in Northern Europe during the Last Glacial-Holocene Transition (14-9 C-14 kyr BP) Interpreted from Coleopteran Assemblages. *Journal of Quaternary Science* 13:419–433.
Eicher, U., and U. Siegenthaler
 1976 Palynological and Oxygen Isotope Investigations on Late-Glacial Sediment Cores from Swiss Lakes. *Boreas* 5:109–117.
Eriksen, B.
 1991 *Change and Continuity in a Prehistoric Hunter-gatherer Society.* Archaeologica Venatoria 12, Tübingen.

Esterhues, K., J. Lechterbeck, J. Schneider, and U. Wolf-Brozio
2002 Late- and Post-glacial Evolution of Lake Steisslingen (I): Sedimentary, History, Palynological Record and Inorganic Geochemical Indicators. *Palaeogeography, Palaeoclimatology, Palaeoecology* 187:341–371.

Firestone, R., A. West, J. Kennett, L. Becker, T. Bunch, Z. Revay, P. Schultz, T. Belgya, D. Kennett, J. Erlandson, O. Dickerson, A. Goodyear, R. Harris, G. Howard, J. Kloosterman, P. Lechler, P. Mayewski, J. Montgomery, R. Poreda, T. Darrah, S. Que Hee, A. Smith, A. Stich, W. Topping, J. Wittke, and W. Wolbach
2007 Evidence for an Extraterrestrial Impact 12,900 Years Ago That Contributed to the Megafaunal Extinctions and the Younger Dryas Cooling. *Proceedings of the National Academy of Sciences* 104:16016–16021.

Fisher, L.
2000 *Land Use and Technology from Magdalenian to Early Mesolithic in Southern Germany.* Unpublished Ph.D. dissertation, University of Michigan, Ann Arbor.

Frenzel, B.
1983 Die Vegetationsgeschichte Süddeutschlands im Eiszeitalter. In *Urgeschichte in Baden-Württemberg*, edited by H. Müller-Beck, pp. 91–165. Konrad Theiss Verlag, Stuttgart.

Hahn, J., and A. Scheer
1983 Das Halga-Abri am Hohlenfelsen bei Schelklingen: Eine Mesolithische Und Jungpaläolithische Schichtenfolge. *Archäologische Korrespondenzblatt* 13:19–28.

Irimoto, T.
1980 *Chipewyan Ecology: Group Structure and Caribou Hunting System.* Senri Ethnological Studies 8. National Museum of Ethnology, Osaka.

Isarin, R., and H. Renssen
1999 Reconstructing and Modeling the Late Weichselian Climates: The Younger Dryas in Europe as a Case Study. *Earth Sciences Review* 48:1–38.

Jochim, M.
1995 Two Late Palaeolithic Sites on the Federsee, South Germany. *Journal of Field Archaeology* 22:263–273.
1998 *A Hunter-Gatherer Landscape.* Plenum, New York.

Jochim, M., M. Glass, L. Fisher, and P. McCartney
1998 Mapping the Stone Age: An Interim Report on the South German Survey Project. In *Aktuelle Forschungen zum Mesolithikum/Current Mesolithic Research*, edited by N. Conard, pp. 121–132. Urgeschichtliche Materialhefte 12. Mo Vince Verlag, Tübingen.

Kind, C.
1987 *Das Felsställe: Eine Jungpaläolithisch-Frühmesolithische Abri-Station Bei Ehingen-Mühlen, Alb-Donau-Kreis.* Forschungen und Berichte zur Vor- und Frühgeschichte in Baden-Württemberg 23. Konrad Theiss Verlag, Stuttgart.

Kind, C.

1995 Ein spätpaläolithischer Uferrandlagerplatz am Federsee in Oberschwaben: Sattenbeuren-Kieswerk. *Fundberichte aus Baden-Württemberg* 20:160–194.

Lais, R.

1929 Ein Werkplatz des Azilio-Tardenoisiens am Isteiner Klotz. *Badische Fundberichte* 11:97–107.

Lang, G.

2006 Late-glacial Fluctuations of Timberline in the Black Forest (SW Germany). *Vegetational History and Archaeobotany* 15:373–375.

Leesch, D.

1997 *Un Campement Magdaleien au Bord du lac de Neuchatel, Cadre Chronologique et Culturel, Mobilier et Structures, Analyse Spatiale.* Musee Cantonal d'Archeologie, Neuchatel.

Magny, M.

2004 Holocene Climate Variability as Reflected by Mid-European Lake-level Fluctuations and its Probable Impact on Prehistoric Human Settlements. *Quaternary International* 113:65–79.

Mieg, M.

1904 Stations Prehistoriques de Kleinkems (Grand-duche de Bade). *Bulletin de la Societe des Sciences de Nancy.* Series III, Tome V:97–108.

Morel, P., and W. Müller

1997 *Un Campement Magdalenien au Bord du lac de Neuchatel, etude Archeozoologique (secteur I).* Musee Cantonal d'Archeologie, Neuchatel.

Nielsen, E.

1992 Paläolithische und Mesolithische Fundstellen im Zentralschweizerischen Wauwilermoos. *Archäologisches Korrespondenzblatt* 22:27–40.

Peyrona, O.

2005 Late-glacial Climatic Changes in Eastern France (Lake Lautrey) from Pollen, Lake-levels, and Chironomids. *Quaternary Research* 62:197–211.

Reinerth, H.

1956 Die älteste Besiedlung des Allgäues. *Vorzeit am Bodensee* Heft 1–4:1–35.

Rösch, M.

1990 Vegetationsgeschichtliche Untersuchungen im Durchenbergried. *Sidelungsarchäologie im Alpenvorland* II:9–64.

Schuler, A.

1994 *Die Schussenquelle: Eine Freilandstation des Magdalenien in Oberschwaben.* Materialhefte zur Archäologie. Landesdenkmalamt Baden-Württemberg. Konrad Theiss Verlag, Stuttgart.

Stapert, D.

2000 The Late Palaeolithic in the Northern Netherlands. *Memoires du Musee d'Ile-de-France* 7:175–195.

Taute, W.

1972 Die spätpaläolithisch-frühmesolithische Schichtenfolge im Zigeunerfels Bei Sigmaringen (Vorbericht). *Archäolotische Informationen* 2/3:59–66.

Taute, W.
1978 *Das Mesolithikum in Süddeutschland, Teil 2: Naturwissenschaftliche Untersuchungen.* Tübinger Monographien zur Urgeschichte 5/2. Archaeologica Venatoria, Tübingen.

Torke, W.
1981 *Fischreste als Quellen der ökologie und ökonomie in der Steinzeit Südwestdeutschlands.* Urgeschichtliche Materialhefte 4. Archaeologica Venatoria, Tübingen.

Weniger, G.
1982 *Wildbeuter und ihre Umwelt.* Archaeologica Venatoria 5. Archaeological Venatoria, Tübingen.

8

EUROPE IN THE YOUNGER DRYAS: ANIMAL RESOURCES, SETTLEMENT, AND FUNERARY BEHAVIOR

Stella M. Blockley and Clive S. Gamble

Introduction

The Younger Dryas (Greenland Stadial 1 [GS1]) was of sufficient climatic severity to have been potentially very disruptive to humans and the faunal populations on which they depended. The Younger Dryas (YD) has been cited as partially responsible for extinctions in North America; although, human influence and other external factors have also been discussed (Firestone et al. 2007; Robinson et al. 2005). Further, the YD has even been put forward as a possible factor in the adoption of agriculture in the Near East (Bar-Yosef and Belfer-Cohen 1992; Byrd 2005; Hole 2007).

In this paper, we will briefly examine the consequences of the YD in Britain and Europe where its effect on climate was marked; January temperatures were up to -30 to $-10\,^\circ$ C below current averages, based on the ECHAM3-T42 atmospheric general circulation model (Renssen et al. 2001) (Figure 8.1). However, despite these extremes, the YD in Europe has not been linked to any extinction events or major changes in human adaptations such as agriculture. Therefore, the question to ask is whether it acted as a determinant factor on human behavior and if so, how?

Hunter-Gatherer Behavior: Human Response during The Younger Dryas, edited by Metin I. Eren, 179–194. © Left Coast Press. All rights reserved.

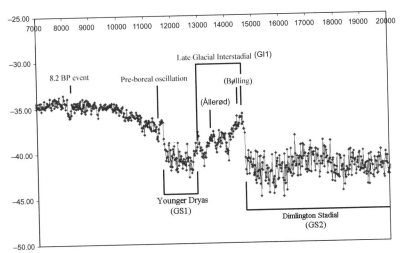

Figure 8.1 Reconstructed temperatures for the Younger Dryas (a) winter and (b) summer (after Renssen et al. 2001).

Key: Bold = °C isotherms; Italics = °C differences from present temperatures.

To examine this question, we will assess the disruption to human and animal populations through an analysis of the radiocarbon evidence that focuses on funerary behavior, animal resources, and settlement patterns. Our approach uses dates-as-data and draws on a radiocarbon database that has been compiled to study the recolonization of Europe after the Last Glacial Maximum (LGM) and to assess if humans had any impact on the demise of the continent's megafauna. The database contains 3,545 audited and calibrated radiocarbon dates (Pettitt et al. 2003), that mainly fall between 8,900 and 34,630 BP (10,000 cal BP and 40,000 cal BP), of which 707 are direct dates on animal taxa; and another 884 direct dates from human skeletal material, artifacts, and cut-marked bone. Charcoal from secure hearth contexts is also included. All radiocarbon dates have been calibrated to 2σ using INTCAL 04 (Stuiver et al. 1998).

Organic materials such as bone and antler offer a particular advantage to an approach where dates-as-data are used to examine the archaeological evidence for the impact of climate change on human adaptations. Because such samples form the material for radiocarbon dating, they provide a direct age estimate rather than a proxy age by association. Furthermore, when the same material is also identified to species, keeping in mind the usual caveats about the radiocarbon method (Brock et al. 2007; Taylor 1992), we can, construct accurate distributions of their location in space and time; a situation that also applies to humans.

The Younger Dryas Climate

The YD (Loch Lomond Stadial/Readvance in Britain, Nanaghan Stadial in Ireland) was a major climate event found in a variety of paleoclimate records from Europe and in the Greenland ice cores (Björk et al. 1998; Lowe et al. 1995; Lowe et al. 2004; Rasmussen et al. 2006; Svensson et al. 2006; Walker et al. 2003). However, the ubiquity of a climate signal does not automatically imply its synchronicity; for example, it cannot be assumed that the cooling was temporally parallel between Greenland and Europe, or indeed across Europe itself (Lowe et al. 2008). To test this, a new ice core record, the NorthGRIP GICC05 oxygen isotope chronology (Lowe et al. 2008; Rasmussen et al. 2006; Svensson et al. 2006) has been developed (Figure 8.2). This record shows a slight offset in timing with the previous stratotype, the GRIP SS08c chronology (Björk et al. 1998; Lowe et al. 2008) (Figure 8.3). The NorthGRIP core is layer-counted and is adopted here as a master chronology.

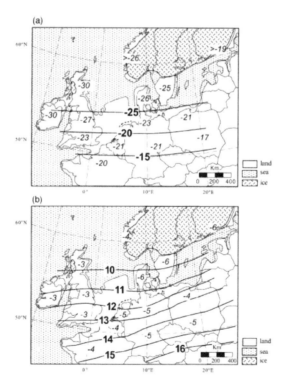

Figure 8.2 The NorthGRIP GICC05, oxygen isotope, chronology SMOW (standard mean of ocean waters) for the last termination (Rasmussen et al. 2006; Svensson et al. 2006).

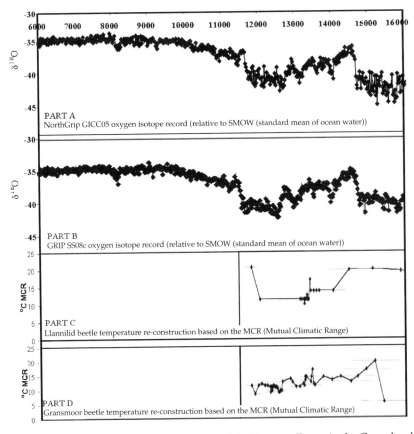

Figure 8.3 Discrepancies in the timings of the Younger Dryas in the Greenland ice core and British climatic records. Part A: the NorthGRIP GICC05 oxygen isotope chronology SMOW (Rasmussen et al. 2006; Svensson et al. 2006). Part B: the GRIP SS08c chronology (Björk et al. 1998; Lowe et al. 2008). Part C: the Gransmoor coleopteran record (Walker et al. 2003). Part D: the Llanilid coleopteran record (Lowe et al. 1995).

However, records from Britain such as the radiocarbon-dated Llanilid Coleoptera, temperature records (Lowe et al. 1995; Walker et al. 2003) show potential for an earlier cooling in Britain (Figure 8.3). This finding indicates that the timings of cooling in Europe attributed to the YD are at best approximate. As the NorthGRIP chronology is a high precision record, these timings will be adopted but it must be remembered that further work may alter these boundaries in different regions (Table 8.1). A reconstruction of the YD ice sheets (Ehlers and Gibbard 2004a, 2004b, 2004c) has been used to show the extent of the ice sheet advance.

Table 8.1 Climatic chronozones based on the NGRIP core (Rasmussen et al. 2006; Svensson et al. 2006).

Chronozone	Start date	Error (+)	End date	Error (+)
Greenland Interstadial 1	14692	186	12896	138
Greenland Stadial 1	12896	138	11703	99
Holocene	11703	99		

Effects on Human Populations

Using the dates-as-data approach, the radiocarbon estimates for humans and other species in Europe have been summed to show their probability distributions during the YD period (Figure 8.4). The sample size of direct dates is, of course, much smaller, but even so, the onset of the YD is marked by a decrease in directly dated human presence with some evidence of a recovery later in the period.

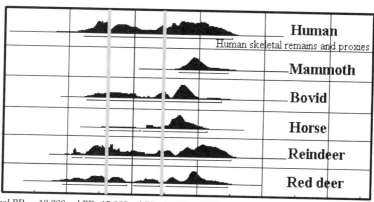

Figure 8.4 Summed radiocarbon dates by species for Europe in the period of study, showing human skeletal remains and human proxies (n = 98); mammoth (n = 5); bovids (n = 29); horse (n = 33); reindeer (n = 30); and red deer (n = 21). The grey box demarcates the period of the Younger Dryas according to the NorthGRIP GICC05, oxygen isotope, chronology SMOW (Svensson et al. 2006).

Funerary Behavior in Britain during the Younger Dryas

Within this general pattern there are notable regional variations. For example, when the directly dated, human skeletal material from Britain is plotted (Figure 8.5) a significant hiatus can be seen during the YD (Blockley 2005, 2008; Chamberlain 1996). However, other evidence for human presence in Britain continues, with radiocarbon-dated human proxies, such as worked and cut marked bone found throughout the YD.

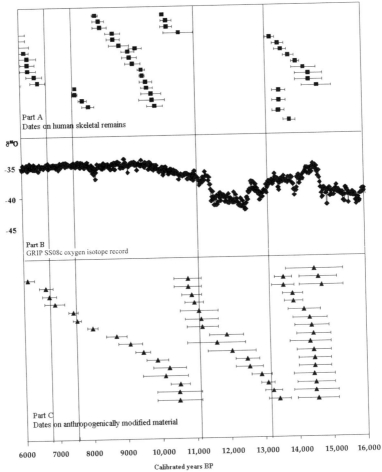

Figure 8.5 Calibrated radiocarbon dates set against the Greenland ice core chronology. The direct dates refer to human skeletal remains (a) and artifact proxies (c) (after Blockley 2005).

A number of hypotheses can be put forward to explain this pattern and which highlight various issues concerning the interpretation of radiocarbon data. These are:

1. The pattern may not be "real" but a function of sampling strategy and incomplete recovery of data. This is a potential problem in all archaeological study and is countered here by the number of radiocarbon dates (Figure 8.5).

2. At a time when Britain was joined to the Continent, humans may have preferentially exploited the coastal areas on the exposed continental shelf. If burials occurred in these areas, then subsequent sea-level rise would have removed them.

3. Funerary behavior may have changed from a pattern of burial in caves to open-air ritual such as excarnation and where survival of the evidence would be poor.

4. Humans may have changed how they used the landscape, potentially in response to movement of fauna.

The well-dated samples of modified material argue against sampling bias for the human skeletal material. Moreover, the presence of these same proxies in inland regions shows that a focused coastal adaptation had not taken place. Nevertheless, there might have been mundane effects of the YD climate downturn on funerary behavior; for example, the difficulty of reaching caves in the cold climate due to ice, or in cases of deliberate deposition that frozen ground prevented the digging of a grave and covering the corpse. Because much of the material from the British caves is fragmentary, it may also be the case that as ice-sheet accumulation occurred, it reduced the flow of rivers and underground swallets so that surface material, including human skeletal remains, was no longer washed into the caves.

Reduced occupation throughout Northern Europe during the YD (Figure 8.4) would impact the archaeological visibility of funerary behavior by simply reducing the number of burials. It is also possible that the lack of burials during the YD reflected a loss of feeling for land, which is not frequently exploited. Britain became a social geography of marginal landscapes for both the living and their dead.

More changes are evident when the examination of funerary behavior is extended to Europe. In the Greenland Interstadial 1 (GI-1), humans practiced a range of funerary behavior that involved deposition in both caves and open-air locations (Orschiedt 1999). During this warm-phase deposition of human skeletal remains, the European data show (Figure 8.6) that humans established an affinity with a region to make

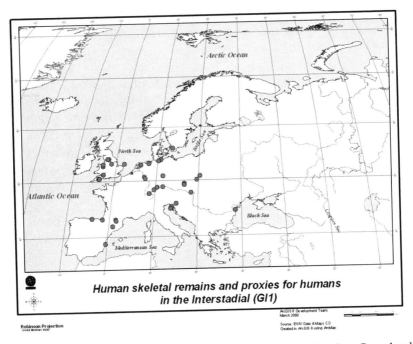

Figure 8.6 Distribution of directly dated humans in the Greenland Interstadial 1.

deposition of the dead both possible and desirable. However, with the onset of the YD (Figure 8.7) there is a reduction in dated, human skeletal remains; the open-air site of Vlasac providing the only evidence of funerary behavior (Blockley 2005). These changes appear to mirror those seen on a smaller scale in Britain.

Animal Resources

The effects of the YD on key animal taxa for human subsistence can be seen in the dates-as-data analysis (Figure 8.4), although small sample size has to be noted. No species remained unaffected by the cold phase as shown by the dip in frequency of the summed radiocarbon dates. The severe cold of the YD in particular affected red deer and a short hiatus is evident at c. 10,200 BP (12,000 cal BP). Mammoth largely disappears before the end of GI1 in Western Europe (Stuart et al. 2004; also see Figure 8.4 here) and horse is much reduced. Red deer and reindeer, and to a lesser extent *Bos*/bison, form a "bridge" of resources for humans through most of the YD.

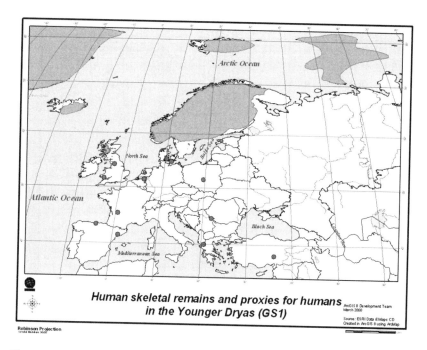

Figure 8.7 Distribution of directly dated humans in the Younger Dryas.

The distribution of directly dated fauna in GI1 and the YD are shown in Figures 8.8 and 8.9. In the GI1, the main resources for humans, horse, reindeer, and red deer are clustered on the North European plain, along the Danube with some important outliers in Western Russia. By contrast the direct dates for human presence (Figure 8.6) show a Western European distribution with a notable scarcity of information from France, although the Iberian Peninsula is represented.

In the YD, there is a contraction of the animal species consistent with a response to the cold phase that shortened the growing season and so curtailed the opportunities for grazing (Figures 8.8 and 8.9). However, the distribution is so restricted that no sensible geographical pattern can be discerned and a sampling bias must be expected. This is also the case with the direct dates for humans seen here in Figure 8.7.

Settlement Patterns

The period leading from GS2 into the early part of GI1 sees a major dispersal of population into Northern Europe in what has been termed Population Event 3 (PE3) in the sequence of late glacial recolonization

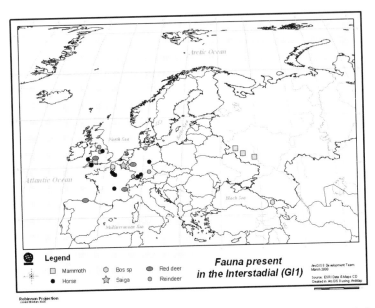

Figure 8.8 Distribution of directly dated fauna in Greenland Interstadial 1.

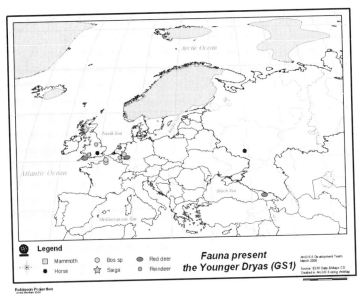

Figure 8.9 Distribution of directly dated fauna in the Younger Dryas (GS1).

(Gamble et al. 2005); an event that is confirmed by genetic data (Soares et al. 2010). It is estimated that population size reached somewhere around 64,000 as the result of this dispersal process from the southern refuges that began some 16,000 cal BP years ago (c. 13,256 BP) (Gamble et al. 2004: Table 6).

In Northern Europe, this demographic expansion of PE3 was marked by a widespread use of caves and rockshelters, as well as open-air sites (Figure 8.10). This dual pattern can best be described as a dispersed settlement pattern and may be linked to the process by which humans recolonized these northern areas. Sheltered sites would have met logistical needs for small hunting parties that needed to move unencumbered. During recolonization, the northern areas may have been used by task groups searching for hunting opportunities. With the climatic amelioration of GI1 range size, these groups would have been reduced as animal biomass increased, and it was this additional packing that led to the higher population numbers for the region. After PE3, as shown in Figure 8.10, there was a significant change in settlement patterns in Northern Europe. Sheltered sites were no longer used at either the same frequency or intensity, and open sites became the norm. The switch to large, open locations points to a nucleated rather than a dispersed pattern of settlement during the latter part of GI1.

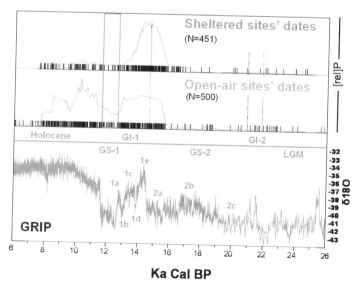

Figure 8.10 Numbers of cave sites and open-air sites through the period of study (from Gamble et al. 2005). GS1 = YD.

However, populations that were well-embedded within regions during GI1 then had to adapt to the extreme climate of the YD. The dates-as-data curve reveals a decline in activity in Northern Europe and the likely return to a dispersed settlement system, but it is one based this time on open rather than cave sites. Here, perhaps, there is a parallel to the effects in the Near East of the YD on sedentism and intensification, although nucleation did not lead in Northern Europe to such fundamental changes in human economy and society. Instead population numbers, as indicated by the dates-as-data curves declined but never to those levels found earlier in the refugia of the LGM.

Conclusion

Did the YD in Europe act as a determinant factor on human behavior? The dates-as-data approach clearly shows that it did; although, its climatic severity did not lead to an abandonment of the northern areas as it had during the LGM. The YD also severely disrupted animal resources. However, for some species, this was a process that began in GI1 when conditions were much warmer. What the dates-as-data analysis shows is that any effects have to be examined on a regional basis. The absence in Britain of any dated human remains for the YD forms a sharp contrast with the evidence from the warmer phases that came before and after. Such changes in funerary behavior most likely reflect the change in settlement pattern from nucleated to dispersed that in turn reflects the smaller populations that existed in this part of the European biotidal zone (Gamble 2009). The presence of directly dated artifacts, charcoal, and cut-marked bone from the YD occupation of Britain points to continuous settlement that used different settlement strategies to cope with a reduced animal resource base. Finally, while intensification did indeed occur during the YD in areas of the Near East, the question then arises whether a comparable process of intensification also occurred far away in Northern Europe. The answer is affirmative when viewed over the long-term of human evolution. The occupation of northwest Europe during the YD was important, because it reversed the pattern of climate determining settlement and led to continued occupation in what for hominids had, up until then, always been ecologically unlikely places.

Acknowledgments

The research was supported by the NERC Megafaunal extinctions project NE/D003105/1. Comments and assistance from Adrian Lister, Tony Stuart, Simon Blockley, and William Davies are gratefully acknowledged.

References

Bar-Yosef, O., and A. Belfer-Cohen

1992 From Foraging to Farming in the Mediterranean Levant. In *Transitions to Agriculture in Prehistory*, edited by A. Gebauer and T. Douglas Price, pp. 21–48. Prehistory Press, Ann Arbor.

Björk, S., M. Walker, L. Cwynar, S. Johnsen, K. L. Knudsen, J. Lowe, and B. Wohlfarth

1998 An Event Stratigraphy for the Last Termination in the North Atlantic Region Based on the Greenland Ice-core Record: A Proposal by the INTIMATE Group. *Journal of Quaternary Science* 13:283–292.

Blockley, S.

2005 Two Hiatuses in Human Bone Radiocarbon Dates in Britain (17,000 to 5000 cal BP). *Antiquity* 79:505–513.

2008 Continuity and Change in Funerary Behaviour in Britain, 16000–6000 cal BP. In *Crossing Frontiers: The Opportunities and Challenges of Interdisciplinary Approaches to Archaeology: Proceedings of a Conference Held at the University of Oxford, 25–26th June 2005*, edited by H. Schroeder, P. Bray, P. Gardener, V. Jefferson, and E. Macaulay-Lewis. Oxford University School of Archaeology Monograph 66. OUSA, Oxford.

Brock, F., C. Ramsey, and T. Higham

2007 Quality Assurance of Ultrafiltered Bone Dating. *Radiocarbon* 49:187–192.

Byrd, B.

2005 Reassessing the Emergence of Village Life in the Near East. *Journal of Archaeological Research* 13:231–290.

Chamberlain, A.

1996 More Dating Evidence for Human Remains in British Caves. *Antiquity* 70:950–953.

Ehlers, J., and P. Gibbard (editors)

2004a *Extent and Chronology of Glaciation. Volume 1: Europe*. Elsevier Science, Amsterdam.

2004b *Extent and Chronology of Glaciation. Volume 2: North America*. Elsevier Science, Amsterdam.

2004c *Extent and Chronology of Glaciation. Volume 3: South America, Asia, Africa, Australia, Antarctica*. Elsevier Science, Amsterdam.

Firestone, R., A. West, J. Kennett, L. Becker, T. Bunch, Z. Revay, P. Schultz, T. Belgya, D. Kennett, J. Erlandson, O. Dickerson, A. Goodyear, R. Harris, G. Howard, J. Kloosterman, P. Lechler, P. Mayewski, J. Montgomery, R. Poreda, T. Darrah, S. Que Hee, A. Smith, A. Stich, W. Topping, J. Wittke, and W. Wolbach

2007 Evidence for an Extraterrestrial Impact 12,900 Years Ago that Contributed to the Megafaunal Extinctions and the Younger Dryas Cooling. *Proceedings of the National Academy of Sciences* 104:16016–16021.

Gamble, C.
   2009 Human Display and Dispersal: A Case Study from Biotidal Britain in
   the Middle and Upper Pleistocene. *Evolutionary Anthropology* 18:144–156.

Gamble, C., W. Davies, P. Pettitt, and M. Richards
   2004 Climate Change and Evolving Human Diversity in Europe during
   the Last Glacial. *Philosophical Transactions of the Royal Society of Biological
   Sciences* 359:243–254.

Gamble, C., S. Davies, M. Richards, P. Pettitt, and L. Hazelwood
   2005 Archaeological and Genetic Foundations of the European Population
   during the Late Glacial: Implications for "Agricultural Thinking".
   Cambridge Archaeological Journal 15:55–85.

Hole, F.
   2007 Agricultural Sustainability in the Semi-arid Near East. *Climate of the
   Past* 3:193–203.

Lowe, J. J., G. Coope, C. Sheldrick, D. Harkness, and M. Walker
   1995 Direct Comparison of UK Temperatures and Greenland Snow
   Accumulation Rates, 15,000 to 12,000 Years Ago. *Journal of Quaternary
   Science* 10:175–180.

Lowe, J., S. Rasmussen, S. Björck, W. Hoek, J. Steffensen, M. Walker, and Z. Yu
   2008 Synchronisation of Palaeoenvironmental Events in the North Atlantic
   Region during the Last Termination: A Revised Protocol Recommended
   by the INTIMATE Group. *Quaternary Science Reviews* 27:6–17.

Lowe, J., M. Walker, E. Scott, D. Harkness, C. Bryant, and S. Davies
   2004 A Coherent High-precision Radiocarbon Chronology for the Late-
   glacial Sequence at Sluggan Bog, Co. Antrim, Northern Ireland. *Journal
   of Quaternary Science* 19:147–158.

Orschiedt, J.
   1999 *Manipulation an Menschlichen Skelettresten: Taphonomische Prozesse,
   Sekundarbestattungen oder Kannibalismus?* Tubingen: Mo Vince Verlag
   Urgeschichtliche Materialhefte 13.

Pettitt, P., S. W. Davies, C. Gamble, and M. Richards
   2003 Radiocarbon Chronology: Quantifying Our Confidence Beyond Two
   Half-Lives. *Journal of Archaeological Science* 30:1685–1693.

Rasmussen, S., K. Andersen, A. Svensson, J. Steffensen, B. Vinther, H. Clausen,
M-L Siggaard-Andersen, S. Johnsen, L. Larsen, D. Dahl-Jensen, M. Bigler,
R. Röthlisberger, H. Fischer, K. Goto-Azuma, M. Hansson, and U. Ruth
   2006 A New Greenland Ice Core Chronology for the Last Glacial Termination.
   Journal of Geophysical Research 111:D06102.

Renssen, H., R. Isarin, D. Jacob, R. Podzun, and J. Vandenberghe
   2001 Simulation of the Younger Dryas Climate in Europe Using a Regional
   Climate Model Nested in an AGCM: Preliminary Results. *Global and
   Planetary Change* 30:41–57.

Robinson, G. S., L. Burney, and D. Burney
   2005 Landscape Paleoecology and Megafaunal Extinction in Southeastern
   New York State. *Ecological Monographs* 75:295–315.

Soares, P., A. Achilli, O. Semino, W. Davies, V. Macaulay, H-J Bandelt, A. Torroni, and M. Richards
2010 The Archaeogenetics of Europe. *Current Biology* 20:174–183.

Stuart, A., P. Kosintsev, T. Higham, and A. Lister
2004 Pleistocene to Holocene Extinction Dynamics in Giant Deer and Woolly Mammoth. *Nature* 431:684–689.

Stuiver, M., P. Reimer, E. Bard, J. Beck, G. Burr, K. Hughen, B. Kromer, G. McCormac, V. der Plicht, and M. Spurk
1998 INTCAL98 Radiocarbon Age Calibration, 24,000–0 cal BP. *Radiocarbon* 40:1041–1083.

Svensson, A., K. Andersen, M. Bigler, H. Clausen, D. Dahl-Jensen, S. Davies, S. Johnsen, R. Muscheler, S. Rasmussen, R. Röthlisberger, J. Steffensen, and B. Vinther
2006 The Greenland Ice Core Chronology 2005, 15–42 ka. Part 2: Comparison to Other Records. *Quaternary Science Reviews* 25:3258–3267.

Taylor, R.
1992 Radiocarbon Dating of Bone: To Collagen and Beyond. In *Radiocarbon after Four Decades an Interdisciplinary Perspective*, edited by R. Taylor, R. Kra, and A. Long, pp. 375–402. Springer, New York.

Walker, M., G. Coope, D. Harkness, J. Lowe, C. Sheldrick, S. Blockley, and C. Turney
2003 Devensian Late-glacial Environmental Changes in Britain: A Multi-proxy Record from Llanilid, South Wales, UK. *Quaternary Science Reviews* 22:475–520.

9

THE YOUNGER DRYAS AND HUNTER-GATHERER TRANSITIONS TO FOOD PRODUCTION IN THE NEAR EAST

Cheryl A. Makarewicz

Introduction

The shift in human approaches to subsistence from gathering unpredictable, wild floral resources to the scheduled production of plant food marks a critical threshold in human prehistory that not only dramatically changed how humans procured food resources, but also contributed to widespread, far-reaching changes in human settlement patterns, social organization, and cultural lifeways. By intentionally planting certain floral types or enhancing wild plant stands selected for their dietary or economic value, forager-gatherers could increase the predictability of their plant food resources and reduce risk to their overall subsistence base. In the Near East, the transition from forager-gatherer lifeways to ones dependent on the use of plant cultivars appears to be intimately tied to the Younger Dryas, a period of global cooling and increased aridity that lasted from 12,900 to 11,700/11,600 cal BP (Alley et al. 1993; Rasmussen et al. 2006).

The prevailing model linking these two phenomena posits that the Younger Dryas caused a significant depletion in wild cereal resources that required the development of new subsistence strategies in order alleviate plant-food, resource stress (Bar-Yosef 2000, 2002; Bar-Yosef

Hunter-Gatherer Behavior: Human Response during The Younger Dryas, edited by Metin I. Eren, 195–230. © Left Coast Press. All rights reserved.

and Belfer-Cohen 2002). More specifically, the warm and humid conditions immediately prior to the Younger Dryas, during the Bølling-Ållerød climatic stage (~14,700 to 12,900 cal BP), were conducive to the expansion of highly productive habitats yielding an abundance of foodstuffs available to hunter-gatherers and, possibly, an increase in microhabitats supporting large-seed C_3 annual grasses such as wild barley and wheat (Hillman et al. 2001; Moore et al. 2000; Weinstein-Evron 1994).

As annual average temperature, precipitation, and atmospheric CO_2 levels decreased with the onset of the Younger Dryas, the geographic distribution and natural productivity of C_3 plants, most notably the cereals, dropped (Bar-Yosef 2002; Sage 1995). In response, hunter-gatherer groups shifted their attention toward intensive manipulation of cereal resources during the penultimate portion of the Younger Dryas in order to revive and expand this limited resource (Bar-Yosef and Belfer-Cohen 2002). The viability of this model is dependent in part on the parallel cultural and paleoenvironmental trajectories spanning the Younger Dryas. Here, the well-documented, but complex and often equivocal, paleoenvironmental record of the Near East during this period of climatic dynamism is closely examined and articulated with the cultural periods encompassing the transition from hunting-gathering to hunting-cultivation, the Natufian, and the Pre-Pottery Neolithic A.

Paleoclimatic Evidence for the Younger Dryas in the Near East

The distribution and predictability of plant and animal resources strongly influence human decision-making processes regarding the scheduling of subsistence activities, the timing of movement, and the distribution of settlements. Consequently, shifts in the availability of foodstuffs can have significant impacts on the character and evolutionary trajectories of human subsistence economies, social organization, and cultural lifeways. Since floral and faunal resources are sensitive to both broad changes in regional climate and fluctuations in local environmental conditions at multiple timescales, high-resolution, paleoenvironmental reconstructions are critical to the identification of potential linkages between environmental change and the emergence of novel food procurement strategies in the archaeological record. Fortunately, late Pleistocene and early Holocene paleoclimates in the Near East are relatively well-documented in multiple, independent data sets, including pollen and lacustrine records, the stable isotopes of various biogenic and pedogenic substrates, and landscape geomorphology (Bar-Matthews et al. 1997, 1999; Baruch and Bottema 1999;

Goldberg 1986, 1994; Rossignol-Strick 1995, 1997). Analyses of these data sets have established the broad impact of regional climate change on various Near Eastern ecological and geological systems, but the high-resolution, environmental archives provided by palynological and stable isotopic records are particularly well-suited to identifying shifts in vegetation distribution, precipitation levels, and temperature levels in prehistory. Here, pollen and speleothem data recovered from the southern Levant, where there is also an extensive archaeological record covering the transition from hunting and gathering to agriculture, are examined (Figure 9.1).

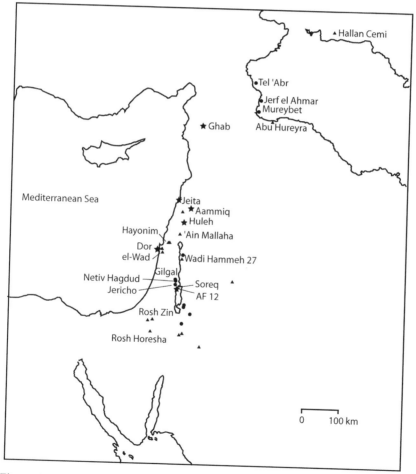

Figure 9.1 Map of the Near East indicating location of sites discussed in the text. ▲ = Natufian; □ = Pre-Pottery Neolithic A; ★ = pollen core or speleothem.

Pollen Cores

The southern Levant is characterized by pronounced topographic variation and a strong precipitation and temperature gradient that, together, influence local vegetational biome composition to produce a great deal of floral variation over relatively short distances. Rainfall levels drop and temperatures increase moving east away from the Mediterranean and south toward the Red Sea (Ben-Gai et al. 1998). Four phytogeographic zones are represented in the southern Levant, including the Mediterranean, Irano-Turanian, Saharo-Arabian, and Sudanian zones (al-Eisawi and al-Oqlah 2000; Zohary 1973).

Analyses of newly extracted pollen cores and reanalyses of existing cores extracted from lake sediments at various locales throughout the Near East are building an increasingly more refined picture of the distribution of vegetation in prehistoric Near Eastern environments. Until quite recently, the pollen cores from the Huleh and Ghab valleys have served as the primary source of regional paleoenvironmental information for late Pleistocene-Holocene timescales in the Levant (Baruch and Bottema 1999; Niklewski and van Zeist 1970; van Zeist and Bottema 1991; Yasuda et al. 2000). Two new pollen cores recovered from the Bekaa Valley and the Carmel Coast complement findings from the Huleh and Ghab cores while filling geospatial gaps in the pollen record and isolating important variations in regional, vegetational paleodistributions and environments (Hajar et al. 2008; Kadosh et al. 2004). However, since each of the four southern Levantine pollen sequences is uniquely problematic in different ways—which can have important implications for understanding the timing, intensity, and impact of the Younger Dryas in the southern Levant—the late Pleistocene and early Holocene portions of each pollen core are discussed in detail below. Revisiting these cores in detail reveals a picture of regional, environmental variation during the Younger Dryas, and highlights uncertainties in the chronology of paleoclimatic reconstructions based on palynological analyses of sediment cores.

The Huleh Core

Lake Huleh is located in the northern Galilee region and is bordered on the east by the Golan Heights and by the hills of the upper Galilee to the west (Figure 9.1). Compared to other pollen cores recovered from Near Eastern Quaternary deposits, the Huleh core is well-dated (Baruch and Bottema 1999), but the original radiocarbon determinations yielded by the Huleh core may be inaccurate due to the carbonate reservoir effects (Cappers et al. 2002; Meadows 2005; see discussion below). The revised dates used here are according to the revised chronology by Cappers et al. (1998).

The Huleh core documents a long history of vegetational change in the southern Levant (Figure 9.2a). At 19,000 cal BP, low arboreal pollen and high Chenopodiacea and *Artemisia* levels mark the Last Glacial Maximum (LGM), but high levels of grasses indicate more temperate conditions existed in the southern Levant compared to inland areas of the Near East (Rosen 2007). At approximately 17,400 cal BP, arboreal pollen, represented by *Quercus ithaburensis* and *Pistacia*, rose to extremely high levels while abundances of grasses and cereals declined. The dominance of deciduous oak and presence of *Pistacia* in the pollen assemblage indicate relatively warm and moist environmental conditions and the expansion of Mediterranean, forest biomes in the southern Levant. Beginning at about 12,800 cal BP, there was a dramatic decline in arboreal pollen (seen in Zone 3), particularly in deciduous oak, which drops from 70% to 30% of the total pollen assemblage, and a significant increase in Cerealia-type and Gramineae pollen grains. The marked shift in the arboreal: nonarboreal, pollen ratio suggests that the forest surrounding Lake Huleh contracted due to increased aridity and decreased temperature levels associated with the cooling and drying effects of the Younger Dryas. The persistence of *Pistacia* during this period may indicate that the Huleh Lake basin was not severely impacted by arid conditions, was buffered by high water tables, or both, and served as a refugia for pistachio trees (Wright and Thorpe 2003). The lack of a simultaneous increase in chenopods and *Artemisia* in the Huleh core during the Younger Dryas, a pattern found in other cores extracted from Near Eastern localities, supports an interpretation of moister conditions in southern Levant and suggests the region may have been characterized by an open oak savanna (Wright and Thorpe 2003). At approximately 10,400 cal BP (Zone 4), arboreal pollen—dominated by deciduous oak—levels rose, and olive made a first appearance in the pollen spectra. The increase in oak suggests a general rise in temperature, while the presence of olive may indicate a rise in winter temperature. Depressed fluctuations of pollen abundances in this portion of the pollen curve relative to chronologically earlier zones may indicate increased climatic stability in Zone 4 (Baruch and Bottema 1999).

There is some disagreement regarding the timing of the observed shifts in pollen spectra in the late Pleistocene–early Holocene portion of the Huleh core. Baruch and Bottema (1999) interpret Zone 3 as representing the Younger Dryas, but Rossignol-Strick (1995) suggests that the slight rise in *Pistacia* seen in Zone 3, which typically grows in warm, moist conditions, points to early Holocene environments and

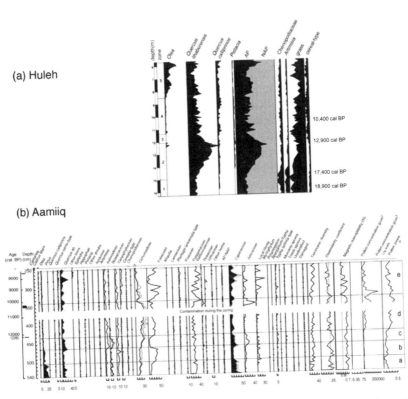

Figure 9.2 Pollen diagrams from a) Huleh and b) Aamiiq (after Baruch and Bottema 1999 and Hajar et al. 2008).

that the lowest portion (Zone 1) of the Huleh core—characterized by very low abundances of *Quercus*, little or no *Pistacia*, and high percentages of chenopods and *Artemisia*—instead represents the Younger Dryas. Similarly, Meadows (2005) suggests hard-water effects have severely impacted the Huleh radiocarbon determinations and proposes an approximately 5,000-year correction of dates, a calibration which would effectively place the Younger Dryas in Pollen Zone 1.

Ghab Core

Several cores extracted from the Ghab Valley, located in the Orontes River valley in northwest Syria, record the composition of prehistoric vegetational biomes in the northern Levant (Figure 9.3) (Niklewski and van Zeist 1970; Yasuda et al. 2000). The original chronological framework used to interpret the first Ghab cores was based on an age-depth

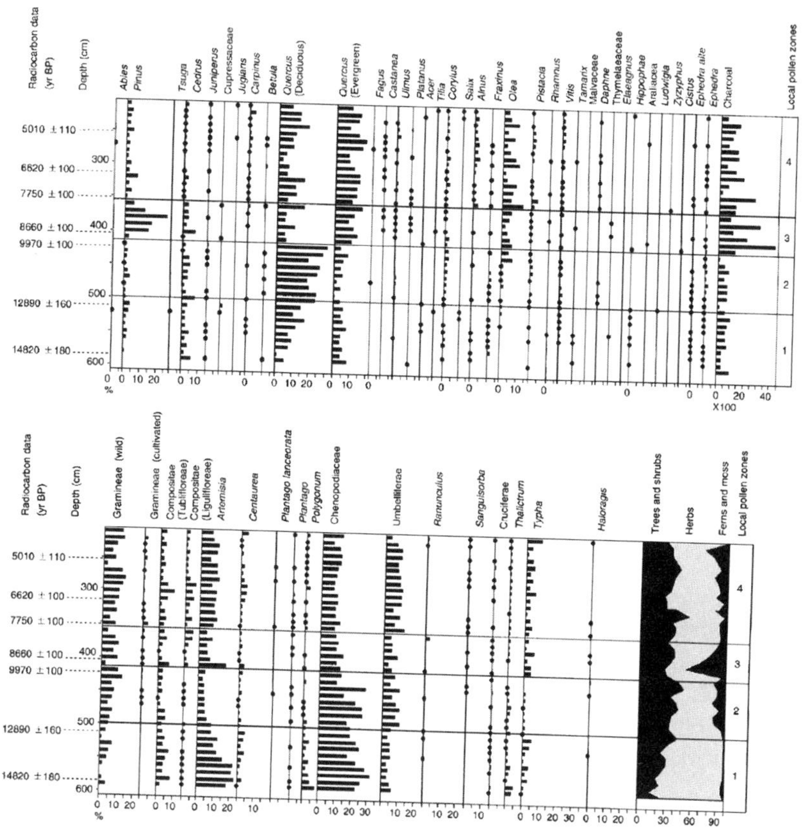

Figure 9.3   Arboreal and nonarboreal, pollen diagrams from Ghab (after Yasuda et al. 2000).

curve calculated from only two radiocarbon dates, one of which is located near the bottom of the core and exhibits a very old date accompanied by a large standard deviation: 45, 650 ± 2000 uncal BP (Niklewski and van Zeist 1970). According to the original chronological framework, the Younger Dryas in the Ghab was characterized by *increased* forest cover and humidity (Baruch and Bottema 1991; van Zeist and Woldring 1980). Given the considerable uncertainty of modeling chronological extrapolations from only two dates, a new relative chronology was established by comparing the major pollen zones observed in the Ghab core with radiometric and palynological data recovered from marine cores (Rossignol-Strick 1995). The marine data suggest that the Younger Dryas is regionally marked by an increase in the Chenopodiaceae. By correlating the "Chenopodiaceae Phase" seen in marine records with the zone of increased chenopod abundances and decrease in forest cover in the Ghab core, Rossignol-Strick (1995) concluded that the Younger Dryas is represented in the Y5 portion of the Ghab core (which had been previously attributed to the Last Glacial Maximum by Niklewski and van Zeist [1970]). In an attempt to gain a better understanding of the composition and timing of the turnover of the vegetational biome in the Ghab region, an additional core with a much longer late Pleistocene–early Holocene sequence yielding nine radiocarbon determinations obtained from freshwater mollusks, was recovered (Yasuda et al. 2000). The general agreement between the observed peak in the *Artemisia* to Chenopodiaceae ratio and interpolated radiocarbon dates consistent with the timing of the Younger Dryas suggest that hard-water effects on the Ghab radiometric dates are small (Yasuda et al. 2000; but see below).

Immediately prior to the Younger Dryas, deciduous oak pollen reaches the highest abundance levels visible in entirety of the Ghab core, and other moisture-dependent taxa including cedar, pistachio, olive, almond, chestnut, and cereals are also well-represented. This pollen distribution suggests a vegetational mosaic of oak forest, cedar forest, and grasslands existed in the Ghab region. The combination of extremely high Chenopodiaceae and grass levels and low total, absolute pollen, concentrations between about 12,800 and 11,500 cal BP likely indicate the onset of the Younger Dryas (Yasuda et al. 2000; duration of Younger Dryas based on interpolation between two radiocarbon determinations of 12,890 +/– 160 cal BP and 9970 +/– 100 cal BP). A return to pluvial conditions is indicated by the expansion of oak forest and the appearance of olive.

As with the Huleh and old Ghab cores, there is disagreement regarding the timing of the Younger Dryas event in the new Ghab core (Meadows 2005; Robinson et al. 2006; Wright and Thorpe 2003). Meadows (2005) asserts that radiometric determinations for the new Ghab core roughly require a 4.5 ka correction since freshwater molluscs obtain their carbonate from dissolved inorganic carbon (DIC). Meadows (2005) also argues that the pollen spectra for the Younger Dryas should exhibit a concurrent rise in both Chenopodiaceae and *Artemesia* abundances, a pattern that is visible only at the very *bottom* of the new Ghab core. However, the increase in chenopods relative to *Artemisia* visible between 13,500 and 11,500 cal BP may indicate exposure of saline soils during a period of low lake levels rather than the initiation of arid environmental conditions (Wright and Thorpe 2003). Wright and Thorpe (2003) suggest that the persistence of oak and the lack of correlation between Chenopodiaceae and *Artemisia* curves in Zone 2 of the new Ghab core indicates that Zone 2 should be assigned to the early Holocene, and that the more conspicuous peak in Chenopodiaceae and *Artemisia* pollen abundances located further down in the core represents the Younger Dryas.

Aamiq Core

A new pollen core obtained from the Aammiq wetland, located in the Bekaa Valley, Lebanon, provides an additional source of information documenting paleoenvironmental conditions and vegetational distributions in the central Levant (Figure 9.2b; Hajar et al. 2008). Four radiocarbon determinations derived from organic material found in sediments were recovered from the Aammiq core. Additional dates were calculated through linear interpolation using an age-depth model, and hard-water effects appear to be negligible. During the Bølling-Allerød (pollen zones a, b, and c), environmental conditions in the Bekaa Valley were relatively dry, but moist enough to support arboreal vegetation, as indicated by high percentages of *Cedrus libani*, *Quercus cerris*, and open-range vegetation including Chenopodiaceae, Apiaceae, Asteroideae, and *Artemisia*. The expansion of cedars and deciduous oaks seen in this portion of the Aamiiq core is similar to patterns observed in the Ghab core (Niklewski and van Zeist 1970; Rossignol-Strick 1995). A significant drop in arboreal pollen and an increase in Chenopodiaceae and Apiaceae at the end of zone c marks a relatively rapid onset of the Younger Dryas (~12,500 to 11,500 cal BP) and indicates a retraction of forest and the growth of Chenopodiaceae steppe; low percentages of cedar suggest that small stands of these trees survived in refugia. *Artemisia* levels in the Aammiq core are even lower than those observed in the Ghab cores for a similar time period and suggest that the effects of the Younger Dryas were relatively mild in this area. A return to moist conditions is indicated by a rapid drop in Chenopodiaceae, high levels of deciduous oak, and herbaceous, vascular plant pollen at roughly 11,400 cal BP, suggesting the expansion of oak forest and the formation of the Aammiq marsh.

D-Dor Core

A core extracted from the Tantura lagoon, located at Dor on the Carmel coastal plain, provides a picture of early Holocene vegetational biomes outside of the Rift Valley (Figure 9.4; Kadosh et al. 2004). The core was dated using two luminescence and six radiocarbon determinations obtained from sand and clay samples, respectively. Pollen Zone 1 is characterized by low, arboreal pollen levels—primarily

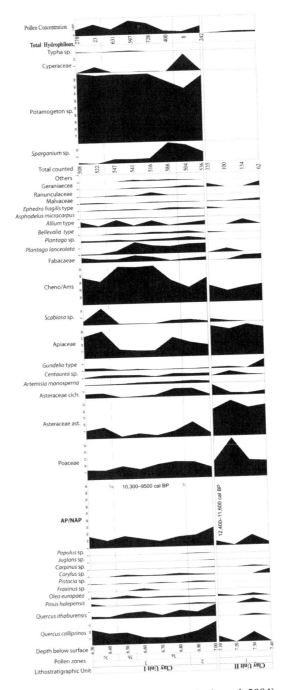

Figure 9.4 Pollen diagram from Dor (after Kadosh et al. 2004).

represented by *Quercus calliprinos*—and high abundances of nonarboreal Chenopodocaeae/Amaranthaceae, Poaceae, Apiaceae, and
Asteroideae, which together suggest generally dry conditions on the
coastal plain between 12,400–11,000 cal BP. The abundance of oak and
the presence of *Pinus* and *Olea* pollens in the lowest portion of pollen
Zone 1 may indicate more humid conditions relative to the uppermost
portion of the zone, where Poaceae, Asteroideae, and *Artemisia* levels are highly abundant and suggestive of dry conditions. However,
the deposition of clays in the uppermost portion of Zone 1 may indicate the formation of wetlands and more humid conditions. It may be
that the pollen spectra for this latest portion of Zone 1, radiocarbon
dated to 12,400–11,600 cal BP, actually represents pollen from Zone 2
that infiltrated through cracks in dried marshy clays (Weinstein-Evron
1998). The depositional gap in the D-Dor core immediately following
the deposition of sediments and pollen in Zone 1 suggests the development of extremely arid conditions were likely associated with the
Younger Dryas (Kadosh et al. 2004). The return to humid conditions
and higher precipitation levels between 10,300–9550 cal BP (pollen
Zone 2) is indicated by the combination of extremely high percentages
of *Quercus calliprinos, Quercus ithaburensis*, and *Populus* and relatively
low representations of Poaceae and Asteraceae. At this time, oak forest
probably covered both the mountains and the coastal plain (Kadosh
et al. 2004).

Speleothems

Speleothems provide a high-resolution, dateable record of paleoclimatic conditions over long time periods, and through oxygen and carbon, stable isotopic analyses of calcitic carbonates, paleo-precipitation
and temperature levels can be directly measured. Multiple speleothems have been identified in the southern Levant, but only those
from Soreq, the West Jerusalem caves, Galilee caves, and Jeitun record
paleoenvironmental inputs for the late Pleistocene and early Holocene;
all others exhibit formation hiatuses during this period. The oxygen
isotopic composition of speleothems is largely controlled by the $\delta^{18}O$
signature of local meteoric waters, rainfall volume, and aridity, so that
an increase in speleothem $\delta^{18}O$ values indicates decreasing precipitation levels, increasing aridity, and/or higher temperatures (Gat 1996).
The modern-day average of precipitation falling on the Levantine
Mediterranean coast is 6.5‰ in oxygen isotopes (Bar-Matthews et al.
1999), and, in general, meteoric waters become increasingly enriched
moving east away from the Mediterranean Sea and south toward
the Red Sea (Gat and Dansgaard 1972). Speleothem $\delta^{18}O$ values are

enriched +1.0‰ to +1.5‰ relative to rainfall due to evaporation of water percolating through the upper vadose, zone sediments (Bar-Matthews et al. 1996). Based on modern-day, weighted average $\delta^{18}O$ values of annual precipitation obtained over a twelve year sampling period at Soreq Cave, a +1‰ shift in speleothem $\delta^{18}O$ values reflects an aprromixate 200mm decrease in precipitation levels (Bar-Matthews et al. 2003). For carbon isotopes, the $\delta^{13}C$ values of speleothems are largely determined by the $\delta^{13}C$ signature of soil CO_2, which is dictated by the proportion of C_3 and C_4 vegetation growing on overlying soils (which exhibit average $\delta^{13}C$ values of −26.0‰ and −12.5‰, respectively), the isotopic composition of dissolved bedrock carbonate, and Rayleigh distillation processes occurring during carbonate precipitation and CO_2 degassing (Bar-Matthews et al. 1996, 1999). Changes over time in the oxygen and carbon isotopic composition of the speleothems discussed here are thus due to a combination in differences in local temperature and precipitation levels, elevation, and latitude.

Soreq Cave

Soreq is a karstic cave located on the westward flank of the Judean Hill anticline (400 m asl) that has produced multiple speleothems, which together, provide a deep and continuous stable isotopic record of southern Levantine paleoclimates (Figure 9.5). The chronological framework of the paleoclimatic data provided by the Soreq speleothems is provided by 53 [230]TH [234]U (TIMS) dates, although only a few dates are available for the late Pleistocene-early Holocene portion of this speleothem. During the Late Glacial Maximum (~19,000 cal BP), speleothems exhibit the highest $\delta^{18}O$ values relative to all subsequent periods, averaging approximately +3‰, indicating extremely cold and arid conditions with annual rainfall of 200–450 mm, and average temperatures of 12–16°C. Carbon isotope values are similarly high, about +4.0‰, and attest to a mixed C_3-C_4 vegetational biome.

From the Late Glacial Maximum to 15,000 cal BP, both oxygen and carbon isotope values of speleothems markedly decrease to approximately −5‰ and −6‰, respectively, indicating an increase in temperature and precipitation levels to 430–530 mm per year, and a shift toward a C_3-dominated floral biome. Immediately prior to the Younger Dryas, from 15,000 to 13,200 cal BP, $\delta^{18}O$ values decrease further to −6.1‰, indicating wet conditions with precipitation levels averaging 550–750 mm. The onset of the Younger Dryas is indicated by the relatively rapid increase in $\delta^{18}O$ and $\delta^{13}C$ values to −5.0‰ and −12.0‰, respectively, between 13,000 and 11,000 cal BP. These isotopic values demonstrate high aridity levels and high abundances of C_4 flora present in local floral

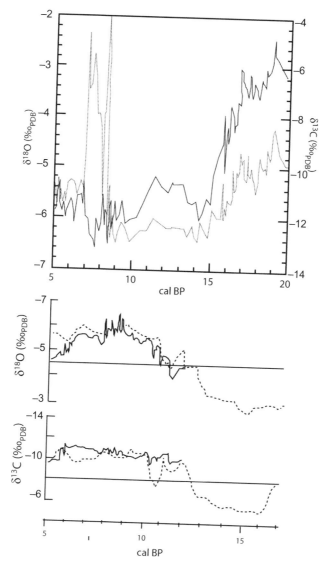

Figure 9.5 Oxygen and carbon isotopic variation over time in speleothems from Soreq Cave; solid line = ¹⁸O, dashed line = ¹³C (after Bar-Matthews et al. 1999). Oxygen and carbon isotopic variation over time in speleothems from Jeita (solid line) and the West Jerusalem caves (dotted line) (after Verheyden et al. 2008 and Frumkin et al. 2000).

biomes (Bar-Matthews et al. 1997). Estimated rainfall levels during the Younger Dryas are not described by Bar-Matthews et al. (1997), but based on calculations converting speleothem $\delta^{18}O$ PDB values to estimated $\delta^{18}O$ SMOW of cave water for other climatic phases (Bar-Matthews et al. 1997: Table 2), precipitation levels during the Younger Dryas likely averaged between 500 mm and 400 mm.

The end of the Younger Dryas in the Soreq speleothem is marked petrographically and isotopically by the formation of speleothems exhibiting thin, irregular, brown-reddish laminae containing extremely high concentrations of oxides and detritus, and a rapid shift to low $\delta^{18}O$ values (range = ca. −6.8‰ to −5.6‰) and low $\delta^{13}C$ values. The oxygen isotopic data indicate a rapid return to warm and moist conditions, with temperatures ranging from 14.5–18.0 °C and precipitation levels from 680–850 mm. Continued depletion in oxygen and carbon isotopes after 10,000 cal BP suggests a further increase in precipitation levels to 680–950 mm during the early Holocene. Spikes observed in carbon isotopic values are likely due to rapid percolation of precipitation through thin soils that result in poor dissolution of soil CO_2, rather than an increase in C_4 vegetation associated with higher aridity levels (Bar-Matthews et al. 1997).

West Jerusalem Cave

The speleothem from West Jerusalem Cave (AF12), located in the Judean Hills (730 m asl) and dated by TIMS U-series, provides additional isotopic evidence for late Pleistocene-early Holocene paleoenvironments in the southern Levant (Figure 9.5; Frumkin et al. 2000). Although the timing of climate shifts observed in the AF12 speleothem differ from those seen at Soreq, there is general agreement between the oxygen and carbon isotopic patterns produced by each speleothem. Given the close geographical proximity of both Soreq and AF12, it is likely that dating lacunae in the late Pleistocene/early Holocene portion of both speleothems explain the observed chronological differences between isotopic trends. The AF12 speleothem exhibits very high $\delta^{18}O$ values (~−3.0‰) at cal 17,000 BP, indicating extremely cold and dry conditions associated with the end of the Late Glacial Maximum. Steady depletion of oxygen isotopes between 17,000 and 13,000 cal BP points to gradual warming and an increase in precipitation. At around 13,000 cal BP, there is a dramatic decrease in $\delta^{18}O$ values from −3.2‰ to −4.5‰ and, a further marked depletion to approximately −5.1‰ at 12,000 cal BP, indicating the onset of very moist conditions. After 12,000 cal BP, oxygen isotopes from the AF12 speleothem become increasingly enriched, up to −4.5‰, and indicate a moderately paced onset of arid conditions associated with the Younger Dryas. The trend of increasing aridity reverses gradually after 11,200 cal BP, indicated by a steady decrease in $\delta^{18}O$ values. The return to pluvial conditions dramatically accelerates at about 10,600 BP, when oxygen isotopes drop to around –5.7‰. It is significant that although there is clear drop-off in precipitation levels during the Younger Dryas, the oxygen isotope values exhibited by the AF12 speleothem during this period never exceed those produced earlier during the Bølling-Allerød.

Jeita

An additional speleothem isotopic record documenting southern Levantine paleoclimate was recovered from Jeita (100 m asl), a cave located on the western flank of Mount Lebanon, approximately 5 km west of the Mediterranean coast and 15 km north of Beirut (Figure 9.5; Verheyden et al. 2008). Eleven U-series determinations were obtained from the Jeita speleothem and additional ages were interpolated or extrapolated from those determinations. The Jeita speleothem record begins at 11,900 cal BP and exhibits high $\delta^{18}O$ values, ranging from –4.5‰ to –3.9‰, consistent with the high aridity levels expected for the Younger Dryas, until roughly 11,200 cal BP. Carbon isotopic values are also high during this period, averaging –9.8‰, and may indicate poor soil formation processes typically associated with dry conditions (Veryheyden et al. 2008), or a high proportion of C_4 vegetation. Despite high $\delta^{18}O$ and $\delta^{13}C$ values in this portion of Jeita speleothem, the continued growth of the speleothem during the Younger Dryas demonstrates that conditions were not so dry as to prevent speleothem deposition. After 11,000 cal BP, oxygen isotope values in the Jeita speleothem quickly drop to c. –4.8‰, suggestive of a rapid return to wetter conditions and increased soil productivity. Continued climatic amelioration during the early Holocene is indicated by additional depletion of $\delta^{18}O$ values to –5.5‰ by 10,000 cal BP (Verheyden et al. 2008).

Late Pleistocene-Early Holocene Environments in the Levant

Pollen and speleothem records summarized here suggest that the impact of the Younger Dryas varied across the region, with some local environments experiencing more arid conditions and greater shifts in the composition of vegetational communities than others. Moisture levels in the Mediterranean zone of the southern Levant were likely higher than those for inland areas of the northern Levant, suggesting that changes in the composition of floral biomes in the southern Levant may have been less pronounced than those in other regions.

In addition, although the Younger Dryas is generally characterized by cool and arid conditions, the pollen core and speleothem stable isotopic data attest to occasional oscillations toward warmer and moister conditions during this climatological event. It is significant that the pollen and speleothem data argue for a spatially and chronologically heterogeneous expression of the Younger Dryas across the Levant, suggesting that cultural responses to this climatic event may also have been diverse.

Transitions to Agriculture: The Natufian and the Pre-Pottery Neolithic A

The transition from foraging and gathering to cultivation and agriculture represents the intersection of multiple shifts in subsistence and social systems that occurred over the course of several thousand years between roughly 14,000 to 8500 cal BP (Bar-Yosef 2001; Kuijt and Goring-Morris 2002). In the Levant, many of these important transformations in human lifeways occurred during the Natufian and the Pre-Pottery Neolithic A (PPNA), two distinct but ontogenetically related cultural periods, against the backdrop of the major climatic shifts of the Younger Dryas and the early Holocene climatic amelioration.

The Natufian

The Natufian marks the consistent appearance of sedentary lifeways in the Near East. The Natufian culture was originally described as occupying a "core area" that corresponded spatially to the resource-rich Mediterranean phytogeographic zone (Bar-Yosef and Belfer-Cohen 1991), but recent excavations demonstrating a sizeable Natufian presence in regions characterized by more steppic vegetational communities has led to the reconceptualization of the central and southern Levant as the "Natufian homeland" (Bar-Yosef 2002). With the exception of Abu Hureyra and Hallan Çemi, which are located in the Euphrates Valley and the foothills of the Taurus mountains respectively, there is currently little archaeological evidence for Natufian or contemporaneous hunter-gatherers in other regions of the Near East.

The Natufian is subdivided chronologically into the early Natufian (ca. 13,000 to 11,000 cal BC) and late Natufian (11,000 to 9,600 cal BC) on the basis of observed variation in lithic techno-typology, such as the presence of Helwan and backed lunates, trapeze-rectangles, and triangles in early Natufian deposits and backed lunates in late Natufian deposits, and differences in settlement organization and occupation intensity (Bar-Yosef 2000). Significantly, the early and late Natufians experienced very different environmental conditions: early Natufian hunter-gatherers enjoyed the warm and moist environments of the Bølling-Ållerød, while the late Natufians grappled with the harsher climatic conditions of the Younger Dryas (Bar-Yosef 2000, 2002).

The Early Natufian

The early Natufian represents an unprecedented development in hunter-gatherer lifeways, distinguished from its Kebaran and Geometric Kebaran predecessors by the first appearance and use of relatively large residential hamlets, cemeteries, and abundant ground stone and mobiliary art. Early Natufian settlements varied in size, with the largest sites reaching 0.2 hectares, and contained substantial, solidly built semisubterranean dwellings with stone foundations ranging in diameter from around 7 to 15 m (Goring-Morris and Belfer-Cohen 2008). These structures were circular or D-shaped in form and were covered by substantial roofs, indicated by numerous postholes arranged in circular patterns inside dwellings (Edwards 1991; Valla et al. 1991). Most constructions served primarily as domestic dwellings, although some structures at some sites appear to have been used for communal or ritual activities (Valla 1988). Storage installations are uncommon in early Natufian sites, represented by only a paved bin at Hayonim Terrace and some plastered pits uncovered at 'Ain Mallaha (Perrot 1966; Valla et al. 1991). Ground stone tools, ornamental art, and human interments are also commonly found at early Natufian settlements (Bar-Yosef and Belfer-Cohen 1989, 1991). The early Natufian dead were buried in abandoned domestic structures, outside houses, or in specific areas reserved for mortuary activities (Bar-Yosef 2002). Corpses were often collectively interred, although singular burials were not uncommon (Belfer-Cohen 1995). A small proportion of the dead, altogether representing a range of age groups, were buried with body ornaments including marine shells, bone pendants, headgear, and belts. These selectively placed adornments may suggest nascent social differentiation or ranking within early Natufian societies (Bar-Yosef 2002; but see Belfer-Cohen 1995; Byrd and Monahan 1995). Interestingly, there are sharp differences in the decorative motifs of body jewelry and patterns on presumably mundane items including bone spatulas, stone bowls, and shaft-straighteners between different sites (Edwards 1991; Kuijt and Goring-Morris 2002; Noy 1991). These patterns, which include net, chevron, and meander motifs, may have functioned as signifiers marking the group affiliation of the user (Belfer-Cohen 1988).

The largest Natufian settlements, such as Mallaha and Wadi Hammeh 27, contain substantial dwellings, ground stone tools, varied lithic and faunal assemblages, and human remains, and are typically interpreted as base camps or "hamlets". In addition to large base camps, the early Natufians frequented raw material, extraction sites, briefly visited stations used for logistical hunting and plant gathering bouts, and inhabited seasonal camps in order to exploit foodstuffs only available during certain parts of the year (Bar-Yosef 2002: Figure 5.13). Although the intensity and duration of occupation of early Natufian settlements remains poorly understood, the presence and relatively high abundance of commensals such as mice and sparrows at early Natufian sites strongly suggests that human groups occupying these settlements were sedentary to some extent (Tchernov 1991, 1993). It may be that entire hamlets were occupied strictly on a seasonal basis and served as logistical encampments for the exploitation of nearby food resources. Alternatively, base camps may have been inhabited year-round, but portions of the settlement were occasionally vacated as certain segments of the community made anticipated moves for subsistence or social activities.

Unfortunately, previous investigations have yet to offer definitive information about seasonality of habitation occupation or mobility during the early Natufian. While analyses of seasonal bands in gazelle tooth cementum suggest a year-round occupation of early Natufian hamlets (Lieberman 1993), diagenetic processes can produce apatitic, crystalline features that mimic cementum increments (Lieberman 1991; Stutz 2002). Isotopic analyses offer similarly ambiguous results. Although the pattern of low variation in the strontium isotopic composition of modern territorial gazelle is also visible in early Natufian faunal and human remains—a result that has been interpreted to indicate hunter-gatherer movement was restricted to base camp areas (Shewan 2004)—other geological and biological factors may be contributing to the strontium isotope signal in modern and prehistoric bone. For example, diagenetic alteration of sampled biological substrates and a homogenous regime of biologically available strontium over large regions may obscure even significant movements of human groups.

The Natufian likely represents a crucial period in the transformation of plant exploitation strategies utilized by prehistoric hunter-gatherers, but our understanding of early Natufian food procurement strategies is largely limited to the animal-based portion of the subsistence economy. Carbonized botanical remains are poorly preserved, if at all, in the *terra rossa* soils covering many Natufian sites, and consequently, macrobotanical remains are available for only Hayonim Cave and Wadi Hammeh 27 (Hopf and Bar-Yosef 1987). Wild barley (*Hordeum spontaneum*) was exploited at both sites. Lupines (*Lupinus pilosus*), peas (*Pisum* sp.), and almond (*Amygdalus communis*) were gathered at Hayonim, and goat-faced grass (*Aegilops* sp.), lentils (*Lens* sp.), and possibly almond, pistachio, hawthorne, buckthorn, and hackberry fruits were collected at Wadi Hammeh 27 (Edwards 2003; Hopf and Bar-Yosef 1987). While it was once thought that the Natufians represented the first Levantine Epipaleolithic hunter-gatherer group to heavily exploit cereals (Bar-Yosef 1998), there is now evidence for intensive use of grasses and cereals during the earliest portion of the Levantine Epipaleolithic at approximately 23,000 cal BP. The large quantities of wild emmer wheat, barley, and small-grained grasses recovered from Ohalo II, located on the Sea of Galilee, indicate grasses and cereals were key dietary components for hunter-gatherers some 10,000 years before the Natufian (Weiss et al. 2004). The exploitation of these foodstuffs may be linked to the "broad spectrum revolution" (Weiss et al. 2004), when hunter-gatherers broadened their subsistence base and placed a new focus on previously under-exploited, low-ranked resources as high-ranked plant and animal resources became increasingly scarce (Flannery 1969).

Much of the evidence for the exploitation of floral resources, including wild cereals, is found in the Natufian chipped-stone and ground stone records. Sickle blades and picks, tools that increase the yields and collection efficiency of plants growing in dense stands (Hillman and Davies 1990), were manufactured for the first time during the Natufian, and experimental studies and use-wear analyses indicate sickles were used to harvest grasses and cereals (Anderson 1994; Yamada 2000). An abundant and varied ground stone assemblage, which includes portable bowls and mortars, cup holes, pestles, and heavy goblet-shaped mortars, also appears. The intensive use of a cohesive food-processing toolkit of sickles, picks, and ground stone almost certainly suggests intensification in the processing of, although not necessarily in the gathering, of wild plant foods (but see Wright 1991).

The Late Natufian

The onset of the Younger Dryas reconfigured the Natufian culture from a collection of largely sedentary hunter-gatherers concentrated primarily within the rich Mediterranean core area to a more mobile society that expanded their overall range to include a variety of ecological zones. Increased human mobility during the late Natufian is suggested by the combination of shifts seen in site size, architectural features, burial practices, and small game use. Several early Natufian base camps, including those at Hayonim Cave and Terrace, 'Ain Mallaha, and el Wad, continued to be inhabited during the late Natufian, but the size and intensity of occupation of these sites diminished markedly (Belfer-Cohen and Bar-Yosef 2000; Valla et al. 1991). The majority of late Natufian sites situated within the Mediterranean zone contain smaller structures (compared to early Natufian ones) characterized by a reduction in the scale of stone foundation construction and fewer postholes, which may be suggestive of a lower level of energetic investment in dwellings (Bar-Yosef and Belfer-Cohen 1991; Grosman 2003; Valla et al. 1991). The decrease in the size of domestic dwellings may also reflect a shift in social structure from extended residential units during the early Natufian to one centered around nuclear families during the late Natufian (Goring-Morris and Belfer-Cohen 2008).

In contrast to their early Natufian predecessors, late Natufian sites located in the more arid ecotones to the south and east of the Mediterranean zone are more substantial than early Natufian settlements located in the same region (Betts 1991; Gebel and Muheisen 1985; Goring-Morris and Horwitz 2000; Henry 1976; Marks and Larson 1977). In the Negev and Sinai, a specialized late Natufian adaptation to the steppic-desertic conditions of the Negev and Sinai, called the Harifian, emerged. Harifian sites include small lowland seasonal camps comprised of stone-built structures approximately 3–5 m in diameter and arranged in a cellular pattern (Henry 1976). Camps located in the highlands are characterized by larger semisubterranean structures spaced apart from each other and they often accommodate bedrock mortars and grinding slabs (Goring-Morris 1991). The geospatial arrangement of Harifian camps suggests extensive movements by hunter-gatherers circulating between the lowlands and the highlands on a seasonal basis (Goring-Morris 1987, 1991).

Late Natufian burial practices appear to have been adjusted to a more mobile lifestyle and are distinguished from early Natufian ones by an increase inhumations containing multiple individuals and secondary burials, as well as the cessation of placing decorative objects and body ornaments with the dead (Belfer-Cohen and Bar-Yosef 2000). These new mortuary practices suggest a revival of more egalitarian social structures and an emphasis on community unity, and in the case of secondary burials, indicate a higher incidence of transporting the remains of the dead back to base camps and territories (Belfer-Cohen and Grosman 1997; Byrd and Monahan 1995; Goring-Morris 1987). Occasionally, skulls were removed from individuals, anticipating a relatively common mortuary custom practiced during the Pre-Pottery Neolithic A (Belfer-Cohen 1988).

Small game indices, which serve as a proxy for establishing site occupation duration by measuring human foraging efficiency in resource patches encompassing habitation sites (Stiner and Munro 2002), also suggest shifts in late Natufian mobility patterns (Munro 2004; Stiner and Munro 2002). Slow-moving game, such as spur-thighed tortoise (*Testudo graeca*), require little energetic investment on the part of humans to gather, while fast-moving game such as cape hare (*Lepus capensis*), the chukar partridge (*Alectoris chukar*), and waterfowl entails increased capture effort and/or, high energetic investment in the use and maintenance of manufactured technologies such as nets, traps, and bows (Stiner et al. 1999, 2000). The exploitation of fast-moving, low-ranked game during the early Natufian indicates that hunting pressure greatly reduced the availability of slow-moving, high-ranked game such as tortoises and, points toward intensive sedentism and site use (Munro 2004). In contrast, high-ranked, slow-moving tortoises dominate late Natufian, small game assemblages and suggests a relaxation of gathering pressure due to increased mobility of human forager groups and lower occupation intensity of habitation sites.

Our understanding of plant use during the critical period of the late Natufian is as limited as that for the early Natufian. However, there is some evidence suggesting that late Natufian gatherers were developing new plant exploitation strategies, perhaps in response to diminishing wild plant resources associated with the onset of the Younger Dryas. At Abu Hureyra, the use of morphologically wild pulses, cereals, and grasses declined dramatically during the initial portion of the Younger Dryas, but domestic type rye (*Secale cereale*) seeds exhibiting plump seeds (but retaining a brittle rachis) appeared during the later portion of the Younger Dryas, as did drought-intolerant weedy taxa typically encountered in rain-fed cultivation plots (Hillman et al. 2001).

Notably, it appears that there were few changes in animal exploitation strategies between the early and late Natufian, despite major shifts in climate and hunter-gatherer mobility patterns. Although there are differences in the exploitation of slow moving vs. fast-moving small game between the two periods as discussed above, early and late Natufian faunal resource use was otherwise the same (Munro 2001). Gazelle continued to serve as the primary game hunted during both periods. Juvenile gazelle were exploited at similarly high levels during both the early and late Natufian, suggesting that prey availability and hunting pressure remained unchanged despite the onset of environmentally challenging conditions associated with the Younger Dryas (Munro 2004). In addition, the absence of differences in relative species abundance, demographic profiles, bone fragmentation, and body-part distribution—zooarchaeological data sets that can be used to measure animal resource extraction levels—suggest that the intensity of animal exploitation remained unchanged throughout Natufian (Munro 2001).

After the Younger Dryas: The Pre-Pottery Neolithic A

The emergence of Pre-Pottery Neolithic A cultures roughly coincided with the end of the Younger Dryas and spanned approximately a thousand years from approximately 9,700 to 8,500/8,300 cal BC. Unlike Natufian sites, which were restricted geographically to the southern and central Levant, PPNA settlements were distributed throughout the Levant, the Taurus and Zagros regions, and Cyprus. The PPNA settlements were generally situated on highly productive alluvial fans, near marshes, or within river valleys, although a number of PPNA sites have now been identified in the arguably more marginal ecotones east of the Levantine Corridor (Bar-Yosef 2000; Kuijt and Goring-Morris 2002). Further, PPNA sites range in size and function from large "villages," to small, seasonal occupations, and to specialized logistical sites that may have been used to provision larger settlements (Goring-Morris and Belfer-Cohen 2008; Kuijt and Goring-Morris 2002). Settlements may have been organized hierarchically (Kuijt 1994), with larger villages serving as regional centers regularly used by visitors for social and economic reasons.

Such PPNA residential dwellings shared many features with those of the Natufian, as domestic architecture from both periods exhibit semi-subterranean construction and round or oval footprints. However, PPNA structures were generally more substantial and elaborate in their construction than their Natufian predecessors, and were constructed of mudbrick or piseé laid over stone foundations with cobbled or prepared earth floors; they contained hearths and inset limestone slabs, and were sometimes divided internally into distinct spaces (Kuijt and Goring-Morris 2002). Significantly, visible storage features are a regular feature of PPNA houses, and, some buildings appear to have been devoted solely to grain storage (Bar-Yosef 2002; Bar-Yosef and Gopher 1997; Kuijt and Finlayson 2009; Weiss et al. 2006). Refuse was disposed of in defined areas separate from domestic spaces during the PPNA, a departure from the Natufian practice of haphazardly discarding waste both inside and outside of houses (Hardy-Smith and Edwards 2004).

While evidence for sizeable Natufian nonresidential architecture is generally lacking, during the PPNA large-scale structures such as the circular benched structure at Jerf el Ahmar (Building EA30), the Jericho tower, and the spectacular Göbekli Tepe complex were constructed. In addition to serving as a central platform through which community members could negotiate mundane and sacred aspects of daily life, these structures suggest that the PPNA societies possessed mechanisms for internal organization that were capable of organizing labor for sustained periods (Bar-Yosef 1986; Verhoeven 2002).

Additionally, PPNA mortuary practices included the primary interment of individual adults and young adults, many with their skulls removed some time after initial burial, and unaccompanied by grave goods (Bar-Yosef 2000). The general homogeneity in burial practices, the absence of grave goods, and low intrasite differences in household size suggests PPNA societies were largely egalitarian, but instances of skull caching and skull display may indicate that social distinctions of some sort existed (Bar-Yosef 2000; Kenyon 1981; Kuijt 1996). It is unclear if the type of low-level social differentiation seen in the PPNA represents a reversion back to the same trajectory of social differentiation that was first expressed during the early Natufian, but interrupted during the Younger Dryas, or, if it represents a new path based upon entirely different social expectations and criteria.

The Pre-Pottery Neolithic A marks a major shift in human approaches to subsistence from plant gathering to the consistent practice of plant cultivation, where wild plant resources were augmented by a more predictable food source in the form of managed plants, particularly cereals and legumes. The intensity of PPNA cultivation practices are unknown, but the targeted exploitation of cereal plants during this period is suggested by the consistent presence of barley and wheat in PPNA deposits (Bar-Yosef 1991; Kislev 1992; Willcox 1996), use of grain silos (Bar-Yosef and Gopher 1997; Stordeur 2000), location of PPNA occupations on rich alluvial fans, and co-occurrence of weedy taxa and cultivars (Bar-Yosef and Belfer-Cohen 1989; Colledge 1998; Kislev 1997). Although it is generally assumed that cultivated cereals were a major component of PPNA plant subsistence strategies, it may be that managed cereals, as well as other cultivars, effectively served only as a dietary supplement and did not entirely replace gathered plant resources. Macrobotanical analyses indicate that PPNA cultivars were morphologically wild (Colledge 1998; Kislev 1989; Zohary 1973), and that not all cultivars initially manipulated by humans became domesticates (Weiss et al. 2006).

New paleobotanical data recovered from PPNA sites have revealed that the early cultivation of local plant species was carried out independently in multiple regions throughout the Levant (Weiss et al. 2006). Wild barley (*Hordeum spontaneum*) and oats (*Avena sterilis*) were cultivated in the southern Levant, which is indicated by the hundreds of thousands of grains recovered from a granary at Gilgal and large quantities of barley at Netiv Hagdud (Kislev 1997; Weiss et al. 2006). High abundances of wild barley at Tell 'Abr, Mureybet, and Jerf el-Ahmar suggest the plant was also brought under cultivation, perhaps independently, in the northern Levant (Willcox et al. 2008).

The consistent appearance and high relative abundance of rambling vetch (*Vicia peregrina*), a slightly toxic legume that is difficult to gather efficiently under wild conditions, at Netiv Hagdud suggest this legume was cultivated as a companion crop to barley (Melamed et al. 2008). Recent genetic analyses of archived modern seeds suggest that initial cultivation of wild einkorn wheat (*Triticum boeticum*) took place in the Karacadağ region of Anatolia (Huen et al. 2008; Kilian et al. 2007); although, an additional independent center of einkorn cultivation in the northern Levant is still a possibility (Willcox 2005, but see Huen et al. 2008). Lentil (*Lens* sp.) appears to have been first cultivated in the middle Euphrates region, indicated by high pulse abundances at multiple PPNA sites in the area, which is well outside habitats naturally favored by pulses (Willcox et al. 2008). Since wild lentils exhibit extremely high seed dormancy (i.e., 90% of seeds fail to germinate after sowing) lentils recovered from the Euphrates regions likely possessed a dormancy-free mutation and represent the first stage of lentil domestication (Ladizinsky 1987; Willcox 2002). The presence of lentils at Netiv Hagdud, a site located outside of the biogeographic distribution of the taxon, indicates that the cultivar spread rapidly south once this important genetic mutation took hold. Intentional planting of fig also took place in the southern Levant at Netiv Hagdud and Gilgal, where hundreds of druplets recovered at the site are characterized by parthenocarpy, a genetic mutation characterized by embryo-less druplets. Figs characterized by the parthenocarpic condition can propagate only with human intervention (Kislev et al. 2006).

Although a nuanced understanding of animal exploitation strategies practiced during the PPNA is still not well defined for the southern Levant, due in part to poor preservation of faunal assemblages, it is clear that gazelle and bird hunting formed the foundation of most PPNA animal-based subsistence economies in the region (Tchernov 1993). The slightly higher proportion of juvenile gazelle present in PPNA faunal assemblages compared to Natufian ones, combined with an intensive focus on low-ranking water fowl, suggests intensified predation pressure on dwindling gazelle herds (Davis 2005). While other ungulate taxa, including goats, fallow deer, cattle, and pigs, were also occasionally exploited, small game, fish, and in particular, avian resources played a newly important and prominent role in PPNA animal exploitation strategies (Tchernov 1994). The intensive use of faunas requiring significant energetic investment for capture for relatively low returns during the PPNA is a similar to exploitation strategies employed by the early Natufians and suggests high human foraging pressures associated with increased sedentism.

The Impact of the Younger Dryas on the Transition from Plant Gathering to Gathering-Cultivation

In the Levant, the origins of plant cultivation as a subsistence practice has generally been conceptualized as an intensification strategy undertaken by hunter-gatherers in response to increasing stress on wild floral resources during the climatic decline of the Younger Dryas (Bar-Yosef 2002; Bar-Yosef and Belfer-Cohen 2002). However, new paleoclimatic and archaeological data suggest that the connection between these two events was more complex and nuanced than previously understood. Although the Younger Dryas likely contributed in major ways to the transition from foraging to farming, a re-evaluation of the underlying mechanisms and processes that contributed to the emergence of cultivation practices in the Near East is necessary.

Current explanatory models describing the emergence of cultivation in the Near East hinge on the Younger Dryas acting as a stressor on a single food resource—cereals. Specifically, the cool and arid climatic conditions of the Younger Dryas selected against C_3 plants, and consequently constricted the geographic distribution and natural productivity of wild cereal stands used by the Natufians (Bar-Yosef 2002). However, the Huleh and new Ghab pollen cores indicate that the availability of cereal and grass resources did not diminish, but actually *expanded* during the Younger Dryas (Bottema 2002; Yasuda et al. 2000). In addition, suggestions that radical shifts in the distribution of wild cereals during the Younger Dryas dramatically constricted the accessibility of these resources may be unfounded (Willcox 2005). Wild wheats and rye stands require specific altitudinal and soil conditions for growth, so that even major climatic change would likely have little impact on the distribution of wild cereals (Willcox 2005). The sustained presence of cereals and grasses on the landscape during the Younger Dryas suggests that—*if* the transition from collecting to cultivation is rooted in a reduction in plant food resources—shifts in hunter-gatherer subsistence strategies were not caused by a decrease in these particular resources, but were prompted by a reduction in the productivity of other floral resources specific to the Mediterranean woodlands.

Most recently, Bar-Yosef and Belfer-Cohen (2002) have suggested that cultivation practices emerged in the Levant during the final portion of the Younger Dryas. Although there is very clear evidence for rye cultivation at Abu Hureyra within this time range (Hillman et al. 2001), it may be that cereal cultivation at Abu Hureyra represents a technological "one-off" within the environmental and cultural context of late Pleistocene hunter-gatherers. Speleothem and pollen records indicate that the Younger Dryas variably impacted different regions of the Levant, with some regions experiencing more arid conditions and greater shifts in the composition of vegetational communities than others. The more intense expression of the Younger Dryas in the northern Levant relative to southerly regions, combined with the retention of largely sedentary lifeways at Abu Hureyra during the late Natufian (Moore et al. 2000), could explain why hunter-gatherers at Abu Hureyra embarked on a different subsistence trajectory than their southern Levantine counterparts. In contrast to the situation at Abu Hureyra, increased mobility associated with the southern Levantine late Natufian represents a successful, enduring local adaptation to the challenging environment conditions imposed by the Younger Dryas in that region (Munro 2003). In the southern Levant, the late Natufians adjusted their settlement patterns from a territorially constricted, sedentary lifestyle centered on base camps to a more flexible, fluid one that took better advantage of seasonal shifts in available food resources in multiple ecotones, presumably in response to hypothesized plant food scarcity resulting from climatic shifts associated with the Younger Dryas. By utilizing elastic mobility and settlement patterns, the Late Natufians could have easily opted out of resource intensification strategies such as cultivation and still maintained suitably high levels of gathered and hunted resources. Interestingly, many radiometric determinations recovered from late Natufian deposits appear to predate the Younger Dryas (Stutz et al. 2009), which may indicate that Natufian foraging behavior re-oriented toward increased mobility and extensive extraction of plant and animal foodstuffs independent of climatic deterioration and hypothesized concomitant decline in floral resources.

Much attention has focused on how hunter-gatherers may have dealt with plant exploitation during the Younger Dryas event itself, but it is not until after this climatic event, during the Pre-Pottery Neolithic A, that the transition from foraging to farming was well underway. The uniquely optimal conditions of early Holocene environments, the wettest on record for the past 15,000 years (Robinson et al. 2006), may have been crucial to the long-term human experimentation with intentional plant cultivation. Warm temperatures would extend the seasonal timeframe during which cultivars could be planted and harvested, while high precipitation levels recharged and maintained soil moisture levels for longer durations. Together, these variables effectively mitigated some of the risks associated with dry-farming at lower temperatures and rainfall levels by expanding the window during which propagules could be planted and still successfully germinate. During those initial stages of the long-term process of growing food plants, when gatherers were still experimenting with the scheduling of planting and harvesting activities and testing the appropriateness of different cultivars to local conditions, the flexibility afforded first cultivators by optimal early Holocene environments was likely a crucial variable that promoted successes and cushioned failures associated with those first attempts to manage cultivars.

Epipaleolithic hunter-gatherers of the Levant successfully negotiated the Younger Dryas in part by shifting their mobility patterns in some regions and adopting the novel subsistence strategy of plant cultivation in others. Paleoenvironmental data suggest that the Younger Dryas impacted different areas of the Levant at varying intensities, and accordingly, there is an expectation that hunter-gatherer groups would have developed an array of plant exploitation strategies that regionally varied according to the predictability and availability of floral resources in local vegetational biomes. The Younger Dryas may have contributed to late Natufian hunter-gatherers decisions to experiment with cultivation, perhaps in the form of low-investment practices such as planting propagules in patches that could later be revisited during the seasonal round, but given that the widespread, polycentric emergence and adoption of cereal, legume, and fruit cultivation in the Near East occurred after the Younger Dryas, during a climatic optimum, it seems unlikely that the Younger Dryas promoted full-scale adoption of this novel subsistence strategy. With the acquisition of new data sets and expansion of analytical approaches to include phytolith, starch grain, and stable isotopic analyses, we may better understand the exact role of the Younger Dryas in sparking the transition from hunting and gathering to food production and canalizing plant cultivation as an intensive, far-reaching subsistence strategy in prehistory.

References

Alley, R., D. Meese, C. Shuman, A. Gow, K. Taylor, P. Grootes, J. White, M. Ram, E. Waddington, P. Mayewski, and G. Zielinski
    1993 Abrupt Increase in Greenland Snow Accumulation at the End of the Younger Dryas Event. *Nature* 363:527–529.

Anderson, P.
    1994 Reflections on the Significance of Two PPN Typological Classes in the Light of Experimentation and Microwear Analysis: Flint "Sickles" and Obsidian "Çayönü Tools". In *Neolithic Chipped Stone Industries of the Fertile Crescent: Proceedings of the First Workshop on PPN Chipped Lithic Industries*, edited by H. Gebel and S. Kozlowski, pp. 61–82. Ex Oriente, Berlin.

Bar-Matthews, M., A. Ayalon, M. Gilmour, A. Matthews, and C. Hawkesworth
    2003 Sea-land Oxygen Isotopic Relationships from Planktonic Foraminifera and Speleothems in the Eastern Mediterranean Region and Their Implication for Paleorainfall during Interglacial Intervals. *Geochimica et Cosmochimica Acta* 67:3181–3199.

Bar-Matthews, M., A. Ayalon, and A. Kaufman
1997 Late Quaternary Paleoclimate in the Eastern Mediterranean Region from Stable Isotope Analysis of Speleothems at Soreq Cave, Israel. *Quaternary Research* 47:155–168.

Bar-Matthews, M., A. Ayalon, A. Kaufman, and G. Wasserburg
1999 The Eastern Mediterranean Paleoclimate as a Reflection of Region Events: Soreq Cave, Israel. *Earth and Planetary Science Letters* 166:85–95.

Bar-Matthews, M., A. Ayalon, A. Matthews, E. Sass, and L. Halicz
1996 Carbon and Oxygen Isotope Study of the Active Water-carbonate System in a Karstic Mediterranean Cave: Implications for Paleoclimate Research in Semiarid Regions. *Geochimica et Cosmochimica Acta* 60:337–347.

Bar-Yosef, O.
1986 The Walls of Jericho: An Alternative Explanation. *Paleorient* 15:57–63.

1991, The Early Neolithic of the Levant : Recent Advances. *Review of Archaeology* 12:1–18.

1998 The Natufian Culture in the Levant, Threshold to the Origins of Agriculture. *Evolutionary Anthropology* 6:159–177.

2000 The World around Cyprus: From Epi-Paleolithic Foragers to the Collapse of the PPNB Civilization. In *The Earliest Prehistory of Cyprus: From Colonization to Exploitation*, edited by S. Swiny, pp. 129–164. American Schools of Oriental Research Archaeological Reports, Boston.

2001 From Sedentary Foragers to Village Hierarchies: The Emergence of Social Institutions. In *The Origins of Social Institutions*, edited by G. Runciman, pp. 1–38. Oxford University Press, Oxford.

2002 The Role of the Younger Dryas in the Origin of Agriculture in West Asia. In *The Origins of Pottery and Agriculture*, edited by Y. Yasuda, pp. 39–54. Lustre Press, Roli Books, Japan.

Bar-Yosef, O., and A. Belfer-Cohen
1989 The Origins of Sedentism and Farming Communities in the Levant. *Journal of World Prehistory* 3:447–498.

1991 From Sedentary Hunter-gatherers to Territorial Farmers in the Levant. In *Between Bands and States*, edited by S. Gregg, pp. 181–202. Center for Archeological Investigations, Occasional Paper No. 9, Southern Illinois University, Carbondale.

2002 Facing Environmental Crisis: Societal and Cultural Changes at the Transition from the Younger Dryas to the Holocene in the Levant. In *The Dawn of Farming in the Near East*, edited by R. Cappers and S. Bottema, pp. 55–66. Studies in Early Near Eastern Production, Subsistence, and Environment 6. Ex Oriente, Berlin.

Bar-Yosef, O., and A. Gopher
1997 *An Early Neolithic Village in the Jordan Valley, Part I: The Archaeology of Netiv Hagdud*. American School of Prehistoric Research Bulletin No. 43. Peabody Museum of Archaeology and Ethnology, Harvard University, Cambridge.

Baruch, U., and S. Bottema

1991 Palynological Evidence for Climatic Changes in the Levant ca. 17,000–9,000 BP. In *The Natufian Culture in the Levant*, edited by O. Bar-Yosef and F. Valla, pp. 11–20. International Monographs in Prehistory, Ann Arbor.

1999 A New Pollen Diagram from Lake Hula: Vegetational, Climatic, and Anthropogenic Implications. In *Ancient Lakes: Their Cultural and Biological Diversity*, edited by H. Kawanabe, G. Coulter, and A. Roosevelt, pp. 75–86. Kenobe Productions, Belgium.

Belfer-Cohen, A.

1988 The Natufian Graveyard at Hayonim Cave. *Paléorient* 14:297–308.

1995 Rethinking Social Stratification in the Natufian Culture: The Evidence from Burials. In *The Archaeology of Death in the Ancient Near East*, edited by S. Campbell and A. Green, pp. 9–16. International Monographs in Prehistory, Ann Arbor.

Belfer-Cohen, A., and O. Bar-Yosef

2000 Early Sedentism in the Near East: A Bumpy Ride to Village Life (13,000–8,000 BP). In *Life in Neolithic Farming Communities*, edited by I. Kuijt, pp. 19–38. Plenum Press, New York.

Belfer-Cohen, A., and L. Grosman

1997 The Lithic Assemblage of Salibiya I. *Mitekufat Haeven* 27:19–42.

Ben-Gai, T., A. Bitan, A. Manes, P. Alpert, and S. Rubin

1998 Spatial and Temporal Changes in Rainfall Frequency Distribution Patterns in Israel. *Theoretical and Applied Climatology* 61:177–190.

Betts, A.

1991 The Epipaleolithic in the Black Desert, Eastern Jordan. In *The Natufian Culture in the Levant*, edited by O. Bar-Yosef and F. Valla, pp. 217–234. International Monographs in Prehistory, Ann Arbor.

Bottema, S.

2002 The Use of Palynology in Tracing Early Agriculture. In *The Dawn of Farming in the Near East*, edited by R. T. J. Cappers and S. Bottema, pp. 27–28. Studies in Near Eastern Production, Subsistence, and Environment 6. Berlin.

Byrd, B., and C. Monahan

1995 Death, Mortuary Ritual, and Natufian Social Structure. *Journal of Anthropological Archaeology* 14:251–287.

Cappers, R., S. Bottema, and H. Woldring

1998 Problems in Correlating Pollen Diagrams of the Near East Preliminary Report. In *The Origins of Agriculture and Crop Domestication*, edited by A. Damania, J. Valkon, G. Willcox, and C. Qualset, pp. 160–169. International Genetic Resources Institute, Rome.

Cappers, R. T. J., S. Bottema, H. Woldring, H. van der Plicht, and H. Streurman

2002 Modeling the Emergence of Farming: Implications of the Vegetation Development of the Near East during the Pleistocene-Holocene

Transition. In *The Dawn of Farming in the Near East*, edited by R. Cappers and S. Bottema, pp. 3–14. Studies in Early Near Eastern Production, Subsistence, and Environment 6. Ex Oriente, Berlin.

Colledge, S.
1998 Identifying Pre-domestication Cultivation Using Multivariate Analysis. In *The Origins of Agriculture and Crop Domestication*, edited by A. Damania, J. Valkoun, J. Willcox, and C. Qualset, pp. 121–131. ICARDA, Syria.

Davis, S.
2005 Why Domesticate Food Animals? Some Zooarchaeological Evidence from the Southern Levant. *Journal of Archaeological Science* 32:1408–1416.

Edwards, P.
1991 Wadi Hammeh 27 An Early Natufian Site at Pella, Jordan. In *The Natufian Culture in the Levant*, edited by O. Bar-Yosef and F. Valla, pp. 123–148. International Monographs in Prehistory, Ann Arbor.

2003 Nine Millennia by Lake Lisan: The Epipaleolithic in the East Jordan Valley between 20,000 and 11,000 Years Ago. In *Studies in the History and Archaeology of Jordan, Vol. VII: Jordan by the Millennia*, edited by G. Bisheh, pp. 85–93. Department of the Antiquities of Jordan, Amman.

al-Eisawi, D. M, A. el-Oqlah, S. Oran, and J. Lahham
2000 *Jordan Country Study on Biological Diversity and Taxonomy*. General Corporation for Environmental Protection, United Nations Environment Programme.

Flannery, K.
1969 Origins and Ecological Effects of Early Domestication in Iran and the Near East. In *The Domestication and Exploitation of Plants and Animals*, edited by P. J. Ucko and G. W. Dimbleby, pp. 73–100. Chicago, Aldine Publishing Co.

Frumkin, A., D. Ford, and H. Schwarcz
2000 Paleoclimate and Vegetation of the Last Glacial Cycles in Jerusalem from a Speleothem Record. *Global Biogeochemical Cycles* 14:863–870.

Gat, J.
1996 Oxygen and Hydrogen Isotopes in the Hydrologic Cycle. *Annual Review of Earth and Planetary Sciences* 23:225–263.

Gat, J., and W. Dansgaard
1972 Stable Isotope Survey of the Fresh Water Occurrences in Israel and the Northern Jordan Rift Valley. *Journal of Hydrology* 16:177–212.

Gebel, H., and M. Muheisen
1985 Note from 'Ain Rahub, a New Late Natufian Site in Jordan. *Paléorient* 11:107–110.

Goldberg, P.
1986 Late Quaternary Environmental History of the Southern Levant. *Geoarchaeology* 1:225–244.

Goldberg, P.

1994 Interpreting Late Quaternary Continental Sequences in Israel. In *Late Quaternary Chronology and Paleoclimates of the Eastern Mediterranean*, edited by O. Bar-Yosef and R. Kra, pp. 89–102. Radiocarbon and ASPR, Tucson and Cambridge.

Goring-Morris, N.

1987 At the Edge: Terminal Hunter-gatherers in the Negev and Sinai. *BAR International Series 361*. British Archaeological Reports, Oxford.

1991 The Harifian of the Southern Levant. In *The Natufian Culture in the Levant*, edited by O. Bar-Yosef and F. R. Valla, pp. 173–216. International Monographs in Prehistory, Ann Arbor.

Goring-Morris, N., and A. Belfer-Cohen

2008 A Roof over One's Head: Developments in Near Eastern Residential Architecture across the Epipaleolithic-Neolithic Transition. In *The Neolithic Demographic Transition and its Consequences*, edited by J-P Bocquet-Appel and O. Bar-Yosef, pp. 239–285. Springer Science+Business Media B.V., New York.

Goring-Morris, N., and L. Horwitz

2000 Fauna from the Early Natufian Site of Upper Besor 6 in the Central Negev, Israel. *Paléorient* 26:111–128.

Grosman, L.

2003 Preserving Cultural Traditions in a Period of Instability: The Late Natufian of the Hilly Mediterranean Zone. *Current Anthropology* 44:571–580.

Hajar, L., C. Khater, and R. Cheddadi

2008 Vegetation Changes during the Late Pleistocene and Holocene in Lebabon: A Pollen Record from the Bekaa Valley. *The Holocene* 18:1089–1099.

Hardy-Smith, T., and P. Edwards

2004 The Garbage Crisis in Prehistory: Artefact Discard Patterns at the Early Natufian Site of Wadi Hammeh 27 and the Origins of Household Refuse Disposal Strategies. *Journal of Anthropological Archaeology* 23:253–289.

Henry, D.

1976 Rosh Zin: A Natufian Settlement near Ein Avdat. In *Prehistory and Paleoenvironments in the Central Negev, Israel. The Avdat/Aqev Area*, Part I, edited by A. Marks, pp. 317–348. SMU Press, Dallas.

Hillman, G., and M. Davies

1990 Domestication Rates in Wild-type Wheats and Barley under Primitive Cultivation. *Biological Journal of the Linnaean Society* 39:39–78.

Hillman, G., R. Hedges, A. Moore, S. Colledge, and P. Pettitt

2001 New Evidence of Late Glacial Cereal Cultivation at Abu Hureyra on the Euphrates. *The Holocene* 11:383–393.

Hopf, M., and O. Bar-Yosef
1987 Plant Remains from Hayonim Cave, Western Galilee. *Paléorient* 13:117–120.

Huen, M., S. Haldorsen, and K. Vollan
2008 Reassessing Domestication Events in the Near East: Einkorn and Triticum Urartu. *Genome* 51:444–451.

Kadosh, D., S. Sivan, H. Kutiel, and M. Weinstein-Evron
2004 A Late Quaternary Paleoenvironmental Sequence from Dor, Carmel Coastal Plain, Israel. *Palynology* 28:143–157.

Kenyon, K.
1981 *Excavations at Jericho. Vol. III: The Architecture and Stratigraphy of the Tell.* British School of Archaeology in Jerusalem, London.

Kilian, B., H. Özkan, A. Walther, J. Kohl, T. Dagan, F. Salamini, and W. Martin
2007 Molecular Diversity at 18 Loci in 321 Wild and 92 Domesticate Lines Reveal no Reduction of Nucleotide Diversity during *Triticum monococcum* (Einkorn) Domestication: Implication for the Origin of Agriculture. *Molecular Biology Evolution* 24:2657–2668.

Kislev, M. E.
1989 Pre-domesticated Cereals in the Pre-Pottery Neolithic A Period. *Symposium on Upper Paleolithic, Mesolithic, and Neolithic Populations of Europe and the Mediterranean Basin. BAR International Series* 580:147–151.

1992 Agriculture in the Near East in the VIIth Millenium BC. In *Préhistoire de L'agriculture: Nouvelles Approaches Expérimentales et Ethnographiques,* edited by P. C. Andersen, pp. 87–93. Monographie 6, Centre de Recherches Archéologiques. CNRS Editions, Paris.

Kislev, M.
1997 Early Agriculture and Paleoecology of Netiv Hagdud. In *An Early Neolithic Village in the Jordan Valley, Part I: The Archaeology of Netiv Hagdud,* edited by O. Bar-Yosef and A. Gopher, pp. 209–236. Peabody Museum of Archaeology and Ethnology, Harvard University, Cambridge.

Kislev, M., A. Hartmann, and O. Bar-Yosef
2006 Early Domesticated Fig in the Jordan Valley. *Science* 312:1372–1374.

Kuijt, I.
1994 Pre-Pottery Neolithic A Period Settlement Systems of the Southern Levant: New Data, Archaeological Visibility, and Regional Site Hierarchies. *Journal of Mediterranean Archaeology* 7:165–192.

1996 Negotiation Equality through Ritual: A Consideration of Late Natufian and Pre-Pottery Neolithic A Period Mortuary Practices. *Journal of Anthropological* Archaeology 15:313–336.

Kuijt, I., and B. Finlayson
2009 Evidence for Food Storage and Predomestication Granaries. *Proceedings of the National Academy of Sciences* 106:10966–10970.

Kuijt, I., and N. Goring-Morris

2002 Foraging, Farming, and Social Complexity in the Pre-Pottery Neolithic of the Southern Levant: A Review and Synthesis. *Journal of World Prehistory* 16:361–440.

Ladizinksy, G.

1987 Pulse Domestication before Cultivation. *Economic Botany* 41:60.

Lieberman, D.

1991 Seasonality and Gazelle Hunting at Hayonim Cave: New Evidence for "Sedentism" during the Natufian. *Paléorient* 17:47–57.

1993 The Rise and Fall of Seasonal Mobility among Hunter-gatherers. *Current Anthropology* 34:599–631.

Marks, A., and P. Larson

1977 Test Excavations at the Natufian Site of Rosh Horesha. In *Prehistory and Paleoenvironments in the Central Negev*, Israel, Vol II., edited by A. Marks, pp. 191–232. Southern Methodist University, Dallas.

Meadows, J.

2005 The Younger Dryas Episode and the Radiocarbon Chronologies of the Lake Huleh and Ghab Valley Pollen Diagrams, Israel and Syria. *The Holocene* 15:631–636.

Melamed, Y., U. Plitmann, and M. Kislev

2008 *Vicia Peregria*: An Edible Early Neolithic Legure. *Vegetation History Archaeobotany* 17 (Suppl 1):S29–S34.

Moore, A., G. Hillman, and A. Legge

2000 Village on the Euphrates: From Foraging to Farming at Abu Hureyra. Oxford University Press, Madison and New York.

Munro, N.

2001 A Prelude to Agriculture: Game Use and Occupation Intensity during the Natufian Period in the Southern Levant. Unpublished Ph.D. dissertation, School of Anthropology, University of Arizona, Tucson.

2003 Small Game, the Younger Dryas, and the Transition to Agriculture in the Southern Levant. *Mitteilungen der Gesselshaft für Urgeschichte* 12:47–71.

2004 Zooarchaeological Measures of Hunting Pressure and Occupation Intensity in the Natufian: Implications for Agricultural Origins. *Current Anthropology* 45:S5–S33.

Niklewski, J., and W. van Zeist

1970 A Late Quaternary Pollen Diagram from Northwestern Syria. *Acta Botanica Neerlandica* 19:737–754.

Noy, T.

1991 Art and Decoration of the Natufian at Nahal Oren. In *The Natufian Culture in the Levant*, edited by O. Bar-Yosef and F. Valla, pp. 557–568. International Monographs in Prehistory, Ann Arbor.

Perrot, J.

1966 Le Gisement Natoufien de Mallaha (Enyan), Israël. *L'Anthropologie* 70:437–484.

Rasmussen, S., K. Andersen, A. Svensson, J. Steffensen, B. Vinther, H. Clausen, M. Siggaard-Andersen, S. Johnsen, L. Larsen, D. Dahl-Jensen, M. Bigler, R. Röthlisberger, H. Fischer, K. Goto-Azuma, M. Hansson, and U. Ruther

2006 A New Greenland Ice Core Chronology for the Last Glacial Termination. *Journal of Geophysical Research* 111:D06102.

Robinson, S., S. Black, B. Sellwood, and P. Valdes

2006 A Review of Palaeoclimates and Palaeoenvironments in the Levant and Eastern Mediterranean from 25,000 to 5000 Years BP: Setting the Environmental Background for the Evolution of Human Civilisation. *Quaternary Science Reviews* 25:1517–1541.

Rosen, A.

2007 *Civilizing Climate: Social Responses to Climate Change in the Ancient Near East.* AltaMira Press, Lanham.

Rossignol-Strick, M.

1995 Sea-land Correlations of Pollen Records in the Eastern Mediterranean for the Glacial-interglacial Transition: Biostratigraphy versus Radiometric Time-scale. *Quaternary Science Reviews* 14:893–915.

1997 Paléoclimate de la Méditerranée oreientale et de L'Asie du Sud-Ouest de 15 000 à 6 000 BP. *Paléorient* 23:175–196.

Sage, R.

1995 Was Low Atmosphere CO_2 during the Pleistocene a Limiting Factor for the Origin of Agriculture? *Global Change Biology* 1:93–106.

Shewan, L.

2004 Natufian Settlement Systems and Adaptive Strategies: The Issue of Sedentism and the Potential of Strontium Isotope Analysis. In *The Last Hunter-gatherer Societies in the Near East*, edited by C. Delage, pp. 55–94. BAR International Series 1320, Oxford.

Stiner, M., and N. Munro

2002 Approaches to Prehistoric Diet Breadth, Demography, and Prey Ranking Systems in Time and Space. *Journal of Archaeological Method and Theory* 9:175–208.

Stiner, M., N. Munro, and T. Surovell

2000 The Tortoise and the Hare: Small Game Use, the Broad Spectrum Revolution, and Paleolithic Demography. *Current Anthropology* 41:39–73.

Stiner, M., N. Munro, T. Surovell, E. Tchernov, and O. Bar-Yosef

1999 Paleolithic Population Growth Pulses Evidenced by Small Animal Exploitation. *Science* 282:190–194.

Stordeur, D.

2000 Les Bâtiments Communautaires de Jerf el Ahmar et Mureybet Horizon PPNA (Syrie). *Paléorient* 26:29.

Stutz, A.

2002 Polarizing Microscopy Identification of Chemical Diagenesis in Archaeological Cementum. *Journal of Archaeological Science* 29:1327–1347.

Stutz, A., G. Bar-Oz, and N. Munro

2009 Increasing the Resolution of the Broad Spectrum Revolution in the Southern Levantine Epipaleolithic (1–12ka). *Journal of Human Evolution* 56:294–306.

Tchernov, E.

1991 Biological Evidence for Human Sedentism in Southwest Asia during the Natufian. In *The Natufian Culture in the Levant*, edited by O. Bar-Yosef and F. Valla, pp. 315–340. International Monographs in Prehistory, Ann Arbor.

1993 The Impact of Sedentism on Animal Exploitation in the Southern Levant. In *Archaeozoology of the Near East*, edited by H. Butenhuis and A. Clason, pp. 10–26. Universal Book Service, Leiden.

1994 *An Early Neolithic Village in the Jordan Valley II: The Fauna of Netiv Hagdud*. American School of Research Bulletin 44, Cambridge.

Valla, F.

1988 Les Premiers Sédentaires de Palestine. *La Recherche* 199:576–584.

Valla, F., F. LeMort, and H. Plisson

1991 Les Natoufiens et les Mallaha et l'Espace. In *The Natufian Culture in the Levant*, edited by O. Bar-Yosef and F. Valla, pp. 111–121. International Monographs in Prehistory, Ann Arbor.

van Zeist, W., and S. Bottema

1991 *Late Quaternary Vegetation of the Near East*. Weisbaden, Dr. Ludwig Reichert Verlag.

van Zeist, W., and H. Woldring

1980 Holocene Vegetation and Climate of Northwestern Syria. *Palaeohistoria* 22:11–125.

Verheyden, S., F. Nader, H. Cheng, L. Edwards, and R. Swennen

2008 Paleoclimate Reconstruction in the Levant Region from the Geochemistry of a Holocene Stalagmite from the Jeita Cave, Lebanon. *Quaternary Research* 70:368–381.

Verhoeven, M.

2002 Ritual and Ideology in the Pre-Pottery Neolithic B of the Levant and Southeast Anatolia. *Cambridge Archaeological Journal* 12:233–258.

Weinstein-Evron, M.

1994 Biases in Archaeological Pollen Assemblages: Case Studies from Israel. *AASP Contributions* 29:193–205.

1998 *Early Natufian el-Wad revisited*. ERAUL 77, Liege.

Weiss, E., M. Kislev, and A. Hartman

2006 Autonomous Cultivation before Domestication. *Science* 312:1608–1610.

Weiss, E., W. Wetterstrom, D. Nadel, and O. Bar-Yosef
2004 The Broad Spectrum Revisited: Evidence from the Plant Remains. *Proceedings of the National Academy of Sciences* 101:9951–9555.

Willcox, G.
1996 Evidence for Plant Exploitation and Vegetation History from Three Early Neolithic Pre-Pottery Sites on the Euphrates (Syria). *Vegetational History and Archaeobotany* 5:143–152.

2002 Charred Plant Remains from a Late Tenth Millennium Kitchen at Jerf el Ahmar (Syria). *Vegetational History and Archaeobotany* 11:55–60.

2005 The Distribution, Natural Habitats and Availability of Wild Cereals in Relation to Their Domestication in the Near East: Multiple Events, Multiple Centres. *Vegetation History and Archaeobotany* 14:534–541.

Willcox, G., S. Fornite, and L. Herveux
2008 Early Holocene Cultivation before Domestication in Northern Syria. *Vegetational History and Archaeobotany* 17:313–325.

Wright, H., Jr., and J. Thorpe
2003 Climatic Change and the Origin of Agriculture in the Near East. In *Global Change in the Holocene*, edited by A. Mackay, R. Battarbee, J. Birks, and F. Oldfield, pp. 49–62. Arnold, London.

Wright, K.
1991 The Origins and Development of Ground Stone Assemblages in Late Pleistocene Southwest Asia. *Paléorient* 17:19–45.

Yamada, S.
2000 Development of the Neolithic: Lithic Use-Wear Analysis of Major Tool Types in the Southern Levant. Unpublished Ph.D. dissertation, Department of Anthropology, Harvard University.

Yasuda, Y., H. Kitagawa, and T. Nakagawa
2000 The Earliest Record of Major Anthropogenic Deforestation in the Ghab Valley, Northwest Syria: A Palynological Study. *Quaternary International* 73/74:127–136.

Zohary, M.
1973 *Geobotanical Foundations of the Middle East*. G. Fischer, Stuttgart.

10

The Younger Dryas in Arid Northeast Asia

Joshua Wright and Lisa Janz

Introduction

In this chapter, we will concentrate on the arid Northeast Asian steppe region east of the Altai mountains, between the forested steppe of Siberia to the north and the loess highlands of eastern Asia to the south. The three primary regions that we will consider are the Khangai mountains in Central Mongolia, the Gobi Desert, and the Ikh Nurruud basin, or Basin of Great Lakes, in western Mongolia (Figure 10.1). The last provides an extensive record of climate proxies from the lakes. Archaeological data, however, comes primarily from the Gobi Desert region.

Why This Region?

The larger issue in the archaeology of this region, and the sites discussed here, is adaptation to climatic fluctuation. Paleoclimatic data show that arid, Northeast Asia has long been a tough environment, and the adaptation to the Younger Dryas by resident hunter-gatherers raises the question of how exceptional the impact of that colder and dryer period might have been on a population already adapted to subsistence on a marginal landscape.

Hunter-Gatherer Behavior: Human Response during The Younger Dryas, edited by Metin I. Eren, 231–248. © Left Coast Press. All rights reserved.

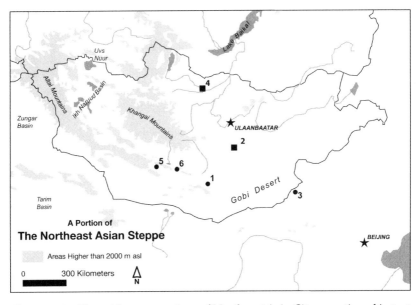

Figure 10.1 The arid steppe regions of Northeast Asia. Sites mentioned in text
are 1) Shabarak-Usu/Bayan Zak; 2) Baga Gazaryn Chuluu; 3) Baron Shabaka
Well; 4) Egiin Gol; 5) Chikhen Agui; and 6) Tsagaan Agui.

As part of the larger East Asian region, the Northeast Asian steppe
was a critical frontier of human activity during the Pleistocene and
Holocene periods. It is tied to greater East Asia by its common chipped-
stone traditions throughout the late Pleistocene and early Holocene,
and by its central role in discussions of the dynamics of human habitation and technological development in Northeast Asia following the
last glaciation (Elston and Brantingham 2002; Goebel 2002). During the
late Pleistocene, there is a noted division between the blade industries
of the western and northern steppe regions of central and Northeast
Asia and the flake and chopper industries associated with the southern
and eastern river drainages and coastal regions of East Asia. During the
terminal Pleistocene, probably beginning around the time of the Last
Glacial Maximum (~21,000 cal BP), a common microblade technology
appeared in much of Northeast Asia, including the north coastal regions and areas previously dominated by flake and chopper, tool traditions. Since the late Holocene, the steppes and deserts of Northeast
Asia have formed a distinct environmental frontier within East Asia
between mobile pastoralists and sedentary agriculturalists.

At the northern extent of the arid reaches of Northeast Asia, the
Khangai mountains (maximum elevation 4,000 m asl) feed rivers that

mostly drain northward as part the Lake Baikal watershed. The western portion of this region is dominated by the eastern edge of the Altai range (maximum elevation 4,200 m asl) and includes many dry, high altitude intermountain plains and a line of shallow lake basins along their northern flanks, which constitutes the Valley of the Gobi Lakes. This valley, extending across the plains that divide the Khangai and Altai ranges, meets the larger Ikh Narruud lake basin (Valley Basin of the Great Lakes, ca. 1,100 m asl) in the west. The lakes across this region are typified by a series of extensive basins that capture drainage from the surrounding highlands. The Gobi Desert, in the south, is the largest Asian desert and the only major, arid region in Northeast Asia. In its eastern reach, the Gobi is characterized by open steppe, while basins and smaller mountain ranges dominate the central and western areas. This latter region forms the central arena for discussion in this chapter because it contains the most well documented archaeological sites.

Climate History

Overall the climate of arid Northeast Asia is dominated by the relationship between the Asian monsoons that bring rain and wet conditions to coastal and southern Asia, and the countervailing westerlies that bring dry conditions to Central Asia. The boundary between these two weather systems shifted back and forth across the Northeast Asian steppe belt throughout the late Pleistocene and Holocene.

The backdrop for the Younger Dryas in arid Northeast Asia is the Last Glacial Maximum of the Sartan glaciation (25,000 cal BP), which brought the snow line down to 2,000–1,800 m asl in this region. By 20,000–18,000 cal BP, higher elevations were deglaciating and warming began throughout the region under discussion (Grunert, Lehmkuhl, and Walther 2000; Horiuchi et al. 2000). Released from periglacial conditions, the warmer succeeding period was one of hyper-aridity in the western basins of Mongolia. Dune fields crossed many of the low-lying basins and loess deposition occurred over wide areas (Lehmkuhl and Lang 2001; Yang et al. 2004). With the warming trend of the Bølling-Ållerød (14,700–13,000 cal BP) (Goldberg et al. 2001; Prokopenko et al. 1999), deciduous forests grew in the northern Khangai and the Selenga river drainage (Feng 2001; Horiuchi et al. 2000).

Typical climatic shifts associated with the cool, dry Younger Dryas have been documented in ice and lake cores recovered in Inner Asia, from the Qinghai plateau (Madsen et al. 1998) and Lake Baikal (Prokopenko et al. 1999). Climate dynamics typical of the late Pleistocene regained some dominance during this interval. During the Younger Dryas, the Northeast Asian steppe and Gobi Desert were outside the reach of the Asian monsoons, as they are today (Feng 2001; Herzschuh 2006; Ilyashuk and Ilyashuk 2007; Zhou et al. 2001). In arid Northeast Asia, this climatic shift toward an exceptionally cool, dry climate was most evident between 12,900 and 11,600 cal BP (see also Herzschuh 2006). Although the snow-line had risen to approximately 3,500 m asl (Lehmkuhl and Lang 2001), extreme aridity and very low lake levels characterized basin and steppe environments (Herzschuh 2006; Huang et al. 2007; Rhodes et al. 1996; Yang et al. 2004). This was not universally the case, and the Uvs Nuur basin in western Mongolia reached its minimum level at 12,200 cal BP. (Yang et al. 2004). Other lake basins all along the eastern face of the Altai began to recover between 12,000 and 10,000 cal BP (Rhodes et al. 1996; Yang et al. 2004). Though some large, arid regions, such as Lake Bosten, in the Zungar basin, did not undergo lake formation until the early Holocene (8000–7000 cal BP) (Huang et al. 2007). Despite this general drying trend, some ambiguities exist in the paleoenvironmental record of the region. Permafrost layers of Gobi Desert soils degraded between 13,000–10,000 cal BP as temperatures consistently warmed (Yang et al. 2004), and some regions saw a rise in lake levels. Around the northwestern edges of the Khangai and the northern area of the Ikh Nurruud basin, lake stands not only increased, but reached their highest recorded levels (Yang et al. 2004). At 11,230 ± 60 cal BP, Uvs Nuur stood forty meters higher than its present level (Grunert, Lehmkuhl, and Walther 2000). Similarly, lake basins all along the eastern face of the Altai began to recover from late glacial aridity between 12,000 and 10,000 cal BP (Rhodes et al. 1996; Yang et al. 2004). These widespread increases in lake levels resulted in huge inflows of water, driving the formation of large alluvial fans at the mountain edges above lakes (Grunert, Lehmkuhl, and Walther 2000). The Lake Baikal drainage, including the northern Khangai mountains, also experienced some increases in aridity and cooling between 13,100 and 12,100 BP (Ilyashuk and Ilyashuk 2007; Prokopenko et al. 1999), but forest cover remained.

In spite of temporary returns to cooler conditions during the Younger Dryas, postglacial, warming trends and deglaciation continued and appear to have moderated the effect of Younger Dryas conditions. Lake levels throughout the Altai region were mostly influenced by long-term warming and deglaciation. In contrast, regions most reliant on precipitation would have been more directly affected by conditions of the arid Younger Dryas. In short, although the Younger Dryas in the Northeast Asian steppe was a continuation of late Pleistocene patterns of widespread aridity, its effect was tempered by high-elevation warming and a concomitant hydrologic dynamism in many lake basins.

Just as the Younger Dryas provides records of tumultuous geomorphological and hydrologic changes, shifting vegetation dynamic provides an important record of early Holocene climatic trends. During the early Holocene, overall conditions remained dry (Chen et al. 2008), but there is a general increase in indicators of wetter conditions (Herzschuh 2006). Lake levels in the Ikh Naruud Basin dropped in the early Holocene, but the shoreline still stood 12–8 meters above modern levels. The dynamics of the streams that fed these lakes changed and they began to down-cut into the large fluvial fans that formed during the Pleistocene and Younger Dryas (Grunert, Lehmkuhl, and Walther 2000; Lehmkuhl and Lang 2001).

Evidence of *Artemisia*-dominated steppe appears throughout the Northeast Asian steppe from the North China Plain (10,000–8000 BP) (Liu, Cui, and Huang 2001) to the Zungar Basin (10,000–6000 cal BP) (Huang et al. 2007; Rhodes et al. 1996). In the Great Lakes region of western Mongolia, and the northern slopes of the Khangai steppe, this *Artemisia*-dominated steppe alternated with periods when forest dominated the ecosystem during the early Holocene (Grunert, Lehmkuhl, and Walther 2000; Lehmkuhl and Lang 2001). In the highlands to the north of the lakes region and the Khangai, an abrupt warming and increase in moisture is indicated by changes in the Chironomid (midge) populations during the early Holocene (Ilyashuk and Ilyashuk 2007). In the Gobi Desert region, low rainfall, desert conditions remained predominant along with unstable lacustrian environments in desert basins (Chen et al. 2008; Herzschuh et al. 2004; Yang et al. 2004); although, by 8000 cal BP there was a widespread high in lake levels throughout the Gobi-Altai region (Harrison, Yu, and Tarasov 1996; Komatsu et al. 2001; Lehmkuhl and Lang 2001). To the south, a monsoon driven wet climate dominated the loess plateau (Chen et al. 2008).

The early Holocene was a climatically rich time in Northeast Asia, vegetation communities rebounded from the arid late Pleistocene, and the environment was characterized by closed woodlands of much more dense vegetation, a situation not typical during the Pleistocene. Despite the potential of the Khangai mountains and Ikh Naruud Basin to support Holocene occupation, thus far the best known archaeological remains from all the periods discussed here come from the less forgiving regions of the Gobi Desert and far eastern spurs of the Altai mountains (Derevyanko and Dorj 1992; Gábori 1963; Okladnikov 1986; Tsybiktarov 2002; Wright 2006; Wright et al. 2007).

Cultural Periods

The discussion of cultural chronology spanning the Younger Dryas is mainly a discussion of chipped-stone tool traditions. Wedge-shaped, microblade cores, small bifaces, and small endscrapers characterize the widespread Northeast Asian microlithic tradition. Microblades were often broken into segments and inserted into hafts, sometimes being retouched along one edge. Intensively retouched microliths are less common in Northeast Asian assemblages, but backed microblades and elaborately retouched small pieces, such as awls, drills, and points produced by pressure flaking do occur (Bettinger, Elston, and Madsen 1994; Bleed 2002; Chen and Wang 1989; Elston and Brantingham 2002; Hayashi 1968; Maringer 1950; Nelson 1926; Tang and Gai 1986; Zheng 2000). Developed microlithic assemblages have been dated as early as the late Pleistocene at sites such as Xueguan, Xiachuan, and Hutouliang on the southern borders of the Gobi Desert (Chen and Wang 1989; Lu 1998) and Verkolenskaya Gora, Ust-Kyakta and Studenoye 1 in South Siberia (Kuzmin and Orlova 2000). Dates for the northern sites reach well into the Younger Dryas. Although the chronology of pottery in Northeast Asia is not well understood (but see Cohen 2003), over much of temperate and coastal, Northeast Asia the use of pottery develops in the late Pleistocene as early as 16,500 cal BP in the Russian Far East (cf. Frink and Harry 2008; Kuzmin and Orlova 2000; Kuzmin and Shewkomud 2003; Wu and Zhao 2003). New dates from the Gobi Desert indicate the use of pottery by at least 9600 cal BP (Janz 2012).

That being said, there is little well-documented evidence for human activity in the Northeast Asian steppes during the Younger Dryas. This is not a dearth of evidence; there are widespread traces of the people using microlithic tools throughout the region (Bettinger, Elston, and Madsen 1994; Derev'anko 1998; Derevyanko and Dorj 1992; Fairservis 1993; Wright et al. 2007), but there is a lack of dates for those sites. Though microlithic technology continued to be used throughout much of the Holocene, the relationship of many of these sites to late Pleistocene geomorphology suggests that they could date to the Younger Dryas. In addition, the few dated sites do support the presence of people during the late Younger Dryas and early Holocene (Table 10.1).

Sites of Younger Dryas and Early Holocene

Although, there are currently no archaeological sites securely dated to the Younger Dryas alone, much of the terminal Pleistocene appears to have been characterized by ephemeral traces of hunter-gatherer occupation. Toolkits uniformly composed of microlithic cores and blades made primarily of colorful jaspers, chalcedonies, and silicified sandstone typify Gobi Desert archaeological sites assigned to the earliest postglacial periods. While there is variation in core types, many were wedge-shaped or heavily reduced on all sides to produce a conical or bullet shape. Various types of expedient, tabular, and intermediate

Table 10.1 Dated late Pleistocene and Holocene sites from the Northeast Asian steppe region.

Site	Conventional ^{14}C age	Calibrated age (2σ range)*	Location latitude longitude	Reference	Climate conditions
Tsagaan Agui	33497 ± 600 33840 ± 640	NA	44.42N 101.10E	(Derevianko et al. 2000)	Last Interstadial
Dörölj (Egiin Gol)	21820 ± 190 31880 ± 800	NA	49.26N 103.34E	(Jaubert et al. 2004)	Last Interstadial
EGS 082 (Egiin Gol)	27000 ± 390	NA	49.44 N 103.64 E	Wright 2006	Last Interstadial
Baron Shabaka Well	12450 ±74 12509 ±59	14.9–14.2 15.1–14.2 KBP	42.51 N 111.06 E	(Janz, Elston, and Burr 2009)	Terminal Pleistocene
Baga Gazaryn Chuluu (BGC 1451)	12,203 ± 73	14.3–13.8 KBP	46.18 N 106.04 E	(Janz, Elston, and Burr 2009)	Terminal Pleistocene
Chikhen Agui	5630 ± 220 11545 ±75	11.5–5.5 KBP	44.46 N 99.04 E	Derevienko et al. 2003 (Janz, Elston, and Burr 2009)	Younger Dryas/Early to Mid-Holocene
Shabarakh-Usu (Bayan-Dzak)	7969 ± 37 8439 ± 60	9.5–9.3 KBP 9–8.7 KBP	44.10 N 103.42 E	(Janz, Elston, and Burr 2009)	Early Holocene

*Calibrations performed using Oxcal 4.0 online tool with IntCal 04 calibration curves.

types are also represented in these collections as well as large cylindrical bladelet cores. The majority of cores produced pointed microblades that were occasionally retouched and hafted either broken into segments or whole (Chard 1974; Derev'anko 1998; Lu 1998).

The occurrence of technology such as pottery, grinding stones, and polished stone tools has been used to identify a "Neolithic" culture (Chard 1974; Kuzmin and Shewkomud 2003; Okladnikov 1990) in the early Holocene or late Pleistocene that is not associated with any of the aspects of sedentism, agriculture, animal domestication, or social differentiation widely understood to be associated with Neolithic people of western Eurasia (for more information see Derevianko et al. 2003; Lu 1998; Weber 1995). Dates from Shabarakh-Usu and sites in the southern Gobi Desert (Elston et al. 1997; Janz et al. 2009) suggest that these technologies were established by the early Holocene as part of an Epipaleolithic or Mesolithic type of economy in which pottery and grinding tools were used as part of foraging activities.

Baron Shabaka Well

Baron Shabaka Well is a terminal Pleistocene site with an assemblage deposited during a time of highly contrasting hyper-aridity and increased fluvial flow-out of deglaciating highlands. The Baron Shabaka Well site (also known as [American Museum of Natural History] AMNH Site 19), discovered in 1928 in eastern Inner Mongolia, is one of numerous postglacial habitation sites discovered by the AMNH's Central Asiatic Expeditions. Artifacts were recovered from several discreet clusters within a sand-dune, covered valley (Fairservis 1993). Clusters of artifacts surrounding hearths typified these localities. Lithic materials included both developed microblade assemblages and coarsely chipped implements, along with bifaces, grinding stones, and polished stone (Fairservis 1993). Some site clusters contained coarse, thick ceramic sherds. The site was recently dated using ostrich eggshell fragments, but it is not clear exactly which occupation assemblages the shells were associated with. Overall, the assemblages suggest the site was periodically occupied by mobile hunter-gatherers, some of whom appear to have been processing grass seeds or other such resources within the dune fields.

Chikhen Agui

Chikhen Agui is a cave site located in a small limestone ridge in the eastern Gobi-Altai. The cave is situated near a narrow canyon and adjacent to a spring-fed stream. This site records hunter-gatherer activity in an arid rocky desert region at end of the Younger Dryas, and early to mid-Holocene. Radiocarbon dates (Table 10.1) on charcoal from several hearth features returned dates ranging from the late Pleistocene (Horizon 4) and the Younger Dryas to the mid-Holocene (Horizons 1–3) (Derevianko et al. 2000; Derevianko et al. 2003). Although the earliest AMS date was 13,400 cal BP (11,545 + 75 BP (uncalibrated), the majority of the dates were from ~9000 cal BP. Ostrich eggshell from Horizon 1 date to 11,500 cal BP (10,060 ± 50 BP)) (Kurochkin et al. 2009).

The lithic assemblage is comprised of microblade cores and tools, as well as endscrapers, retouched flake points, and other retouched flakes. Tools were made from reddish- and yellowish-brown jasper or chalcedony, as well as dark siliceous sandstone. Chikhen Agui contained numerous hearths and concentrations of grass, interpreted as the remains of bedding (Derevianko et al. 2003). There is no evidence for pottery, grinding stones, bifaces, or similar technologies at Chikhen Agui (see Janz 2006). The locale would have been an ideal place for hunting large and medium-sized ungulates (Derevianko et al. 2003) and may have been a seasonal hunting camp reoccupied throughout the Pleistocene and Holocene.

Shabarakh-Usu (Bayan-Dzak)

The Shabarakh-Usu, or Bayan-Dzak as it is called today, is a complex of sites in the central Gobi Desert in southern Mongolia that is mainly the remains of a post-Younger Dryas, early Holocene adaptation to increased effective moisture in Pleistocene dune formations and lake or playa environments (Janz 2006, 2012). A series of sites were discovered at this locale by both Soviet (Gábori 1962; Okladnikov 1962) and American (Berkey and Nelson 1926; Maringer 1963) archaeologists. These sites were found amidst extensive dune accumulations that were associated with a small playa in an internally drained basin. Numerous dates on ostrich eggshell fragments and beads from the two sampled sites were closely clustered around 9000 cal KBP (8439 ± 60 to 7969 ± 37 BP) (Janz et al. 2009).

This locale is considered of primary importance, because it produced remains from stratified sites during several sets of excavations in the early twentieth century. While Nelson and Gábori believed there to be both an aceramic Mesolithic as well as a Neolithic (see above) component, Okladnikov found chronologically divergent types of pottery throughout all levels. The recent ostrich eggshell dates were taken from two of Nelson's differing stratigraphic levels but returned dates that were not significantly different (Janz et al. 2009) suggesting relative contemporaneity between aceramic and ceramic locales.

The ubiquity of food processing tools such as pottery, large retouched tools, and grinding stones around the playas, stream edges, and dune fields of Bayan-Dzak suggests that those artifacts are the remains of various activities at task specific locales related to those particularly productive environments. Similar data from Pigeon Spring, in the southern Gobi Desert, suggests that dune regions around springs and playas may have been occupied regularly following the Younger Dryas and before the early Holocene period of increased humidity (Bettinger et al. 2007; Elston et al. 1997). This would support that notion that conditions of the Younger Dryas may have tied foragers to areas where water was more readily available.

Baga Gazaryn Chuluu

Baga Gazaryn Chuluu is a range of rocky hills in the northern Gobi Desert (between 1,400–1,700 m asl). The area has been intensively surveyed, and a pattern of artifact scatters was recorded. These scatters include microblade debris, ceramics, and grinding stones. Occupants made use of the typical cryptocrystalline raw materials of the Gobi Desert for their microblade industries. Based on their geomorphological and archaeological contexts, these chipped-stone artifacts appear to range in time from the end of the late Pleistocene until the early Bronze Age (approximately 3000 cal BP). In general the activity patterns are focused on better watered areas within the hills and the surrounding dry steppes. The position of some sites along dry channels and around dry playa basins suggests an adaptive system that, for some of its history, was developed in wetter than current conditions (Wright et al. 2007).

The dated assemblage reported here is from BGC 1451, and it consists of a scatter of microblade debris, ceramics, and ostrich eggshell that was found on the outwash fan of a small erosion channel. The site had been sealed by colluvium and cut into by the active erosion channel. Stratigraphically, the artifacts are from the first soil formation above the fine-grained loess that underlies much of the soil and surface sediment in the region. In other places at BGC 1451, this loess, and sometimes the first soil, show signs of solifluction suggesting cold conditions after its formation. The chipped-stone assemblage is a typical Gobi Desert, microblade assemblage, with a few retouched bladelets and scrapers. Excavation recovered several dozen, small bladelets and fragments from one small area. In total, this assemblage contains 157 items; the great majority (95.8%) is lithic debitage.

Discussion

The climate in Northeast Asia is mainly determined by the interplay between the northernmost edge of the humid East Asian monsoon regime and the dry air of western Central Asia. The manifestation of the Younger Dryas in the Inner Asian Steppe, Eastern Altai, and the north Gobi Desert is an expression of this relationship following the last glacial. The late Pleistocene to the initial Holocene was a period in which aridity dominated the local climate despite progressive climatic amelioration. As post-glacial increases in precipitation and average temperatures began to transform many highly arid environments into more habitable steppe and desert-steppe, the Younger Dryas temporarily slowed, was interrupted or, in some cases, caused the regression of this process. By the early Holocene, however, much of the arid Northeast Asia had been transformed; steppe and desert-steppe environments were increasingly appealing for hunter-gatherer occupation as Pleistocene dune-fields and small playas or lakes were filled and grasslands expanded. By the end of the early Holocene mosaic steppe vegetation in the southern and northernmost reaches of the region had been transformed into woodlands.

The handful of known, dated, sites in arid, Northeast Asia suggest an adaptive continuity of material culture across the Gobi Desert and surrounding highlands throughout the terminal Pleistocene, Younger Dryas, and early Holocene. However, not enough is known about any one site or area to discuss specific local dynamics. In order to develop a more detailed understanding of subsistence and social organization in the Gobi, Eastern Altai, and Inner Asian steppe, additional sites must be dated, and ancient landscapes must be recovered and documented. The central question that remains to be addressed is how the dynamics of environmental change and dramatic fluctuations in the climate of this region were related to changes in technology, subsistence, and culture throughout the late Pleistocene and early to middle Holocene.

The evidence that we have today suggests a very limited technological impact from the Younger Dryas. It was simply one of several climatic reorientations to which people adapted their existing technologies—microlithic toolkits, ceramics, and ground stone. Furthermore, in as much as the few sites recorded here demonstrate—setting aside the lacunae in the data—regional site distribution, the nature of the landscape and the human ecology of the region during this time suggest that, in an echo of subsistence adaptations that emerged by the end of the Holocene, population mobility would provide a major means of adaptation to shifting environmental conditions.

References

An, Z.
1992 Neolithic Communities in Eastern Parts of Central Asia. In *History of Civilizations of Central Asia, Volume I, The Dawn of Civilization: Earliest Times to 700 B.C.*, edited by A. Dani and V. Masson, pp. 153–168. UNESCO Publishing, Paris.

Berkey, C., and N. Nelson
1926 Geology and Prehistoric Archaeology of the Gobi Desert. *American Museum Novitates* 222:1–16.

Bettinger, R. L., L. Barton, P. J. Richerson, R. Boyd, H. Wang, and W. Choi
2007 The Transition to Agriculture in Northwestern China. In *Late Quaternary Climate Change and Human Adaptation in Arid China*, Developments in Quaternary Science, Vol. 9, edited by D. B. Madsen, F. H. Chen, and X. Gao, pp. 83–101. Developments in Quaternary Science. Elsevier, Amsterdam.

Bettinger, R., R. Elston, and D. Madsen
1994 Prehistoric Settlement Categories and Settlement Systems in the Alashan Desert of Inner Mongolia, PRC. *Journal of Anthropological Archaeology* 13:74–101.

Bleed, P.
2002 Cheap, Regular, and Reliable: Implications of Design Variation in Late Pleistocene Japanese Microblade Technology. In *Thinking Small: Global Perspectives on Microlithization*, Vol. 12, edited by R. Elston and S. Kuhn, pp. 95–102. Archaeological Papers of the American Anthropological Association: American Anthropological Association.

Chard, C.
1974 *Northeast Asia in Prehistory*. University of Wisconsin Press, Madison.

Chen, C., and X. Wang
1989 Upper Paleolithic Microblade Industries in North China and Their Relationships with Northeast Asia and North America. *Arctic Anthropology* 26:127–156.

Chen, F., Z. Yu, M. Yang, E. Ito, S. Wang, D. Madsen, X. Huang, Y. Zhao, T. Sato, H. John, B. Birks, I. Boomeri, J. Chen, C. An, and B. Wünnemann
2008 Holocene Moisture Evolution in Arid Central Asia and its Out-of-phase Relationship with Asian Monsoon History. *Quaternary Science Reviews* 27:351–364.

Cohen, D.
2003 Microblades, Pottery, and the Nature and Chronology of the Palaeolithic-Neolithic Transition in China. *Review of Archaeology* 24:21–36.

Derev'anko, A.
1998 *The Paleolithic of Siberia*. University of Illinois Press, Champaign.

Derevyanko, A., and D. Dorj

1992 Neolithic Tribes in Northern Parts of Central Asia. In *History of Civilizations of Central Asia, Volume I, The Dawn of Civilization: Earliest Times to 700 B.C.*, edited by A. Dani and V. Masson, pp. 169–189. UNESCO Publishing, Paris.

Derevianko, A., S. Gladyshev, T. Nohrina, and J. Olsen

2003 The Mongolian Early Holocene: Excavations at Chikhen Agui Rockshelter in the Gobi Altai. *The Review of Archæology* 24:50–56.

Derevianko, A., J. Olsen, D. Tseveendorj, A. Krivoshapkin, V. Petrin, and P. Brantingham

2000 The Stratified Cave Site of Tsagaan Agui in the Gobi Altai (Mongolia). *Archaeology, Ethnology, and Anthropology of Eurasia* 1:23–36.

Elston, R., and P. Brantingham

2002 Microlithic Technology in Northern Asia: A Risk-minimizing Strategy of the Late Paleolithic and Early Holocene. In *Thinking Small: Global Perspectives on Microlithization*, Vol. 12, edited by R. Elston and S. Kuhn, pp. 103–116. Archaeological Papers of the American Anthropological Association: American Anthropological Association.

Elston, R., X. Chang, D. Madsen, K. Zhong, R. Bettinger, J. Li, P. Brantingham, H. Wang, and J. Yu

1997 New Dates for the North Chinese Mesolithic. *Antiquity* 71:985–993.

Fairservis, W.

1993 *Archaeology of the Southern Gobi of Mongolia*. Carolina Academic Press, Duham.

Feng, Z-D

2001 Gobi Dynamics in the Northern Mongolian Plateau during the Past 20,000+ yr: Preliminary Results. *Quaternary International* 76/77:77–83.

Frink, L., and K. Harry

2008 The Beauty of "Ugly" Eskimo Cooking Pots. *American Antiquity* 73:103–120.

Gábori, M.

1962 Beiträge zur Typologie und Verbreitung der Shabarakh-Kultur. *Archaeologica Polona* 1:159–174.

1963 Gisements et Industries de l'âge de la pièrre en Mongolie. *Acta Archaeologica*: 11–32.

Goldberg, E., M. Grachev, M. Phedorin, I. Kalugin, O. Khlystov, S. Mezentsev, I. Azarova, S. Vorobyeva, T. Zheleznyakova, G. Kulipanov, V. Kondratyev, E. Miginsky, V. Tsukanov, K. Zolotarev, V. Trunova, Y. Kolmogorov, and V. Bobrov

2001 Application of Synchrotron X-ray Fluorescent Analysis to Studies of the Records of Paleoclimates of Eurasia Stored in the Sediments of Lake Baikal and Lake Teletskoye. *Nuclear Instruments and Methods in Physics Research A* 470:388–395.

Goebel, T.

2002 The "Microlithic Adaptation" and Recolonization of Siberia during the Late Upper Pleistocene. In *Thinking Small: Global Perspectives on*

Microlithization, Vol. 12, edited by R. Elston and S. Kuhn, pp. 117–131. Archaeological Papers of the American Anthropological Association: American Anthropological Association.

Grunert, J., F. Lehmkuhl, and M. Walther
2000 Paleoclimatic Evolution of the Uvs Nuur Basin and Adjacent Areas (Western Mongolia). *Quaternary International* 65/66:171–192.

Harrison, S., G. Yu, and P. Tarasov
1996 Late Quaternary Lake-level Record from Northern Eurasia. *Quaternary Research* 45:138–159.

Hayashi, K.
1968 The Fukui Microblade Technology and its Relationships in Northeast Asia and North America. *Arctic Anthropology* 1:128–190.

Herzschuh, U.
2006 Palaeo-moisture Evolution in Monsoonal Central Asia during the Last 50,000 Years. *Quaternary Science Reviews* 25:163–178.

Herzschuh, U., P. Tarasov, B. Wünnemann, and K. Hartmann
2004 Holocene Vegetation and Climate of the Alashan Plateau, NW China, Reconstructed from Pollen Data. *Palaeogeography, Palaeoclimatology, Palaeoecology* 211:1–17.

Horiuchi, K., K. Minoura, K. Hoshino, T. Oda, T. Nakamura, and T. Kawai
2000 Palaeoenvironmental History of Lake Baikal during the Last 23,000 Years. *Palaeogeography, Palaeoclimatology, Palaeoecology* 157:95–108.

Huang, X., F. Chen, Y. Fan, and M. Yang
2007 Dry Late-glacial and Early Holocene Climate in Arid Central Asia Indicated by Lithological and Palynological Evidence from Bosten Lake, China. *Quaternary International* 194:19–27.

Ilyashuk, B., and E. Ilyashuk
2007 Chironomid Record of Late Quaternary Climatic and Environmental Changes from Two Sites in Central Asia (Tuva Republic, Russia)—Local, Regional or Global Causes? *Quaternary Science Reviews* 26:705–731.

Janz, L.
2006 Shabarakh-Usu and the Dune-Dwellers of the Gobi: Explanations for Lithic Assemblage Variability in the Gobi Desert, Mongolia. Master's theses. School of Anthropology, University of Arizona, Tucson.

2012 Chronology of Post-Glacial Settlement in the Gobi Desert and the Neolithization of Arid Mongolia and China. Unpublished Ph.D. dissertation. School of Anthropology, University of Arizona.

Janz, L., R. Elston, and G. Burr
2009 Radiocarbon Evidence for the Holocene Survival of the East Asian Ostrich and Implications for Dating Surface Assemblages in the Gobi Desert. *Journal of Archaeological Science* 36:1982–1989.

Jaubert, J., P. Bertran, M. Fontugne, M. Jarry, S. Lacombe, C. Leroyer, E. Marmet, Y. Taborin, and B. Tsogtbaatar
2004 Le Paleolithique Superieur Ancien de Mongolie: Dorolj 1 (Egiin Gol). Analogies Avec les Donnees de l'Altai et de Siberie. In *Section 6: Le Paléolithique Supérieur/The Upper Palaeolithic. General Sessions and Posters. Acts of the XIVth UISPP Congress, University of Liège, Belgium, 2–8 September 2001. Vol. 1240,* edited by L. Congrès, pp. 225–242. BAR Archaeopress, Oxford.

Komatsu, G., P. Brantingham, J. Olsen, and V. Baker
2001 Paleoshorline Geomorphology of Böön Tsagaan Nuur, Tsagaan Nuur and Orog Nuur: The Valley of Lakes, Mongolia. *Geomorphology* 39:83–98.

Kurochkin, E. N., Y. V. Kuzmin, I.V. Antoshchenko-Olenev, V. I. Zabelin, S.K. Krivonogov, T. I. Nohrina, L.V. Lbova, G. S. Burr, and R. J. Cruz
2009 The Timing of Ostrich Existence in Central Asia: AMS [14]C Age of Eggshell from Mongolia and Southern Siberia (a pilot study). *Nuclear Instruments and Methods in Physics Research Section B: Beam Interactions with Materials and Atoms* 268(7–8):1091–1093.

Kuzmin, Y., and L. Orlova
2000 The Neolithization of Siberia and the Russian Far East: Radiocarbon Evidence. *Antiquity* 74:356–364.

Kuzmin, Y., and I. Shewkomud
2003 The Palaeolithic-Neolithic Transition in the Russian Far East. *The Review of Archæology* 24:37–45.

Lehmkuhl, F., and A. Lang
2001 Geomorphological Investigations and Luminescence Dating in the Southern Part of the Khangay and the Valley of the Gobi Lakes (Central Mongolia). *Journal of Quaternary Science* 16:69–87.

Liu, H., H. Cui, and Y. Huang
2001 Detecting Holocene Movements of the Woodland-steppe Ecotone in Northern China Using Discriminant Analysis. *Journal of Quaternary Science* 16:237–244.

Lu, L.
1998 The Microblade Tradition in China: Regional Chronologies and Significance in the Transition to Neolithic. *Asian Perspectives* 37:84–112.

Madsen, D., L. Jingzen, R. Elston, X. Cheng, R. Bettinger, G. Kan, P. Brantingham, and Z. Kan
1998 The Loess/Paleosol Record and the Nature of the Younger Dryas Climate in Central China. *Geoarchaeology* 13:847–869.

Maringer, J.
1950 Contribution to the Prehistory of Mongolia. In *Reports from the Scientific Expedition to the North-western Provinces of China under the Leadership of Sven Hedin.* Sino-Swedish Expedition Publication 34(7), Tryckeri and Thule, Stockholm.

Maringer, J.
1963 Mongolia before the Mongols. *Arctic Anthropology* 1:75–85.

Nelson, N.
1926 The Dune Dwellers of the Gobi. *Natural History* 222:246–251.

Okladnikov, A.
1962 Novoe v Izuchenii Drevneyshikh kul'tur Mongolii (po rabotam 1960 g.). *Sovetskaya Etnografiya* 1:83–90.

1986 *Paleolit Mongolii*. Izdatelstvo "NAUKA" Sibirskogo Otdeleniya, Novosibirsk.

1990 Inner Asia at the Dawn of History. In *The Cambridge History of Early Inner Asia*, edited by D. Sinor, pp. 41–96. Cambridge University Press, Cambridge.

Prokopenko, A., D. Williams, E. Karabanov, and G. Khursevich
1999 Response of Lake Baikal Ecosystem to Climate Forcing and pCO_2 Change over the Last Glacial/Interglacial Transition. *Earth and Planetary Science Letters* 172:239–253.

Rhodes, T., F. Gasse, L. Ruifen, J. Fontes, W. Keqin, P. Bertrand, E. Gibert, F. Mélières, P. Tucholka, W. Zhixiang, and C. Zhi-Yuan
1996 A Late Pleistocene-Holocene Lacustrine Record from Lake Manas, Zunggar (Northern Xinjiang, Western China). *Palaeogeography, Palaeoclimatology, Palaeoecology* 120:105–121.

Tang, C., and P. Gai
1986 Upper Paleolithic Cultural Traditions in North China. *Advances in World Archaeology* 5:339–364.

Tsybiktarov, A.
2002 Eastern Central Asia at the Dawn of the Bronze Age: Issues in Ethno-cultural History of Mongolia and the Southern Trans-Baikal Region in the Late Third-early Second Millennium BC. *Archaeology, Ethnology, and Anthropology of Eurasia* 3:107–123.

Weber, A.
1995 Neolithic and Early Bronze Age of the Lake Baikal Region: A Review of Recent Research. *Journal of World Prehistory* 9:99–165.

Wright, J.
2006 The Adoption of Pastoralism Northeast Asia: Monumental Transformation in the Egiin Gol Valley, Mongolia. Unpublished Ph.D. dissertation, Harvard University.

Wright, J., W. Honeychurch, and C. Amartuvshin
2007 Initial Findings of the Baga Gazaryn Chuluu Archaeological Survey (2003–2006). *Antiquity* 81(313): Project Gallery.

Wu, X., and C. Zhao
2003 Chronology of the Transition from Palaeolithic to Neolithic in China. *The Review of Archæology* 24:15–20.

Yang, X., K. Rost, F. Lehmkuhl, Z. Zhenda, and J. Dodson
    2004 The Evolution of Dry Lands in Northern China and in the Republic of Mongolia since the Last Glacial Maximum. *Quaternary International* 118–119:69–85.
Zheng, S.
    2000 The Epipaleolithic in China. *Journal of East Asian Archaeology* 2:51–66.
Zhou, W., M. Head, Z. An, P. Deckker, Z. Liu, X. Liu, X. Lu, D. Donahue, A. Jull, and J. Beck
    2001 Terrestrial Evidence for a Spatial Structure of Tropical-polar Interconnections during the Younger Dryas Episode. *Earth and Planetary Science Letters* 191:231–239.

11

Looking for the Younger Dryas

David J. Meltzer and Ofer Bar-Yosef

The Younger Dryas has been known since the mid-twentieth century as a distinctive climatic phenomenon of Late Glacial Europe; but by the 1990s, it had gone global. Evidence across the northern hemisphere, along with a few hints from the southern hemisphere, seemed to indicate this was a widespread, abrupt, and possibly quite severe cold snap that for a geologically brief period dating between approximately 11,000 and 10,000 years ago (12,900–11,700 calendar years before present [Steffensen et al. 2008]), which reversed the trend of postglacial warming (e.g., Alley 2007).

It is not uncommon in archaeology for distinctive climatic episodes such as this one to be marshaled into service to help explain concurrent cultural changes and patterns (see, for example, the literature surrounding the Altithermal/mid-Holocene Climatic Optimum [Meltzer 1999]). Thus, and not surprisingly, soon after the extent and apparent severity of the Younger Dryas became known, it was introduced into archaeological discussions of terminal Pleistocene human adaptations (e.g., Haynes 1991). Its ostensibly, severely cold climate was variously invoked to explain "the demise of the Clovis way of life, the emergence of subregional cultural traditions, [and] the extinction of the megafauna" in North America (Anderson and Faught 2000:512). It has also been considered to have had an influence on migration patterns in northern

Hunter-Gatherer Behavior: Human Response during The Younger Dryas, edited by Metin I. Eren, 249–268. © Left Coast Press. All rights reserved.

Eurasia (Dolukhanov 1997) and to have helped explain cultural changes leading to the archaeologically distinctive Late Natufian changes of settlement pattern of the Levant (Bar-Yosef 1998, 2010)—among other cultural phenomena.

Efforts to link climate change and culture change are hardly unreasonable, although the initial enthusiasm for a causal relationship often outpaces the empirical evidence linking the two. Hence, we spot what we believe are clear-cut archaeological consequences of climatic and attendant ecological changes, but on closer examination of the evidence—both archaeological and environmental—we ultimately (and perhaps even inevitably) come to realize that the supposed links between the climatic mechanism and the human response(s) are not as straightforward as they first appeared (see also Dillehay, this volume[1]).

We are now in that corrective phase in regard to the Younger Dryas, and not just because the links between climate and culture are less apparent, but also because our understanding of the Younger Dryas period itself has become more nuanced. Over the last two decades, there has been considerable research into the geographic extent, timing and rapidity, and severity and seasonality of climate changes during this period, as well as how those changes played out in atmospheric, oceanic, and terrestrial environments, via greenhouse gases (including carbon dioxide and methane), and the effects of those on radiocarbon dating during this period (summarized in Alley 2007; Meltzer and Holliday 2010). It is now evident that the Younger Dryas, or more properly, the Younger Dryas Chronozone (YDC) is a chronostratigraphic unit that does not coincide everywhere with a particular climatic or ecological signal; in fact, climate and environment during the YDC is proving to be variable across space and through time.

Cooling during the YDC was dominantly a northern hemispheric phenomenon, with severely cold conditions limited to localized, high-latitude regions. Yet even for areas that experienced severe cold during the YDC, this was not a "dramatic return to near glacial conditions" (cf. Rick and Erlandson, this volume) of the Last Glacial Maximum (LGM). By the YDC, the chilling orographic and thermal effects of the continental ice sheets were much diminished; northern hemisphere insolation and atmospheric CO_2 levels had climbed to near interglacial levels (and YDC summer insolation was higher in the mid to high latitudes than at any time over the preceding 70,000 years [data from Berger and Loutre 1991]); and, seasonality was greatly amplified, compared to the LGM or even later Holocene times. This created conditions that were essentially without a modern equivalent (Cole and Arundel 2005; Denton et al. 2005; Dyke 2004; Monnin et al. 2001; Shuman et al. 2002).

In North America, for example, the climate during the YDC was cool and wet in some places, cool and dry in others, and in a few spots warm and wet; no area, as yet, appears to have been warm and dry (see geographic summary in Meltzer and Holliday 2010: Figure 1; Grimm et al. 2006; Shuman et al. 2002; Yu and Wright 2001). And in some areas it was wet early on then became drier; in other areas the reverse is in evidence (Anderson et al. 2002; Holliday 2000; Huckleberry 2001; Mann and Meltzer 2007; Polyak et al. 2004; Quade et al. 1998; Yu and Wright 2001; cf. Haynes 2008).

Furthermore, it now appears that the onset of YDC cooling and other changes were gradual, rather than abrupt as was previously supposed. Moreover, there was necessarily a temporal lag between any changes in climate, and subsequent changes in vegetation, and then in turn changes in local faunas. Moreover, plant and animal responses to YDC climates were species-specific, highly individualistic, and played out at different rates, at different times and places (Eren 2009; see also Cannon 2004; FAUNMAP 1996; Grimm and Jacobson 2004). Gradual change on a time scale of centuries may not have been visible to human populations on the ground at that time, even over several generations. Only at the close of this episode, there apparently was a rapid, "ultra-sharp" stepped change in climate (Broecker et al. 2010:1079).

Finally, although the uniqueness of this episode in the geological record has long been stressed—Broecker had described it as "a freak event rather than . . . something common to each glacial termination" (Broecker 2006a:1147)—he and colleagues now argue that YDC climate changes may not have been all that unusual. As they put it, "when viewed in the context of the last four terminations, cold reversals equivalent to the YD seem to be integral parts of global switches from glacial to interglacial climate" (Broecker et al. 2010:1080). Their conclusion is in large part driven by the apparent gradualness of the onset of YDC climate changes, along with an inability to find the geological evidence demanded by the long-hypothesized catastrophic mechanism behind those changes. For example, a supposed sudden release of freshwater from glacial Lake Agassiz eastward via the St. Lawrence seaway into the North Atlantic where, cooling or perhaps even freezing in winter, was hypothesized to have shut down meridional overturning circulation, preventing the movement of warm Gulf Stream water north, and thereby bringing cold and dry climates to northern regions (Alley 2007; Broecker et al. 1989).[2] Had the proposed eastward drainage of Lake Agassiz's occurred, it ought to have carved an outlet channel or scattered substantial debris in what must have been an outflow of considerable magnitude; yet no such evidence has been found (Broecker 2006a, 2006b; Fisher et al. 2006, 2008; Lowell et al. 2005;

Teller et al. 2005). The debate over that evidence (or lack thereof) is ongoing (e.g., Carlson et al. 2007, 2009; Lowell et al. 2009; see also Murton et al. 2010). But even if an outlet channel and accompanying flood debris is found, oceanographers (e.g., Wunsch 2010) are highly skeptical that a release of freshwater into the North Atlantic would have had the profound climatic effects that have been proposed.

In any case, and in regard to YDC climate and climate change, the devil is in the details; and, recent overviews of pollen, chronomid, isotope, ice core, dust and sediment, and other climate proxies have shown that within those broad brush strokes, the climate (temperature, precipitation, seasonality) during the YDC likely varied considerably, even on a sub-continental and regional scale (Meltzer and Holliday 2010; Yi and Saito 2004; cf. Haynes 2008) as several of the papers in this volume attest (e.g., Dillehay, Eren, Jochim, Makarewicz).

So what does this mean for those of us who are understandably curious about the effects of climate change on Late Glacial human populations? We certainly don't need to involve ourselves in the debate among Quaternary scientists over the cause and consequences of YDC climate changes. Few of our archaeological records have data that bear on those issues, and one must use caution in treating floral or faunal remains from archaeological sites as proxies of climate or environment; people are selective in what they exploit on a landscape (Dillehay, this volume), and there are often scale mismatches in the records.

What we can do is ask whether the changes in climate and environment during the YDC exhibited anything "out of the ordinary" from the point of view of human adaptations, especially for mobile hunter-gatherers, whose movements into different habitats and patches across space may have presented greater adaptive challenges than what the YDC produced over time. We know, of course, that humans adapt to environments and that cultures change over time. But in order to forge viable links between specific climatic and cultural changes, we cannot simply invoke global climate patterns to explain particular cultural changes or patterns. We must carefully assess at a scale-appropriate level the ecological and climatic conditions specific to a place and time that *could* have had a real-time impact on contemporary groups if climatic changes were happening fast enough that they would have been detectable to humans over the course of just several generations, such that grandparents would have noticed a difference they could tell their grandchildren. Or perhaps that such changes led to longer-term cultural adjustments that ultimately prompted a shift in adaptation.

Further, we must explain why any identified changes *would* have had an impact on human groups—here careful attention to the nature of contemporary human adaptations is obviously relevant. And, of course, we cannot assume that having identified climatic or environmental patterns (or changes) that occurred during the YDC, necessarily had *any* bearing at all on contemporary human populations. After all, and as has been noted elsewhere, cultural change can occur independent of climate change, and climate change need not trigger cultural change (Meltzer and Holliday 2010). In brief, climate changes of the YDC should be considered innocent of causing cultural change until such time as proven guilty.

The papers in this volume largely follow this precept (see also the papers from a recent symposium on human adaptations during the YDC [Straus and Goebel 2011]); the pendulum of enthusiasm for the YDC as a cause of cultural change having now swung toward a more circumspect assessment of links between climate and culture(s). This yields not only a much more sophisticated understanding of the changes during this period, it also helps identify where we need to redirect our thinking to other causal factors that might also be in play.

This volume's regional coverage appropriately extends from the Americas, both North (LaBelle, Rick, and Erlandson) and South (Borrero, Dillehay), to Europe (Jochim, Blockley, and Gamble), and with a few areas of western (Makarewicz) and northeastern Asia (Wright and Janz) put in for good measure. As such, the papers provide useful overviews of climatic conditions and cultures in very different settings. Each deals directly or indirectly with a series of questions that are appropriately asked in any attempt to understand the possible impact of YDC climatic and environmental changes on contemporary human populations. Namely, is there evidence in that region of severe or rapidly changing climatic or environmental conditions specifically assignable to the YDC? Were there changes in technology, subsistence, or settlement patterns and land use during the YDC? And, finally, are those climatic and environmental changes occurring at a relevant temporal and spatial scale? We organize our discussion by addressing, briefly, each of these questions, and then summarizing what we see as some of the salient lessons drawn from this volume.

In regard to YDC climatic conditions, it is clear that much of the Americas' climatic changes during the YDC were relatively insignificant (though perhaps not so for far northern North America, as Graf and Bigelow [2011] elsewhere suggest). This was especially the case in South America, where "the YD was not a widespread climatic event" (Dillehay), or at best "would have been of minor significance" (Borrero). In North America, even in northern latitudes, Eren's (2009) analysis of the pollen record indicates that in the lower Great Lakes, biotic change over the course of the YDC was gradual, spatially variable, and relatively insignificant in real time. Others looking at the adjacent New England-maritimes region reach a somewhat different conclusion (e.g., Lothrop et al. 2011); however, this may reflect the use of different proxy indicators, and differences that would have emerged in regions progressively "downstream" from the Atlantic maritimes region.

Likewise, in the steppe region of northern Asia, Wright and Janz highlight the lack of change in YDC climate. Although, they note there was a general cooling and drying trend through the YDC (a function of the weakening of the Asian monsoon, see Denton et al. 2010), it did not get cold. Even though precipitation declined during this span, its impact on people may have been relatively inconsequential in areas where continued deglaciation kept lake levels relatively high. But most importantly, perhaps, they observe that this was already a region of widespread aridity during the late Pleistocene, so the conditions of the YDC may not have been noticeably worse than what had come before.

Younger Dryas climates appear to have been somewhat more complicated in Europe and the Middle East. In the Levant, Makarewicz highlights the "spatially and chronologically heterogeneous expression of the Younger Dryas," where some settings experienced more arid conditions and greater shifts in vegetation than others. Increasing aridity was more pronounced in the already, semiarid/steppic, eastern and southern Levant, but was less consequential in Levant's western region. Jochim reports that in Europe, cooling was more pronounced in northern latitudes, which resulted in the southward retreat of forest and woodlands and concomitant expansion of tundra in northern Europe. However, cooler conditions were not sufficiently widespread as to have had an impact in central and southern Europe where, despite somewhat cooler temperatures, vegetation communities "were not drastically disrupted." Rather, over time in those regions, forests became more open, resulting in gradually changing habitats and prey abundance (also Blockley and Gamble).

Only for far northeastern Europe do Blockley and Gamble assert changes during the YDC were of sufficient severity to be "potentially highly disruptive." They base that conclusion primarily on the ice-core records of Greenland (which is not inappropriate, given the proximity of the region to Greenland), local proxies (beetles), and modeled temperature changes. They make the important observation that YDC climate changes may not have been synchronous across the region, though leave unanswered the question of whether such changes were also of comparable *severity* across the region.

One important point emphasized in virtually all these chapters is that climates and environments of the YDC were not significantly different from the climatic and environmental conditions to which hunter-gatherers on the contemporary landscape would have already been adapted (e.g., Borrero, Dillehay; see also Eren 2009). Coastal areas were apparently something of an exception to this trend, as Rick and Erlandson indicate that cooling sea surface temperatures had an obvious impact on the marine fauna. Yet, as observed elsewhere (Reeder et al. 2011), such changes were perhaps not as important a factor as the unrelated but ongoing major changes in shoreline position and coastal habitats (see also Fedje et al. 2011).

As to what cultural responses may have been occurring in real-time response to YDC changes, few of the chapters report significant technological change that might have been triggered by changing YDC conditions. As Wright and Janz observe, the microblade and microcore technology of earlier late Pleistocene times continues without interruption through the YDC and even into the Holocene in Mongolia and north China (Elston et al. 2011; Shizitan Archaeological Team 2010). A similar lack of technological change is apparent in other regions (Borrero, Dillehay). Borrero, in fact, makes the telling observation that not only is there little apparent technological change, there is "nothing in the archaeological record [that] indicates any sort of specific adaptation to cold." Namely, no evidence of bone technology for making clothing, limited evidence for shelter, no use of bone as fuel, no evidence of intensive use of faunal remains, and "no specialization in the tool kit" (Borrero).

There *is* technological change in the Great Lakes and New England region during the YDC, but the change that occurs is relatively insignificant, namely an adjustment in hafting technology, from fluted to nonfluted, projectile points (Eren 2009; Lothrop et al. 2011; Newby et al. 2005). However, Eren rightly wonders why "technologically flexible, highly mobile late Pleistocene foragers could not have hunted moose or deer with fluted points (or caribou with nonfluted points)," and raises the intriguing—though as yet untested—hypothesis that the change could simply reflect cultural drift rather than an adaptive response (cf. Newby et al. 2005; see also Lothrop et al. 2011; Meltzer 2009). That hypothesis warrants further investigation, and it may likewise bear on appearance of new projectile point styles on the Great Plains in YDC times, as reported by LaBelle, or the contemporaneous Fishtail and Paijan forms seen in Andean South America (which as Dillehay observes cannot be a result of their function or environmental conditions, since both were used in similar settings).

Whether one can take the appearance of those new styles a step further and suggest, as LaBelle does, that this indicates an "increasing definition of the group identity, first beginning during the Younger Dryas" is unclear, as is the question of whether the onset of the YDC was in any way responsible. But LaBelle appropriately steps back from making any causal connection, noting that a concomitant increase in relative size of the human populations may be a more likely cause. This is an issue Dillehay explores as well; however, the claim has recently been made that there was a decline in human populations at the onset of the YDC (Anderson et al. 2011), which is intended to bolster the hypothesis that there was an extraterrestrial impact which decimated human populations. There are reasons to be suspicious of that claim, as Holliday and Meltzer (2010) discuss.

The lack of technological change signals that a significant change in subsistence during YDC would not be expected, and the papers in this volume indicate that is the case as well. Moreover, common to several of the regions discussed here are two observations, which were likely related: the changes in subsistence during this period are subtle, and secondly, they only take place gradually over time. Thus, the nature of the prey species may have remained relatively constant over time in various regions of Europe and Asia (Blockley and Gamble, Jochim, Makarewicz), but as Jochim put it in regard to Europe, "What *was* new was the gradually changing habitat in which these prey were found, the slowly differing relative proportions of each, and the changing behavior of each in the new landscape" (see also LaBelle). What this suggests is that the *cumulative* changes in climate and environment over the course of the YDC created conditions that at the end of the YDC were very different from those at the beginning, and it is to those that humans ultimately adapted (Meltzer and Holliday 2010). That frames the question of whether humans had to respond to YDC climatic changes in a very different way (i.e., not the real-time response that was traditionally envisioned).

Even if there was neither significant technological or subsistence change taking place in response to subtle changes in local climatic and environmental conditions, there remains the possibility that human responses played out in terms of settlement patterns and land use. Mobile hunter-gatherers (as most groups around the globe were during the YDC), often respond to even subtle perturbations by dispersing to other habitats, or changing the manner in which they distributed themselves seasonally or annually on the landscape (Jochim, Wright, and Janz). To this point, Makarewicz suggests that the "onset of the Younger Dryas reconfigured the Natufian culture from a collection of largely sedentary hunter-gatherers concentrated primarily within the rich Mediterranean core area to a more mobile society that expanded their overall range to include a variety of ecological zones." But whether those changes were a direct result of YDC changes is unclear.

Both Borrero and Dillehay see settlement changes in South America during the YDC, notably in patterns of discontinuous landscape use, depositional gaps in the record, and/or decreases in mobility. Yet, neither argues climate was demonstrably (or even likely) the cause of those changes. Moreover, Borrero makes the important observation that even if conditions were colder in South America at that time (which he does not think is the case), that might have been helpful in facilitating movement over frozen rivers that might not have been as easy to traverse in warmer times. Obviously, the "benefits" of cooler climates will vary depending on the setting. As LaBelle observes, cooling in high-elevation settings might have rendered mountain routes impassable, particularly in areas (primarily in the more northern reaches of the Rockies), where glacial ice might have readvanced.

Indeed, LaBelle suggests that the presence of Folsom houses, at sites such as Agate Basin (Frison 1982), Barger Gulch (Surovell and Waguespack 2007), and Mountaineer (Stiger 2006) indicates "an adaptation to colder Younger Dryas settings or to investment in certain locales." Perhaps, but rather than as a response to colder, YDC conditions, they may simply reflect winter occupations in those settings, which even today experience cold, harsh winters.

It is harsher YDC winters that Blockley and Gamble suggest are behind a significant settlement-related change during the YDC: a downturn in the number of burials. They suggest as one possible explanation that this scarcity was due to a "loss of feeling for land which is not frequently exploited." It is an interesting, albeit untestable hypothesis, but also one seemingly at odds with their observation that this ostensibly "marginal landscape" for the living and their dead nonetheless shows evidence of continuity in other cultural indicators (notably artifacts). Another, more testable alternative is their suggestion that the dearth of YDC burials is due to the difficulty of reaching caves in cold YDC climates owing to ice, or the struggle to bury a body in frozen ground. Of course, it is doubtful such problems would have been faced year-round, for it is always important to bear in mind that for every YDC winter, there was a YDC summer. And there is evidence to indicate that in the northern latitudes, YDC winters were quite severe, but not YDC summers. Denton et al. (2005) put YDC winter temperatures in Greenland at 24° C-cooler than present, and YDC summer temperatures a relatively balmier 5–6° C-colder than present, which is the rough equivalent of today's southern Scandinavian summers. The challenging prospect of digging a grave in frozen ground could have easily been circumvented by delaying the burial, a hypothesis that could be tested from evidence in the interment itself.

Ultimately, none of the authors in this volume see strong links between time-specific aspects of YDC climate, climate change, and human responses. But that comes as little surprise. Any YDC changes played out over decades and centuries. Humans respond to the weather over days, weeks, and months. Dillehay puts it well when he observes that the

> long-time frame of most climatic changes [which includes those of the YDC] may not be directly relevant . . . because they occurred so slowly compared to the likely more rapid rate at which humans were adapting through sociocultural mechanisms. However, short-term, climatic changes (e.g., excessive drought, El Nino flooding) may have been relevant but are currently difficult to identify and correlate in local archaeological and paleoecological records.

To amplify Dillehay's point, environments by the end of the YDC were in many places very different than they had been at the outset, and humans ultimately had to adjust to those changes: but is a cumulative adaptation over forty generations a response to the YDC? Or is it just humans doing what they do? Unless YDC changes were truly abrupt, severe, and presented conditions and adaptive challenges well outside the range that these groups had to cope with previously, which they apparently were not for much of the earth's inhabited regions, it is unlikely that responses to it were likewise abrupt or significant.

Moreover, as several of the volume's authors (e.g., Eren, Jochim, Wright, and Janz) emphasize, Old World Paleolithic and New World Paleoindian groups were highly mobile, had developed adaptive strategies to meet multiple contingencies, had yet to experience relatively *stable* climates or environments (and in some places were occupying already-harsh settings [Borrero, Wright, and Janz]), and were neither fully settled in nor dependent on particular resources in specific environments. Adapting to changing environmental conditions was nothing new to them. As Borrero puts it, these groups "had a veritable library of tactics and strategies for survival under a variety of environments. . . . And [they] were probably prepared with a flexible suite of technological and subsistence strategies to deal with climatic instability." In effect, human groups on the YDC landscape were essentially preadapted to coping with changing and even harsh, cold environments (Borrero, Eren, Wright, and Janz).

Even if little happened at the outset, or even through most of the YDC, significant changes did occur toward the end of the YDC in certain regions, such as the Zana valley (Dillehay) and the Levant (Makarewicz). In those settings, groups were moving into cultivation and agriculture by terminal YDC times, and certainly by the early Holocene. The YDC provided a context for those changes, though it was not necessarily the cause. For also apparent in the archaeological record through the terminal Pleistocene, more broadly, were long-term changes in human population densities. By terminal Pleistocene times, some areas, particularly in the Old World, had in both absolute and relative terms a greater number of people on the landscape. That was not true across much of contemporary Asia and the Americas (save, of course, in more ecologically restrictive settings) where human population numbers likely remained relatively low, and foragers continued to have access to large amounts of uninhabited territory.

Such differences in population parameters establish various "pre-existing" conditions, which implies that the *cumulative* consequences of a millennium of climatic and environmental change could ultimately have had very different and more significant consequences. In much of the New World and Asia, the YDC was hardly noticed, as people had the option of moving—and would continue to have that option—well into the Holocene (Borrero, Eren). In other parts of the New and Old Worlds, rising population densities increasingly restricted mobility, led to fewer adaptive options, which in turn led to changes in subsistence and settlement strategies. For example, the appearance of systematic cultivation in the Levant in PPNA times, which must have developed during the final Natufian. The change in subsistence strategy and settlement pattern occurred in the Levant, an ecological mosaic bordered by the Taurus mountains in the north, the Syro-Arabian deserts in the east, the Mediterranean in the west and the Sinai arid, peninsula in the south. The ameliorated climatic conditions following the LGM led to population increase that caused foragers to spread across the entire Levant. Under such circumstances, even short-term fluctuations of annual precipitation depleted certain habitats and required either increasing mobility across the land or sedentism in well-watered, rich environments, to secure resources for local populations. Cultivation of wild annuals is no more than controlled intensification or "Low Level Food Production" (Smith 2001). It is an economic, risk-minimization approach that could have been adopted by only a portion of the total Levantine population. Once successful, cultivation of cereals with the addition of legumes, accompanied by gathering and hunting, population growth would inevitably result in what is now called "the Neolithic Demographic Transition" (e.g., Bouqeut-Appel and Bar-Yosef 2008).

To echo a statement made elsewhere (Straus and Goebel 2011), the Younger Dryas was not a catastrophe for hunter-gatherers. Had groups at the time been less mobile and more tightly tied to their particular habitats, conditions during this time might have presented more of an adaptive challenge (Straus and Goebel 2011). But then it might not have, as several of the salient points that emerge from this volume make clear.

1. The YDC climatic conditions and changes were not globally synchronous or severe; the stereotype of an abrupt return to harsh and glacially cold conditions is just that—a stereotype. Instead, climatic and environmental changes and conditions during the YDC were quite variable, playing out in different ways in different places and times. Those changes were subtle in many areas, nonexistent in others (notably the southern hemisphere). And there is evidence to indicate that in some areas, YDC conditions were better rather than worse than those that occurred before—or after (Fedje et al. 2011; Goebel et al. 2011).

2. Likewise, there were often only subtle changes (or none at all) that took place in the archaeological record in many regions during the YDC; *continuity* is more apparent in the archaeological record than is change. And where changes occurred, there is little to indicate they were necessarily caused by or were a consequence of YDC climatic variation. Such changes may simply be coincidental, a consequence of the fact that cultures change regardless of climatic triggers. It is an open question as to how much more significant those changes would have been, had this "experiment" played out at a time when agriculturalists were widespread.

3. Because there is considerable variability both in terms of YDC, climatic and environmental conditions and potential (or actual) human responses, in order to fully address the question of the impact of the Younger Dryas on humans, we must refrain from drawing our own stereotypes. Instead, we must investigate the archaeology of this time period on a regional basis across the globe.

4. That will require considerably finer-scale, paleoenvironmental and archaeological data than we now possess. Amassing those records will be a challenge, because, as Makarewicz observes, the resources on which humans depend respond to "both broad changes in regional climate and fluctuations in local environmental conditions at multiple timescales," and which as Dillehay notes, we are attempting to link to an archaeological record that has a "discontinuous nature of archaeological time and space gaps in both local and regional records." And once

those records have been properly synced in time and space, we must then determine whether the archaeological elements "are associated with social changes or short-term climatic change and thus possible shifts in local resource structures" (Dillehay).

5. The cumulative changes that took place over the course of the YDC ultimately set the environmental stage for what came afterward. Yet, in that sense, the YDC is not so much cause as it is context, and to speak of human responses to YDC changes or conditions likely gives more credit to this particular interval of global climate change than it warrants. Other factors, natural and cultural, were also in play in terminal, Pleistocene times (such as constraints in terms of geography and increasing human population density), and are likely no less significant in helping us understand human adaptations during this time period. Moreover, the YDC was but one phase in a series of "profound environmental modifications" that were taking place in post-LGM times as the world warmed (as Dillehay rightly notes).

6. There is, however, one element of the YDC that does have a profound impact, at least on *our* efforts as archaeologists to understand potential human responses to changes and conditions during this period. It is not once discussed at length in this volume, and hence warrants brief mention here. During the YDC, there were rapid changes in amounts of atmospheric radiocarbon (Hua et al. 2009), which complicates efforts to date samples from this span, as well as calibrate the resulting ages (Meltzer and Holliday 2010). Even if we can overcome the dearth of radiocarbon dates seen in many of these regions and sites, efforts to pin down the timing of cultural changes and their possible cause(s) will require a far more reliable understanding of changes during this period, and a better radiocarbon calibration than now exists.

Notes

1. Henceforth, citations without an accompanying year refer to papers in this volume.
2. The more recent claim that the Younger Dryas climatic changes had an extraterrestrial cause (Firestone et al. 2007) has so far failed every empirical test; see the summary in Pinter et al. 2011 (also Haynes et al. 2010; Paquay et al. 2009; Surovell et al. 2009).

References

Alley, R.

2007 Wally was Right: Predictive Ability of the North Atlantic "Conveyor Belt" Hypothesis for Abrupt Climate Change. *Annual Review of Earth and Planetary Sciences* 35:241–272.

Anderson, D., and M. Faught

2000 Paleoindian Artifact Distribution: Evidence and Implications. *Antiquity* 74:507–513.

Anderson, D., A. Goodyear, J. Kennett, and A. West

2011 Multiple Lines of Evidence for Possible Human Population Decline/ Settlement Reorganization during the Early Younger Dryas. *Quaternary International* 242:570–583.

Anderson, R., B. Allen, and K. Menking

2002 Geomorphic Expression of Abrupt Climate Change in Southwestern North America at the Glacial Termination. *Quaternary Research* 57:371–381.

Bar-Yosef, O.

1998 The Natufian Culture in the Levant, Threshold to the Origins of Agriculture. *Evolutionary Anthropology* 6:159–177.

2010 Farming, Herding, and the Transformation of Human Landscapes in Southwestern Asia. In *Handbook of Landscape Archaeology*, edited by B. David and J. Thomas, pp. 315–327. Left Coast Press, Walnut Creek.

Berger, A., and M. Loutre

1991 Insolation Values for the Climate of the Last 10 Million Years. *Quaternary Science Reviews* 10:297–317.

Bouquet-Appel, J., and O. Bar-Yosef

2008 *The Neolithic Demographic Transition and its Consequences.* Springer, New York.

Broecker, W.

2006a Was the Younger Dryas Triggered by a Flood? *Science* 312:1146–1148.

2006b Abrupt Climate Change Revisited. *Global and Planetary Change* 54:211–215.

Broecker, W., G. Denton, R. Edwards, H. Cheng, R. Alley, and A. Putnam

2010 Putting the Younger Dryas Cold Event into Context. *Quaternary Science Reviews* 29:1078–1081.

Broecker, W., J. Kennett, B. Flower, J. Teller, S. Trumbore, G. Bonani, and W. Wolfli

1989 Routing of Meltwater from the Laurentide Ice Sheet during the Young Dryas Cold Episode. *Nature* 341:318–323.

Cannon, M.

2004 Geographic Variability in North American Mammal Community Richness during the Terminal Pleistocene. *Quaternary Science Reviews* 23:1099–1123.

Carlson, A., P. Clark, B. Haley, G. Klinkhammer, K. Simmons, E. Brook, and K. Meissner

2007 Geochemical Proxies of North American Freshwater Routing during the Younger Dryas Cold Event. *Proceedings of the National Academy of Sciences* 104:6556–6561.

Carlson, A., P. Clark, and S. Hostetler

2009 Comment: Radiocarbon Deglaciation Chronology of the Thunder Bay, Ontario Area and Implications for Ice Sheet Retreat Patterns. *Quaternary Science Reviews* 28:2546–2547.

Cole, K., and S. Arundel

2005 Carbon Isotopes from Fossil Packrat Pellets and Elevational Movements of Utah Agave Plants Reveal the Younger Dryas Cold Period in Grand Canyon, Arizona. *Geology* 33:713–716.

Denton, G., R. Alley, G. Comer, and W. Broecker

2005 The Role of Seasonality in Abrupt Climate Change. *Quaternary Science Reviews* 24:1159–1182.

Denton, G., R. Anderson, J. Toggweiler, R. Edwards, J. Schaefer, and A. Putnam

2010 The Last Glacial Termination. *Science* 328:1652–1656.

Dolukhanov, P.

1997 The Pleistocene-Holocene Transition in Northern Eurasia: Environmental Changes and Human Adaptations. *Quaternary International* 41–42:181–191.

Dyke, A.

2004 An Outline of North American Deglaciation with Emphasis on Central and Northern Canada. In *Quaternary Glaciations—Extent and Chronology Developments in Quaternary Science*, Vol 2b, edited by J. Ehlers and P. Gibbard, pp. 373–424. Elsevier, Amsterdam.

Elston, R., G. Dong, and D. Zhang

2011 Late Pleistocene Intensification Technologies in Northern China. *Quaternary International* 242:401–415.

Eren, M.

1996 Spatial Response of Mammals to Late Quaternary Environmental Fluctuations. *Science* 272:1601–1606.

2009 Paleoindian Stability during the Younger Dryas in the North American Lower Great Lakes. In *Transitions in Prehistory: Papers in Honor of Ofer Bar-Yosef*, edited by J. Shea and D. Lieberman, pp. 389–422. American School of Prehistoric Research Press and Oxbow Books, Oxford. FAUNMAP working group

FAUNMAP Working Group

1996 Spatial Response of Mammals to Late Quaternary Environmental Fluctuations. *Science* 272:1601–1606.

Fedje, D., Q. Mackie, T. Lacourse, and D. McLaren

2011 Younger Dryas Environments and Archaeology on the Northwest Coast of North America. *Quaternary International* 242:452–462.

Firestone, R., A. West, J. Kennett, L. Becker, T. Bunch, Z. Revay, P. Schultz, T. Belgya, D. Kennett, J. Erlandson, O. Dickerson, A. Goodyear, R. Harris, G. Howard, J. Kloosterman, P. Lechler, P. Mayewski, J. Montgomery, R. Poreda, T. Darrah, S. Que Hee, A. Smith, A. Stich, W. Topping, J. Wittke, and W. Wolbach

2007 Evidence for an Extraterrestrial Impact 12,900 Years Ago that Contributed to the Megafaunal Extinctions and the Younger Dryas Cooling. *Proceedings of the National Academy of Sciences* 104:16016–16021.

Fisher, T., T. Lowell, and H. Loope

2006 Comment on "Alternative Routing of Lake Agassiz Overflow during the Younger Dryas: Dew Dates, Paleotopography, and a Re-evaluation" by Teller et al. (2005). *Quaternary Science Reviews* 25:1137–1141.

Fisher, T., C. Yansa, T. Lowell, K. Lepper, I. Hajdas, and A. Ashworth

2008 The Chronology, Climate, and Confusion of the Moorhead Phase of Glacial Lake Agassiz: New Results from the Ojata Beach, North Dakota, USA. *Quaternary Science Reviews* 27:1124–1135.

Frison, G.

1982 *The Agate Basin Site.* Academic Press, New York.

Goebel, T., B. Hockett, K. Adams, D. Rhode, and K. Graf

2011 Climate, Environment, and Humans in North America's Great Basin during the Younger Dryas, 12,900–11,600 Calendar Years Ago. *Quaternary International* 242:479–501.

Graf, K., and N. Bigelow

2011 Human Response to Climate during the Younger Dryas Chronozone in Central Alaska. *Quaternary International* 242:434–451.

Grimm, E., and G. Jacobson

2004 Late Quaternary Vegetation History of the Eastern United States. In *The Quaternary Period in the United States,* edited by A. Gillespie, S. Porter, and B. Atwater, pp. 381–402. Elsevier Science, New York.

Grimm, E., W. Watts, G. Jacobson, B. Hansen, H. Almquist, and A. Dieffenbacher- Krall

2006 Evidence for Warm Wet Heinrich Events in Florida. *Quaternary Science Reviews* 25:2197–2211.

Haynes, C. Vance

1991 Geoarchaeological and Paleohydrological Evidence for a Clovis-age Drought in North America and its Bearing on Extinction. *Quaternary Research* 35:438–450.

Haynes, C. Vance

2008 Younger Dryas "Black Mats" and the Rancholabrean Termination in North America. *Proceedings of the National Academy of Sciences* 105:6520–6525.

Haynes, C. Vance, J. Boerner, K. Domanik, D. Lauretta, J. Ballenger, and J. Goreva

2010 The Murray Springs Clovis Site, Pleistocene Extinction, and the Question of Extraterrestrial Impact. *Proceedings of the National Academy of Sciences* 107:4010–4015.

Holliday, V.

2000 Folsom Drought and Episodic Drying on the Southern High Plains from 10,900–10,200 ^{14}C yr BP. *Quaternary Research* 53:1–12.

Holliday, V., and D. Meltzer

2010 The 12.9ka ET Impact Hypothesis and North American Paleoindians. *Current Anthropology* 51:575–607.

Hua, Q., M. Barbetti, D. Fink, K.F. Kaiser, M. Friedrich, B. Kromer, V. Levchenko, U. Zoppi, A. Smith, and F. Bertuch

2009 Atmospheric ^{14}C Variations Derived from Tree Rings during the Early Younger Dryas. *Quaternary Science Reviews* 28:2982–2990.

Huckleberry, G.

2001 Archaeological Sediments in Dryland Alluvial Environments. In *Sediments in Archaeological Contexts*, edited by J. Stein and W. Farrand, pp. 67–92. University of Utah Press, Salt Lake City.

Lothrop, J., P. Newby, A. Spiess, and J. Bradley

2011 Paleoindians and the Younger Dryas in the New England-Maritimes Region. *Quaternary International* 242:546–569.

Lowell, T., T. Fisher, G. Comer, I. Hajdas, N. Waterson, K. Glover, H. Loope, J. Schaeffer, V. Rinterknecht, W. Broecker, G. Denton, and J. Teller

2005 Testing the Lake Agassiz Meltwater Trigger for the Younger Dryas. *Eos* 86:365–373.

Lowell, T., T. Fisher, I. Hajdas, K. Glover, H. Loope, and T. Henry

2009 Radiocarbon Deglaciation Chronology of the Thunder Bay, Ontario Area and Implications for Ice Sheet Retreat Patterns. *Quaternary Science Reviews* 28:1597–1607.

Mann, D., and D. Meltzer

2007 Millennial-scale Dynamics of Valley Fills over the Past 12,000 ^{14}C Years, Northeastern New Mexico, USA. *Geological Society of America Bulletin* 119:1433–1448.

Meltzer, D.

1999 Human Responses to Middle Holocene (Altithermal) Climates on the North American Great Plains. *Quaternary Research* 52:404–416.

2009 *First Peoples in a New World: Colonizing Ice Age America.* University of California Press, Berkeley.

Meltzer, D., and V. Holliday
  2010 Would North American Paleoindians Have Noticed Younger Dryas Age Climate Changes? *Journal of World Prehistory* 23:1–41.

Monnin, E., A. Indermuhle, A. Dallenbach, J. Fluckiger, B. Stauffer, T. Stocker, D. Raynaud, and J-M Barnola
  2001 Atmospheric CO_2 Concentrations over the Last Glacial Termination. *Science* 291:112–114.

Murton, J., M. Bateman, S. Dallimore, J. Teller, and Z. Yang
  2010 Identification of Younger Dryas Outburst Flood Path from Lake Agassiz to the Arctic Ocean. *Nature* 464:740–743.

Newby, P., J. Bradley, A. Spiess, B. Shuman, and P. Leduc
  2005 A Paleoindian Response to Younger Dryas Climate Change. *Quaternary Science Reviews* 24:141–154.

Paquay, F., S. Goderis, G. Ravizza, F. Vanhaeck, M. Boyd, T. Surovell, V. Holliday, C. Vance Haynes, Jr., and P. Claeys
  2009 Absence of Geochemical Evidence for an Impact at the Bølling-Allerød/Younger Dryas Transition. *Proceedings of the National Academy of Sciences* 106:21505–21510.

Pinter, N., A. Scott, T. Daulton, A. Podoll, C. Koeberl, R. Anderson, and S. Ishman
  2011 The Younger Dryas Impact Hypothesis: A Requiem. *Earth-Science Reviews* 106:247–264.

Polyak, V., J. Rasmussen, and Y. Asmerom
  2004 Prolonged Wet Period in the Southwestern United States through the Younger Dryas. *Geology* 32:5–8.

Quade, J., R. Forester, W. Pratt, and C. Carter
  1998 Black Mats, Spring-fed Streams, and Late-glacial-age Recharge in the Southern Great Basin. *Quaternary Research* 49:129–148.

Reeder, L., J. Erlandson, and T. Rick
  2001 Younger Dryas Environments and Human Adaptations on the West Coast of the United States and Baja California. *Quaternary International* 242:463–478.

Shizitan Archaeological Team
  2010 The Excavations of Locality S9 of the Shizitan Site in Jixian County, Shanxi. *Kao-Gu (Archaeology)* 10:871–881.

Shuman, B., T. Webb, P. Bartlein, and J. Williams
  2002 The Anatomy of a Climatic Oscillation: Vegetation Change in Eastern North America during the Younger Dryas Chronozone. *Quaternary Science Reviews* 21:1777–1791.

Smith, B.
  2001 Low-level Food Production. *Journal of Archaeological Research* 9:1–43.

Steffensen, J., K. Andersen, M. Bigler, H. Clausen, D. Dahl-Jensen, H. Fischer, K. Goto-Azuma, M. Hansson, S. Johnsen, J. Jouzel, V. Masson-Delmotte,

T. Popp, S. Rasmussen, R. Rothlishberger, U. Ruth, B. Stauffer, M-L Siggaard-Anderson, A. Sveinbjornsdottir, A. Svensson, and J. White
    2008 High-resolution Greenland Ice Core Data Show Abrupt Climate Change Happens in Few Years. *Science* 321:680–684.

Stiger, M.
    2006 A Folsom Structure in the Colorado Mountains. *American Antiquity* 71:321–351.

Straus, L., and T. Goebel
    2011 Humans and Younger Dryas: Dead End, Short Detour, or Open Road to the Holocene? *Quaternary International* 242:259–261.

Surovell, T., V. Holliday, J. Gringerich, C. Ketron, C. Vance Haynes, Jr., I. Hilman, D. Wagner, E. Johnson, and P. Claeys
    2009 An Independent Evaluation of the Younger Dryas Extraterrestrial Impact Hypothesis. *Proceedings of the National Academy of Sciences* 106:18155–18158.

Surovell, T., and N. Waguespack
    2007 Folsom Hearth-centered Use of Space at Barger Gulch, Locality B. In *Emerging Frontiers in Colorado Paleoindian Archaeology*, edited by R. S. Brunswig and B. Pitblado, pp. 219–259. University of Colorado Press, Boulder.

Teller, J., M. Boyd, Z. Yang, P. Kor, and A. Fard
    2005 Alternative Routing of Lake Agassiz Overflow during the Younger Dryas: New Dates, Paleotopography, and a Re-evaluation. *Quaternary Science Reviews* 24:1890–1905.

Wunsch, C.
    2010 Towards Understanding the Paleocene. *Quaternary Science Reviews* 29:1960–1967.

Yi, S., and Saito, Y.
    2004 Latest Pleistocene Climate Variation in the East Asian Monsoon from Pollen Records of Two East China Regions. *Quaternary International* 121:75–87.

Yu, Z., and H. Wright, Jr.
    2001 Response of Interior North America to Abrupt Climate Oscillations in the North Atlantic Region during the Last Deglaciation. *Earth-Science Reviews* 52:333–369.

INDEX

ABOUT THE AUTHORS

David G. Anderson is a Professor in the Department of Anthropology at the University of Tennessee, Knoxville. He received his Ph.D. from the University of Michigan in 1990, having earlier received an M.A. from the University of Arkansas in 1979 and a B.A. from Case Western Reserve University in 1972. All three degrees were in anthropology. He has conducted archaeological fieldwork in the Southeastern, Southwestern, and Midwestern United States, and in the Caribbean. His work includes some 350 publications and meeting papers and some 45 books and technical monographs. Professional interests include exploring the development of cultural complexity in eastern North America from initial colonization onwards, climate change, and its impact on human societies, teaching, and developing technical and popular syntheses of archaeological research. He is the founding director of the Paleoindian Database of the Americas (PIDBA), which is available online at http://pidba.utk.edu/. Additional biographical data is also available on the web at http://web.utk.edu/~anthrop/faculty/anderson.html and at http://en.wikipedia.org/wiki/David_G._Anderson

Ofer Bar-Yosef is the George G. and Janet G. B. MacCurdy Professor of Prehistoric Archaeology, Department of Anthropology, Harvard University. He has extensive field experience excavating sites dated to the lower through the terminal Pleistocene and early Holocene in Israel, Turkey, Georgia, and China. He has published extensively on issues related to cultural evolution, interactions of humans with their environments, and in particular about the apparent relationship between the YD and the origins of sedentism, territoriality, and the emergence of intentional systematic cultivation in West and East Asia. He is a member of the U. S. National Academy of Sciences.

Stella M. Blockley holds a BSc in Archaeology and an MSc in Human Osteology and Palaeopathology from the University of Bradford. Her Ph.D. was concerned with the relationship between climate, funerary behavior, and diet during periods of climatic change, focusing on the

Pleistocene-Holocene transition in Britain. Her research interests include the study of diet through isotopic analysis, effects of climatic change on population movement, skeletal changes, funerary behavior, and the identification of social differences within and between populations.

Luis Alberto Borrero is a Professor at the Universidad de Buenos Aires. Vice-Director of the Instituto Multidisciplinario de Historia y Ciencias Humanas (CONICET, Argentina). He is involved in archaeological fieldwork and laboratory projects concerning the peopling of southern South America. Dr. Borrero is Vice-President of the INQUA commission on Humans and the Biosphere. He has long-term research interests in the archaeology of hunter-gatherer societies and in the taphonomy of ungulates, pinnipeds, and whales.

Tom D. Dillehay, Rebecca Webb Wilson University Distinguished Professor in Anthropology, Religion, and Culture at Vanderbilt University and Profesor Extraordinario at the Universidad Austral de Chile, has carried out numerous archaeological and anthropological projects in Peru, Chile, Argentina, other South American countries, and the United States. His main interests are migration, the long-term transformative processes leading to political and economic change, and the interdisciplinary and historical methodologies designed to study those processes. He has been a visiting professor at several universities around the world, including the Universidad de Chile; Universidad Nacional Mayor de San Marcos, Lima; Universidade de São Paulo; Universidad Nacional Autónoma de México; Cambridge University; University of Tokyo; and the University of Chicago. Dillehay has published fifteen books and more than two hundred refereed journal articles. He currently codirects an interdisciplinary project focused on long-term human and environmental interaction on the north coast of Peru, where he has also recently begun an excavation project at the site of Huaca Prieta. He also directs a project sponsored by the Guggenheim Foundation and the National Science Foundation on the political identity of the Araucanians in Chile and Argentina. Dillehay has received numerous international and national awards for his research, books, and teaching. He is a member of the American Academy of Arts and Sciences.

Metin I. Eren is a Leverhulme Early Career Fellow in the Department of Anthropology at the University of Kent, Canterbury, U.K. He has a degree in Anthropology from Harvard College (A.B.), and as a National Science Foundation Graduate Research Fellow, he received degrees in Anthropology from Southern Methodist University (M.A., Ph. D.), as well as in Experimental Archaeology from the University of Exeter, U.K. (M.A.). He is an experienced flintknapper and has conducted research in, and published numerous papers on, the Stone Age of North America, Europe, Asia, and Africa.

Jon M. Erlandson is an archaeologist who directs the Museum of Natural and Cultural History at the University of Oregon (UO), where he is also a Professor of Anthropology and the Knight Professor of Arts and Sciences. He earned his Ph.D. from the University of California, Santa Barbara, in 1988 and taught at the University of Alaska-Fairbanks before joining the UO faculty in 1990. With seventeen books and over 200 scholarly articles published, Erlandson focuses on the origins and development of maritime societies, human migrations, the peopling of the Americas, and the historical ecology of marine fisheries and coastal ecosystems.

Clive S. Gamble is Professor of Geography in the Center for Quaternary Research at Royal Holloway, University of London. He spent many years at the University of Southampton, where he founded the Center for the Archaeology of Human Origins. He is author of several books, including *In Search of the Neanderthals* with Christopher Stringer (1993), *Timewalkers: The Prehistory of Global Colonisation* (1993), and *The Palaeolithic Societies of Europe* (1999), which won the Society for American Archaeology Book Award in 2000, and most recently *Origins and Revolutions* (2007). He is a codirector of the British Academy Centenary research project, Lucy to Language—the Archaeology of the Social Brain.

Lisa Janz (M.A., 2003, University of Arizona) is a Ph.D. Candidate in the School of Anthropology at the University of Arizona. Her current research is focused on establishing a foundational chronology of hunter-gatherer technology and organizational strategies from the Epipalaeolithic to the initial Bronze Age across three key Gobi Desert regions. Her work explores how preferences in technology and land-use are culturally-driven, adaptive mechanisms used to maintain group health and sustainability. Her Research interests include radiocarbon dating of pottery, pottery use among hunter-gatherers, exploitation of dune fields and wetlands in arid environments, hunter-gatherer adoption of herd animals, ostrich ecology in northern Asia, and the effective use of existing museum collections, including developing responsible and more conservative methods for destructive analysis. Publications include "Dating Northeast Asian Surface Assemblages with Ostrich

Eggshell: Implications for Palaeoecology and Extirpation" (*Journal of Archaeological Science*, 2009).

Michael Jochim is Professor of Anthropology at the University of California, Santa Barbara. His interests in hunter-gatherers, human ecology, and European prehistory combine his research in the late Pleistocene and early Holocene of central Europe. For the past thirty years, he has carried out surveys and excavations in southern Germany and is currently conducting NSF-sponsored fieldwork focused on discovering and excavating late Palaeolithic and early Mesolithic wet sites in that region.

Jason M. LaBelle serves as an Assistant Professor in the Department of Anthropology at Colorado State University. He is an archaeologist interested in Native American foragers inhabiting the Great Plains and Rocky Mountains of North America, with research spanning several periods over the last 13,000 years. His current work involves landscape level survey and testing of prehistoric and protohistoric sites surrounding the Lindenmeier Folsom site, a National Historic Landmark. His research aims to identify temporal shifts in subsistence and settlement patterns, especially those that might be related to regional fire histories. In addition to teaching and research, he serves as the Director of the Laboratory of Public Archaeology (LOPA), which houses archaeological collections and associated data from academic and contract projects located within Colorado. Dr. LaBelle is currently serving on the Board of Directors of the Plains Anthropological Society and is past President of the Colorado Archaeological Society.

Cheryl A. Makarewicz is a Professor of Zooarchaeology and Stable Isotope Science at the Chistian Albrechts University in Kiel, Germany. Makarewicz is involved in several research projects that examine the role of animals in complex societies in the Near East and Inner Asia. Her research focuses in particular on animal domestication processes, the evolution of pastoral economies, and how animals and their products can be used to facilitate social relationships. In addition to her work in Mongolia with modern pastoral nomads, Makarewicz leads excavations at the Pre-pottery Neolithic site of el-Hemmeh, Jordan, where she is investigating the origins of agriculture and village life.

Scott C. Meeks is a Ph.D. student in the Department of Anthropology at the University of Tennessee, Knoxville. He received an M.A. in Anthropology from the University of Alabama in 1998. His thesis was entitled "The Use and Function of Late Middle Archaic Projectile Points in the Midsouth." The author of a number of papers and monographs on the prehistoric archaeology of the Midsouth, his research interests include linking paleoclimatology and archaeology, cultural resource management, and lithic technology. He is currently employed by Tennessee Valley Authority.

David J. Meltzer is Henderson-Morrison Professor of Prehistory, Southern Methodist University. His research focuses on North American, late Pleistocene environments and hunter-gatherer adaptations, as well as the history of American archaeology. Among his many published works are *First Peoples in a New World: Colonizing Ice Age America* (2009) and *Folsom: New Archaeological Investigations of a Classic Paleoindian Bison Kill* (2006). He is a member of the U.S. National Academy of Sciences.

Torben C. Rick is Curator of North American Archaeology and Director of the Program in Human Ecology and Archaeobiology in the Department of Anthropology, National Museum of Natural History, Smithsonian Institution. He received his Ph.D. in Anthropology from the University of Oregon (2004). His research focuses on the archaeology and historical ecology of coastal and island peoples, especially on the North American Pacific and Atlantic Coasts. He has active field projects on California's Channel Islands and the Chesapeake Bay, which are collaborative with researchers from a variety of disciplines (anthropology, biology, ecology, etc.). He focuses on ancient and modern human environmental interactions.

Joshua Wright is a postdoctoral fellow at Stanford University. He holds his Ph.D. from Harvard University (Anthropology, 2006), and an M.Phil. from Cambridge University (East Asia Archaeology, 1995). His research focuses on cultural landscapes in transition, the impact of mobility, and monumental landscapes. He has carried out two major landscape archaeology projects in Mongolia, including one at Baga Gazaryn Chuluu in the North Gobi desert. Currently he conducts research in Mongolia and Xinjiang, China.